Regency II Edition

prNpls v spdri*

JOE M. PULLIS, Ed.D.

Professor, Department of Office Administration
and Business Communication
College of Administration and Business
Louisiana Tech University

CHERYL D. PULLIS, M.Ed.
Educational Consultant

GLENCOE/McGRAW-HILL
A Macmillan/McGraw-Hill Company
Mission Hills, California

*PRINCIPLES OF
SPEEDWRITING

Linda Bippen
Lesson/Exercise Writer

Cheryl D. Pullis, M.Ed.
System Consultant

Send all inquiries to:
Glencoe/McGraw-Hill
15319 Chatsworth Street, P.O. Box 9509
Mission Hills, California 91395-9509

Printed in the United States of America

1 2 3 4 5 6 7 8   94 93 92 91 90

ISBN 0-02-685680-8

Speedwriting is a registered trademark of Glencoe Publishing Company.

CONTENTS

SECTION TWO   SKILL BUILDING AND REINFORCEMENT

Appendix

TEXT

Organization of Principles Text

The seven chapters of the principles text for *Speedwriting, Regency II Edition* are organized into 50 lessons that contain principles, words illustrating each new principle, lists of brief forms and abbreviations, and Reading and Writing Exercises containing new vocabulary and reinforcement of vocabulary previously studied. The Reading and Writing Exercises contain thousands of words of practice material presented in spiral notebook format. The key following each Reading and Writing Exercise is marked in 20-word intervals for ease in timing reading or giving dictation.

Order of Principles Presentation

The order of presentation of the principles is arranged to distribute the learning load equitably and to allow the introduction of realistic, business-related connected matter in the very early lessons.

Every seventh lesson is a review of the previous six lessons, with extensive word development activities providing reinforcement.

Lessons 43–50 are primarily for speed building and serve as a review of the brief forms and abbreviations of the system.

The English language consists of sounds that may be pronounced differently in various parts of our country. In order to have one standard pronunciation, the *Second College Edition* of *The American Heritage Dictionary* was used.

Transcription Skills

Because the transcription of mailable letters is a primary objective of *Speedwriting* instruction, pre-transcription skills are introduced early in the *Speedwriting* principles text. In each lesson beginning with Lesson 8, one or more business vocabulary words are defined. These words are then used in context in the Reading and Writing Exercises for that lesson.

Spelling and Punctuation

Beginning with Lesson 16, commonly misspelled words are presented.

Punctuation rules begin with Lesson 22. Research has indicated that relatively few rules of punctuation account for the overwhelming majority of usage in typical business correspondence. The eight comma rules taught in the

Speedwriting principles text account for the majority of all commas used in business correspondence.

After a comma rule has been introduced, examples of that rule are highlighted in the Reading and Writing Exercises and reinforced with notations. The highlighting gives the instructor a valuable resource for expanding the classroom emphasis on punctuation.

Appendix Materials

The appendix of the text contains a reading-rate chart; tables and keys of brief forms, abbreviations, and phrases; abbreviations of the states, U.S. possessions, and Canadian provinces; an index of city names; abbreviations of metric terms; lists of spelling words; and the principles by order of presentation and system category.

WORKBOOK

Organization of Workbook

A workbook, correlated by lesson, is available to accompany the *Speedwriting* principles text. The primary purpose of the workbook is the reinforcement of theory and princples, brief forms, and abbreviations. The workbook is structured with drills designed to help the student:

1. Review *Speedwriting* principles by writing words that have been studied.
2. Develop the ability to write new *Speedwriting* words from words that have already been learned.
3. Increase business and *Speedwriting* vocabulary.
4. Improve the ability to read from *Speedwriting* notes and to transcribe them accurately.
5. Review language arts elements needed in transcription.

The last eight lessons of the workbook are designed specifically to review previously covered material as follows:

Lesson 43 reviews Lessons 1–7
Lesson 44 reviews Lessons 8–14
Lesson 45 reviews Lessons 15–21
Lesson 46 reviews Lessons 22–28
Lesson 47 reviews Lessons 29–35
Lesson 48 reviews Lessons 36–42
Lesson 49 reviews word beginnings
Lesson 50 reviews word endings

Utilization of Workbook

The workbook may be used as a homework device, as a daily classroom activity, or as a remedial exercise. Keys to the worksheets are printed at the end of each lesson so that students may check their mastery of the material presented in that lesson.

INSTRUCTION TAPES

Cassette Tape Contents

A set of 50 instruction tapes is available for the *Speedwriting* principles text. Each tape corresponds to a lesson in the principles text.

The format for the tapes follows this general outline:
1. A presentation of new theory and principles from the corresponding lesson.
2. A presentation of brief forms and/or abbreviations from the corresponding lesson.
3. Warm-up dictation, beginning with Tape 2, usually related to previously studied business letters in the text.
4. A review of the theory and principles from the *preceding* lesson.
5. A review of brief forms and/or abbreviations from the preceding lesson.
6. Dictation of letters from the preceding lesson, in speed-building format.

Tapes are 30 minutes per lesson. Approximately the last 15 minutes of each tape is dictation for speed development. Dictation speeds begin at 40 words per minute and progress to 90 words per minute.

Utilization of Instruction Tapes

Tapes may be used for review of previously introduced lessons or for review of principles from the previous lesson. In addition, the tape lessons strongly reinforce the brief forms and abbreviations introduced in the correspondingly numbered text and workbook lessons. Another primary use of the tapes is to provide practice dictation to increase dictation-recording speeds. One other benefit is that if students miss a lesson, the tapes may be used to introduce the theory, principles, brief forms, and abbreviations that were missed since the tapes are of an instructional nature.

DICTIONARIES

Two dictionaries are available for use as references. The *Speedwriting Abridged Dictionary* contains over 6,000 of the most frequently used words in business communications. The *Speedwriting Comprehensive Dictionary* contains approximately 22,000 words.

Each volume provides a list of rules for word division, and all places where the words can be correctly divided in keyboarding/transcription applications are shown.

The appendix of each dictionary contains a summary of brief forms, abbreviations, and phrases; abbreviations of the states, U.S. possessions, and Canadian provinces; and abbreviations of metric terms. The Abridged Dictionary presents the principles by order of presentation. The Comprehensive Dictionary provides the principles by system category and a list of major American and Canadian cities in *Speedwriting*.

SPEEDWRITING VOCABULARY BUILDER

The *Speedwriting Vocabulary Builder* consists of the most frequently used 2,000 words in business communication arranged alphabetically by lesson and sound-spelled in *Speedwriting, Regency II Edition*. Mastery of these high-frequency words will enable one to write automatically approximately 90 percent of all words used in contemporary business communications.

INSTRUCTOR'S GUIDE

The Instructor's Guide provides teaching methodology, with specific suggestions for teaching procedures, motivating students, testing and evaluation, and learning the system.

The guide also presents comprehensive lesson plans for all 50 lessons of the text. The plans for Lessons 28–50 contain supplementary drill letters or memos with preview words.

The guide's testing material includes 12 *Speedwriting* vocabulary tests, 2 for each of the text's first 6 chapters; 3 brief form tests; an abbreviation test; and a phrase test. For dictation-recording tests, the guide provides 4 sets of 3-minute takes, which may be dictated at speeds of 50, 60, 70, and 80 words per minute.

Computer-controlled lesson indexes for every lesson in the textbook are provided in the Instructor's Guide.

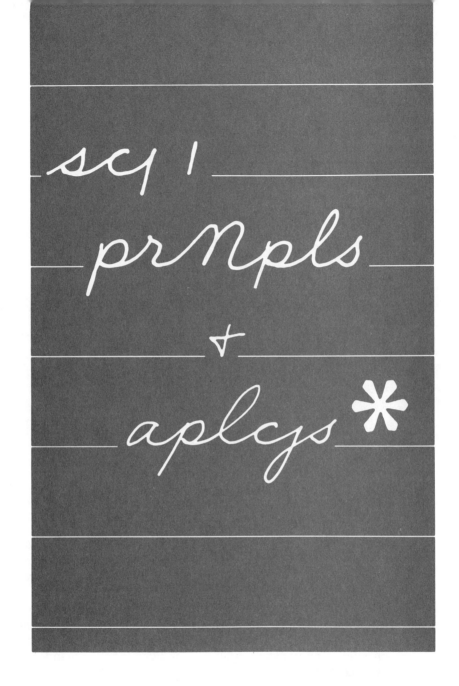

sci 1

prNpls

+

aplcjs

*SECTION ONE
PRINCIPLES AND
APPLICATIONS

Cplr 1

You are about to study *Speedwriting*, a writing system that is based primarily on what you already know—the alphabet—to represent the sounds that make up our language. As a result, taking notes, building speed, and transcribing are accelerated in *Speedwriting*.

The *Speedwriting* system covers all words in the English language. Words used in business, law, medicine, science, and the arts all fall under a *Speedwriting* principle you will study in this course. You will learn to apply these principles as easily and naturally as you now write longhand.

As you study the *Speedwriting* system, you will also learn techniques for practicing and writing your notes quickly and successfully. Begin today to develop good writing and study habits.

*Chapter One

Before You Begin

Choose your pens carefully. Use a good ball-point pen that glides easily across the paper. If the pen glides easily, you'll save time and energy with each stroke. And always have more than one pen ready—just in case the first one stops during dictation.

Use a spiral-bound pad. Use a notebook that is spiral bound at the top so that pages will flip easily and the book will lie flat while you are writing.

A line down the center divides the page in half. Write on only one side of the page until that side is filled. Then move to the top of the other side of the same page. When you have filled the entire page, flip the paper and continue writing on the completely new page that follows.

When you've reached the last page, turn the pad over and begin writing from back to front using the same procedure.

LESSON 1

Streamline letters as you write. Every time you lift your pen to cross a *t* or dot an *i*, you lose valuable time and reduce your speed. *Speedwriting* eliminates extra strokes by avoiding loops, dots, and crosses whenever possible. As you practice, you will become comfortable with this technique, and you will find that streamlining letters makes writing faster, easier, and just as easy to read. Look at these examples:

t	l	b	b
f	b	i	ι
j	1	y	4
g	9	p	p
h	h	z	3

1. Write what you hear. The English language contains many silent letters. In longhand, we write h-i-g-h even when we hear only the sound *hi* and k-n-o-w when we hear only *no*. In *Speedwriting* we write what we hear: *hi* and *no* .

fee, f-e	fe	tie, t-i	li
free, f-r-e	fre	tray, t-r-a	lra
view, v-u	vu	ate, a-t	al
knew, n-u	nu	sigh, s-i	si

Using this principle, then, how would you write the words *see*, *pay*, *low*, and *fly*?

see, s-e	se	pay, p-a	pa
low, l-o	lo	fly, f-l-i	fli

2. Drop medial vowels. Omit vowels that fall in the middle of the word.

build, b-l-d *bld*

save, s-v *sv*

*legal, l-guh-l *lgl*

*glass, guh-l-s *gls*

did, d-d *dd*

bulletin, b-l-t-n *blln*

budget, b-j-t *bjt*

*grade, guh-r-d *grd*

*In *Speedwriting*, the letter g is pronounced *guh*; guh-l-s for glass; guh-r-d for grade; l-guh-l for legal.

Using Principle 2, then, how would you write the words *given*, *said*, *visit*, and *paper*?

given, guh-v-n *gvn*

said, s-d *sd*

visit, v-z-t *vzt*

paper, p-p-r *ppr*

3. Write initial and final vowels. Write the vowels you hear at the beginning and end of the word.

office, o-f-s *ofs*

easy, e-z-e *eze*

ahead, a-h-d *ahd*

ready, r-d-e *rde*

*do, d-u *du*

often, o-f-n *ofn*

follow, f-l-o *flo*

*few, f-u *fu*

*Note that *u* is used for the long vowel sounds of $\overline{oo}$ and $\overline{u}$.

Using Principle 3, how would you write *value*, *enough*, *open*, and *happy*?

value, v-l-u *vlu*

enough, e-n-f *enf*

open, o-p-n *opn*

happy, h-p-e *hpe*

The three principles you have just learned will allow you to write many words you will encounter on your job. In the remaining lessons, you will learn additional principles that will enable you to write other sounds quickly and easily.

Before going on, practice these additional words. First, read the word aloud and spell it according to its sound: grow, guh-r-o. Then sound-spell the word as you write it: grow, guh-r-o *gro* .

deposit, d-p-z-t *dpzt*   type, t-p *tp*

news, n-z *nz*   *review, re-v-u *rvu*

sell, s-l *sl*   knowledge, n-l-j *nlj*

written, r-t-n *rtn*   apply, a-p-l-i *apli*

lease, l-s *ls*   *reason, re-z-n *rzn*

benefit, b-n-f-t *bnfl*   unit, u-n-t *unt*

*Since medial vowels are omitted, the word beginning *re* is represented by an *r*.

Punctuation Symbols.   Use quick, distinct symbols to show punctuation in *Speedwriting* notes. To show capitalization, draw a small curved line under the last letter of the word: Bill, *bl* .

Sue, s-u *su*   Ed, e-d *ed*

Dallas, d-l-s *dls*   Debbie, d-b-e *dbe*

Ted, t-d *td*   New Haven, n-u h-v-n *nu hvn*

To indicate a period at the end of a sentence, write ＼ .

Let Bill know. *ll bl no ＼*

To indicate a question mark, write × .

Does Bill know? *dz bl no ×*

To indicate the end of a paragraph, write ＞ .

Bill does know. *bl dz no ＞*

Brief Forms. You will use some words so often that you will find it helpful to write shortened forms for them. We call these shortened forms **brief forms.** Since brief forms are not written in full, you should commit them to memory. Study and practice the brief forms until you can write them as quickly, easily, and accurately as you write your own name—without hesitation.

More than one word can be represented by the same brief form. When read in context, however, only one meaning will make sense.

a, an	*·*	we	*ℓ*
will, well	*ℓ*	the	*⌐*
it, at	*/ ↗*	is, his	*) ↓*
to, too	*ℓ*	in, not	*m*

PRINCIPLES SUMMARY

1. Write what you hear: know, n-o *no*
2. Drop medial vowels: build, b-l-d *bld*
3. Write initial and final vowels: office, o-f-s *ofs* ; ready, r-d-e *rde* .

Vocabulary Builder. Practice writing these frequently used words:

policy, p-l-s-e	*plse*	believe, b-l-v	*blv*
hope, h-p	*hp*	let, l-t	*lt*
year, y-r	*yr*	offer, o-f-r	*ofr*
help, h-l-p	*hlp*	plan, p-l-n	*pln*
above, a-b-v	*abv*	life, l-f	*lf*
give, guh-v	*gv*	people, p-p-l	*ppl*
city, s-t-e	*ste*	here, h-r	*hr*
feel, f-l	*fl*	price, p-r-s	*prs*

Reading and Writing Exercises

You will find that reading and writing *Speedwriting* is easy as well as fun, and fluency in reading and writing will develop with practice.

The following steps should assist you in studying each of the *Speedwriting* lessons:

1. Study the principles and the words illustrating each principle at the beginning of each lesson.
2. Sound-spell (aloud if possible) as you write and pronounce each word. Write each word (while sound-spelling) two or three times, or until you feel comfortable writing the word.
3. Read the Reading and Writing Exercises, using the key as necessary until the material can be read fluently. Beginning with Lesson 3, each letter and memorandum is marked in groups of 20 standard words (28 syllables). Small, consecutive numbers are placed in the key after each group of 20 standard words; therefore, if while reading you are able to reach the number 4 in one minute, you would be reading at the rate of 80 words per minute (20 x 4); if you reach the number 5, you would be reading at the rate of 100 words per minute, etc. As a general rule, you should be able to read about twice as fast as you expect to write from dictation. A reading-rate chart has been provided in the Appendix to assist you in determining your reading rate.
4. After writing the exercises initially from the *Speedwriting* plate material, then write the Reading and Writing Exercises from the key while self-dictating.
   (a) Read several words from the key.
   (b) Write the words while sound-spelling and saying each word aloud. Normally, it is not necessary to sound-spell the brief forms.
   (c) Repeat this procedure until a letter or memorandum has been written, remembering to check the *Speedwriting* notes in the textbook for any words you may not know how to write.
   (d) Read back the letter or memorandum from your own *Speedwriting* notes.

You now know enough *Speedwriting* to read and write complete sentences. Read the sentences on page 9 aloud. When you encounter an unfamiliar *Speedwriting* word, sound-spell the word. If the correct word still does not come to mind, read on to the end of the sentence. The context, or meaning, of the sentence will help you identify the unfamiliar *Speedwriting* word. If you are still unable to read the *Speedwriting* word, look in the printed key that follows the Reading and Writing Exercises.

SERIES A

1. *[shorthand]*
   [shorthand]
2. *[shorthand]*
   [shorthand]
3. *[shorthand]*
   [shorthand]
4. *[shorthand]*
   [shorthand]
5. *[shorthand]*
   [shorthand]

SERIES B

1. *[shorthand]*
   [shorthand]
2. *[shorthand]*
   [shorthand]
3. *[shorthand]*
   [shorthand]
4. *[shorthand]*
   [shorthand]
5. *[shorthand]*
   [shorthand]

SERIES C

1. *[shorthand]*
   [shorthand]
2. *[shorthand]*
   [shorthand]
3. *[shorthand]*
   Sue will grade it.
4. *[shorthand]*
   Is the new budget ready to review
5. *[shorthand]*
   [shorthand]
   [shorthand]
   [shorthand]
   [shorthand]
   [shorthand]
   [shorthand]

Key

SERIES A
1. We hope to see you soon.
2. Will you pay a fee?
3. It is a new file unit.
4. Is the unit too tall?
5. Sue will not fly to Dallas.

SERIES B
1. Ed is in his office.
2. Did you receive a bill?
3. Tell Debbie to pay it.
4. You will do well in an office job.
5. We will give you a raise in pay.

SERIES C
1. Is Bill at the office?
2. The review is easy to type.
3. Sue will grade it.
4. Is the new budget ready to review?
5. We did not receive it.

Four Steps to Follow in Learning Speedwriting

As you work through each lesson, use these steps as a study plan:

1. *Read the principle and think about it.* How does it apply to each of the words listed under it?

2. *Practice each word listed under the principle.* First, say the word aloud: *glass*. Then sound-spell the word aloud as you would write it in *Speedwriting*: guh-l-s. Then sound-spell and write the word in *Speedwriting*: guh-l-s *gls* .

3. *Read the Speedwriting exercises aloud.* If the correct *Speedwriting* word does not immediately come to mind, sound-spell the word. If the translation is not readily apparent, read on to the end of the sentence. The context, or meaning, of the sentence will help you identify the unfamiliar *Speedwriting* words. Consult the key if you cannot determine the correct word with the help of sound-spelling and context.

4. *Write the Speedwriting exercises.* After you have read the exercises, write them. Writing the *Speedwriting* words will help you develop reading skill as well as an accurate writing style.

LESSON 2

1. Write   *c*   for the sound of *k*.

copy, k-p-e *cpe*   school, s-k-l *scl*

like, l-k *lc*   clerk, k-l-r-k *clrc*

package, p-k-j *pcj*   desk, d-s-k *dsc*

2. Write a capital   *C*   for the sound of *ch*, *cha* (pronounced *chay*).

change, chay-n-j *Cnj*   teach, t-chay *tC*

such, s-chay *sC*   check, chay-k *Cc*

chosen, chay-z-n *Czn*   church, chay-r-chay *CrC*

More about writing. To write *m* and *w* with ease and speed, streamline the letters.

3. Write   ⌒   for the sound of *m*.

may, m-a *⌒a*   much, m-chay *⌒C*

name, n-m *n⌒*   my, m-i *⌒i*

mail, m-l *⌒l*   same, s-m *s⌒*

4. Write   ⌣   for the sound of *w* and *wh*.

way, w-a *⌣a*   week, w-k *⌣c*

when, w-n *⌣n*   wage, w-j *⌣j*

what, w-t *⌣t*   where, w-r *⌣r*

winner, w-n-r *⌣nr*   which, w-chay *⌣C*

5. To add *ing* or *thing* as a word ending, underscore the last letter of the *Speedwriting* word.

billing, b-l-ing *bl*

*paying, p-a-ing *pa*

something, s-m-thing *s⌢*

attaching, a-t-chay-ing *alC*

watching, w-chay-ing *⌣C*

*saying, s-a-ing *sa*

*Note: Always write long vowels before marks of punctuation.

6. To form the plural of any *Speedwriting* word ending in a mark of punctuation, double the last mark of punctuation.

billings, b-l-ings *bl*

savings, s-v-ings *sv*

7. *Adding s.* Write *s* to form the plural of any *Speedwriting* word ending in a letter: books, b-k-s *bcs* . Write *s* to form possessives: girl's, guh-r-l-s *grls* . Write *s* to add *s* to a verb: runs, r-n-s *rns* . Add *s* even though the final sound of such words may be *z*.

checks, chay-k-s *Ccs*

hopes, h-p-s *hps*

helps, h-l-p-s *hlps*

jobs, j-b-s *jbs*

Bill's, b-l-s *bls*

gives, guh-v-s *gvs*

An *s* is also used in the writing of proper nouns ending in *s*, even though the final sound may be *z*.

James, j-m-s *jms*

Ames, a-m-s *a⌣s*

Burns, b-r-n-s *brns*

Charles, chay-r-l-s *Crls*

Practice writing these additional words:

care, k-r	*Cr*	claim, k-l-m	*cl*
games, guh-m-s	*gs*	course, k-r-s	*Crs*
room, r-m	*r*	units, u-n-t-s	*unts*
truck, t-r-k	*lrc*	match, m-chay	*C*
buildings, b-l-d-ings	*bld*	each, e-chay	*eC*
training, t-r-n-ing	*lrn*	coverings, k-v-r-ings	*Cvr*

Abbreviations.   Many abbreviations are so common that they come to mind automatically. *Speedwriting* makes use of these abbreviations. Since you already know many of these abbreviations, you will be able to write them quickly from the beginning.

company	*co*	president	*P*
information	*inf*	and	*�送*
vice president	*VP*	return	*rel*
catalog	*cal*		

Brief Forms

are, our	*n*	can	*C*
for, full	*b*	us	*s*
of, have, very	*V*		

PRINCIPLES SUMMARY

1. Write   c   for the sound of *k*: copy, k-p-e   *cpe*   .
2. Write a capital   C   for the sound of *ch, cha*: check, chay-k   *Cc*   .
3. Write   ⌒   for the sound of *m*: may, m-a   *⌒a*   .
4. Write   ⌣   for the sound of *w* and *wh*: way, w-a   *⌣a*   ; when, w-n   *⌣n*   .
5. To add *ing* or *thing* as a word ending, underscore the last letter of the *Speedwriting* word: billing, b-l-ing   *bl*   ; something, s-m-thing   *⌒*   .
6. To form the plural of any *Speedwriting* word ending in a mark of punctuation, double the last mark of punctuation: billings, b-l-ings   *bl*   .
7. Write   *ᔥ*   to form the plural of any *Speedwriting* word ending in a letter, to form possessives, to add *s* to a verb: jobs, j-b-s   *jbs*   ; Bill's, b-l-s   *bls*   ; gives, guh-v-s   *gvs*   ; or to write the final *s* of a proper noun: James, j-m-s   *jms*   .

Reading and Writing Exercises

SERIES A

1. ∧ u ∧de l du   ∧ln .
   ∧ lp .

5. ⊂ ⌣c ∧ u
   pln l vzl ∧ ofs .

2. e l hlp u yf e c ,
   ∧ , ∧ jb .

SERIES B

3. ∧ P ⊹ VP v ∧ co
   l se ᔥ n · ⌣c ,

1. ll ⌒e no ⌣n
   ∧ inf arvs .

4. du u v ∧ nu
   blln , ∧ , v l

2. ι l ⌒l · f dpzl ,

3. *u l rsv . fre gfl b eC sv dpzl.*

2. *e l u . cpe v sn.*

4. *i l rel Cc l co.*

3. *e r alC . cpe v bl. n c u l s . Cc.*

5. *hr . Cc l cvr fe n f.*

4. *bl nds l no s v sn.*

SERIES C

1. *e r c Cnys n r co cal.*

5. *i l lv inf dsc.*

Key

SERIES A
1. Are you ready to do some typing?
2. We will help you if we can. It is our job.
3. The president and vice president of our company will see us in a week.
4. Do you have the new bulletin? It is very well written.
5. Which week are you planning to visit the office?

SERIES B
1. Let me know when the information arrives.
2. I will mail a full deposit.
3. You will receive a free gift for each savings deposit.
4. I will return the check to the company.
5. Here is a check to cover the fee in full.

SERIES C
1. We are making changes in our company catalog.
2. We will mail you a copy very soon.
3. We are attaching a copy of the bill. When can you mail us a check?
4. Bob needs to know something very soon.
5. I will leave the information at his desk.

LESSON 3

1. Write *m* for the blended sounds of *m-m* (*mem* and *mum*). Write *m* also for the blended sounds of *m-n* (*men/min, mon, mun*).

remember, re-mem-b-r *rmbr*　　mental, men-t-l *mll*

memory, mem-r-e *mre*　　menu, men-u *mu*

memorize, mem-r-z *mrz*　　mineral, min-r-l *mrl*

memo, mem-o *mo*　　monetary, mon-t-r-e *mlre*

mumps, mum-p-s *mps*　　money, mun-e *me*

2. Write *m* for the word ending *ment*. Write *m* also for the word ending *m-nd*, (*mand, mend, mind*).

settlement, s-t-l-ment *sllm*　　demand, d-mand *dm*

replacement, re-p-l-s-ment *rplsm*　amend, a-mend *am*

*payment, p-a-ment *pam*　　recommend, r-k-mend *rcm*

*agreement, a-guh-r-e-ment *agrem*　remind, re-mind *rm*

*Always write the final root-word vowel when adding word endings.

3. Write a capital *n* for the sound of *ent, nt* (pronounced *ent*).

sent, s-nt *sN*　　entry, nt-r-e *Nre*

wants, w-nt-s *Ns*　　renting, r-nt-ing *rN*

center, s-nt-r *sNr*　　current, k-r-nt *crN*

Use *n* to form contractions.

don't, d-nt *dN*　　couldn't, k-d-nt *cdN*

can't, k-nt *cN*　　doesn't, d-z-nt *dzN*

Practice these additional words:

maximum, m-x-mum *~xm*   central, s-nt-r-l *sNrl*

minimum, min-mum *mm*   assignment, a-s-n-ment *asnm*

minutes, min-t-s *mls*   didn't, d-d-nt *ddN*

agent, a-j-nt *ajN*   different, d-f-r-nt *dfrN*

apparent, a-p-r-nt *aprN*   documents, d-k-ment-s *dcms*

PRINCIPLES SUMMARY

1. Write *m* for the blended sounds of *m-m* (*men* and *mum*): members, mem-b-r-s *mbrs* ; mumps, mum-p-s *mps* . Write *m* also for the blended sounds of *m-n*, (*men/min, mon, mun*): menu, men-u *mu* ; mineral, min-r-l *mrl* ; monetary, mon-t-r-e *mlre* ; money, mun-e *me* .
2. Write *m* for the word ending *ment*: settlement, s-t-l-ment *sllm* . Write *m* also for the word ending *m-nd* (*mand, mend, mind*): demand, d-mand *dm* ; amend, a-mend *am* ; remind, re-mind *rm* .
3. Write a capital *N* for the sound of *ent, nt*: sent, s-nt *sN* ; and for contractions: don't, d-nt *dN* .

Vocabulary Builder. Practice writing these frequently used words:

event, e-v-nt *evN*   country, k-nt-r-e *cNre*

front, f-r-nt *frN*   recent, re-s-nt *rsN*

merchant, m-r-chay-nt *~rCN*   rental, r-nt-l *rNl*

movement, m-v-ment *~vm*   retirement, re-t-r-ment *rlrm*

plant, p-l-nt *plN*   terminals, t-r-min-l-s *lrmls*

pleasant, p-l-z-nt *plzN*   tremendous, t-r-men-d-s *lrmds*

printing, p-r-nt-ing *prN_*   won't, w-nt *N*

Reading and Writing Exercises

SERIES A

1. *[shorthand]*
2. *[shorthand]*
3. *[shorthand]*
4. *[shorthand]*
5. *[shorthand]*

SERIES B

1. *[shorthand]*
2. *[shorthand]*
3. *[shorthand]*
4. *[shorthand]*
5. *[shorthand]*

-1-

-2-

Key

SERIES A

1. Do you have plans for retirement? We have a new policy which pays very well.
2. The agent sent us a memo reminding us to mail our payment.
3. We are paying too much money for the policy. May we look for a new agent?
4. We could file a new claim. We will let you know if we reach a settlement.
5. We are seeing a high demand for the new policy.

SERIES B

1. We recommend using our new checks.
2. We will print new checks for you. Do you want us to mail the checks to you at home?
3. You will have to pay a minimum fee and make a deposit if you want to use our new checks.
4. The president wants a copy sent to each of the board members.
5. The desk clerk will return the deposit to you.

1

MEMO TO: Melvin Carter

I can give you the information you need to make the changes in our sales plan. I[1] have a copy of the new plan which gives full details.

At the current time, our office is keeping a very busy[2] schedule. We are making plans for some big events for the weeks ahead. In case you try to reach me at my office,[3] I will leave the copies you need at the front desk.

Feel free to call me for help in the future if you need it.[4] (80)

2

MEMO TO: Judy Jackson

My memo is to remind you of our plans to hold budget hearings in the near future.[1]

The reason for the hearings is to review new budget items and the money we will need to pay for such[2] entries. We are making a schedule for each office. You will receive a notice assigning you a definite[3] time.

If you have new items or replacements, plan to give a brief summary of each at the hearing. (78)

LESSON 4

1. Write ⟋ for the sound of *ish* or *sh*.

finish, f-n-ish *⟋n⟋*   show, ish-o *⟋o*

machine, m-ish-n *⌒⟋n*   wish, w-ish *⌣⟋*

should, ish-d *⟋d*   issuing, i-ish-u-ing *⟋⟋u*

2. Write a capital *a* for the word beginnings *ad* and *al* (pronounced *add*, *al*, or *all*).

admit, ad-m-t *a⌐⟍*   advice, ad-v-s *avo*

advise, ad-v-z *av₃*   album, al-b-m *ab⌐*

admire, ad-m-r *a⌐⟍*   also, al-s-o *aso*

If a word begins with the letters a-d or a-l but does not incorporate the blended sounds of *ad* or *al* in the same syllable, write the word according to the sound.

adopt, a-d-p-t *adpl*   align, a-l-n *aln*

3. Write *n* for the initial sound of *en* or *in* (pronounced *n*).

anything, en-e-thing *ne*   engine, en-j-n *njn*

indent, in-d-nt *ndN*   engineers, en-j-n-r-s *njnrs*

involve, in-v-l-v *nvlv*   intent, in-t-nt *nlN*

Brief Forms

from *⟋⌐*   letter *L*

manage *⌒⟋*   would *d*

firm *⟋r*   perhaps *Ph*

on, own *o*   market *⌒⟍*

part, port *pl*   your *u*

Brief Form Development.   Use brief forms and abbreviations to build related words. For instance:

Brief Form: *for*

Brief Forms: *can* and *not*

form, for-m	$\int$
inform, in-for-m	$n\int$
formal, for-m-l	$\int l$
formula, for-m-l-a	$\int la$
fortune, for-chay-n	$\int Cn$

cancel, can-s-l	csl
cannot, can-not	cn
Abbreviation: *company*	
accompanying, a-company-ing	aco
accompaniment, a-company-ment	$acom$

Write some *Speedwriting* words according to the rule to avoid possible reading and transcribing problems.

William, w-l-y-m ly mechanical, m-k-n-k-l $\sim cncl$

New Brief Form Development

management	ym
manager	yr
managing	y
marketing	r
letters	Ls

yours	us
wouldn't	dN
report	rpl
depart	dpl
letterhead	Lhd

Abbreviations

Mr. $\sim r$ Ms. $\sim s$

Mrs. $\sim rs$ Miss M

Salutations

Dear Mr. Gray	*d·r gra*	Dear Ms. Miller	*d·ro ·lr*
Dear Mrs. Chase	*d·rs Cs*	Dear Miss Temple	*d M Lpl*
Dear Ed	*d ed*	Dear Sue	*d su*

Complimentary Closes

Sincerely yours	*su*	Very truly yours	*vlu*
Cordially yours	*cu*	Yours truly	*ul*
Sincerely	*s*	Yours very truly	*uvl*
Cordially	*c*	Respectfully yours	*ru*

PRINCIPLES SUMMARY

1. Write *A* for the sound of *ish*, *sh*: show, ish-o *Ao* .
2. Write a capital *a* for the word beginnings *ad* and *al*: advice, ad-v-s *avo* ; also, al-s-o *aso* .
3. Write *n* for the initial sound of *en* or *in*: entire, en-t-r *nlr* .

Vocabulary Builder.   Practice writing these frequently used words:

she, ish-e	*Ae*	indeed, in-d-d	*ndd*
entire, en-t-r	*nlr*	support, s-port	*spl*
sure, ish-r	*Ar*	effort, e-for-t	*efl*
increase, in-k-r-s	*ncrs*	brochure, b-r-ish-r	*brAr*
shown, ish-n	*An*	foreign, for-n	*fn*
cash, k-ish	*cA*	furnish, f-r-n-ish	*frnA*

Reading and Writing Exercises

-1-

-2-

-3-

-4-

mo l M su grn
ι sN. nf l L
L r P v r fr asc
l se. cpe v r
nu r rpl. l
nlg e du n
yl v. rpli, du
aso rm r P e
d v C lc l
no, plns f opn
r nu ofss. /
l l dsd o C
frns e l nd. e d
lc l v u Avs l,
ll e no n
u c r lrp
l r nu plN. ι
sl lru l se u /
r ofs n u
arv.

-5-

d s hrpr Ph u
v n sn r nu
cal. f n l u
lc. fu mls l rd
r f e r alc.
u l se e r so
me nu drs, f
u d lc l rsv.
cpe v r cal sn
r f + rel / l
r ofs. e l rs r
cal l u, me ppl
lc l uz r cal l
sp / hr. Nu
Cz r eze al
sp l. cu

-6-

mo l bl dvdsn
e du n v. pln f

lrn r ppl l rn	l u l s. cpe
r nu ans. Ph	v u nu byl x e
r plN yr + r	nd l rvu //
Cf nynr c hlp	ym pln L.
dzn. pln e cd	Ph e c sv me n
uz f r ntr co.	r fCr y e lc
ll s no l u	L l lc / eC
pln l du, Aso	pl v r byl.

Key

1

MEMO TO: Charles Gray

Our rental buildings need repair. We should paint the walls and replace the floor coverings in each[1] room. We should also replace the washing machines in each unit.

Our leasing agent doesn't want us to raise the[2] rent. Each lease is current. She is hoping to keep the buildings full.

What is Ed's advice? I will ask the agent to[3] give you a call to set a time to show you each building. (70)

2

Dear Mrs. Chase:

We have your letter applying for a job in our firm.

Will you also mail us a letter which[1] gives us information on the typing and filing classes you have taken? We may have an opening in our[2] office soon.

For your information, we are attaching a copy of our company's hiring policies. Let[3] us know when you can visit our firm. We hope to hear from you soon.

Yours truly, (74)

3

Dear Mr. Parker:

I forgot to mail my payment to your firm. I hope you will forgive the delay. Here is a[1] check covering part of the bill. I will pay the entire bill very soon.

Sincerely, (35)

4

MEMO TO: Miss Sue Green

I sent an informal letter to the president of the firm asking to see a copy[1] of the new marketing report. To my knowledge, we do not yet have a reply.

Would you also remind the[2] president we would very much like to know his plans for opening our new offices? It is time to decide[3] on which furnishings we will need. We would like to have your advice too.

Let me know when you can make the trip to our[4] new plant. I shall try to see you at the office when you arrive. (91)

5

Dear Ms. Harper:

Perhaps you have not seen our new catalog. If not, will you take a few minutes to read the form[1] we are attaching? You will see we are showing many new items.

If you would like to receive a copy of[2] the catalog, sign the form and return it to our office. We will rush the catalog to you.

Many people[3] like to use our catalog to shop at home. Won't you choose the easy way to shop too?

                              Cordially yours, (78)

6

MEMO TO: Bill Davidson

We do not have a plan for training our people to run our new machines. Perhaps the[1] plant manager and our chief engineer can help design a plan we could use for the entire company. Let us[2] know what you plan to do.

Also, will you mail us a copy of your new budget? We need to review it at[3] management planning time. Perhaps we can save money in the future if we take time to look at each part of our[4] budget. (81)

LESSON 5

You will not have to change your basic handwriting style for *Speedwriting*. However, it is important to develop writing habits that clearly distinguish one *Speedwriting* word from another.

Take a moment now to review your writing style. Do you omit unnecessary loops, crosses, dots, and initial and final strokes where appropriate? Compare the following examples with the *Speedwriting* words you have written so far.

Streamlining *m* and *w*:
Write *m* and *w* with a swift, smooth sweep of the pen.

m	⌒	me	
w	⌣	way	

Loops and Solid Lines:
Write *l* with a clearly defined loop; write *t* with a solid stem. Your stroke for *t* should be clearly taller (about twice the height) than your *i*. The same is true for *l* and *e*, *nt* and *n*, *chay* and *k*.

l		*t*	
t		*i*	
l		*e*	
nt		*n*	
chay		*k*	

Closed Circles:
It is important to close the circles in *s*, *d*, *p*, *guh*, and *a*.

s		sell	
d		due	
p		pay	
guh		get	
a		aim	

Stems on Tall Letters:
Develop the habit of writing the stem long enough to distinguish *d* from *a*.

d		do	
a		ache	

Writing s, ish, and (ampersand):
Develop a curve in the s to distinguish it clearly from the *ish*.

s	*ʌ*	so	*ʌo*
ish	*ʌ*	show	*ʌo*
ampersand	*Ⴑ*	and	*Ⴑ*

Streamline Letters:
Omit loops and upward strokes for *h, t, b, f, u,* and *i* when these letters occur at the beginning of a *Speedwriting* word. Omit tails at the end of a *Speedwriting* word.

h	*h*	hope	*hp*
t	*l*	take	*lc*
b	*ь*	big	*bq*
f	*ɓ*	fine	*fn*
u	*u*	unit	*unl*
i	*ι*	item	*ιᴖ*

Writing v and u:
The letter *v* ends with a brief tail at the top; *u* ends in a swift downward stroke. Write *v* with a sharp point to distinguish it from *u*.

v	*v*	save	*ʌv*
u	*u*	view	*vu*

Final guh and j:
These end in a swift, solid downward stroke.

guh	*q*	dog	*dq*
j	*1*	judge	*ji*

Final o:
This ends at the top of the circle; *a* ends in a downward stroke.

o	*o*	low	*lo*
a	*a*	say	*ʌa*

1. Write *o* for the sound of *ow* (ou). The sound of *ow* is a special vowel called a *diphthong*. Always write this sound in a *Speedwriting* word.

allow, a-l-ow *alo*   doubt, d-ow-t *dol*

now, n-ow *no*   out, ow-t *ol*

proud, p-r-ow-d *prod*   town, t-ow-n *lon*

2. Write a printed capital *S* (joined) for the word beginnings *cer, cir, ser, sur* (pronounced *sir*).

certain, cer-t-n *Sln*   serve, ser-v *Sv*

survey, sur-v-a *Sva*   certificate, cer-t-f-k-t *Slfcl*

service, ser-v-s *Svo*   sermon, ser-mun *Sm*

circle, cir-k-l *Scl*   surprise, sur-p-r-z *Sprz*

Salutations

Gentlemen *1*   Dear Sir *dS*

Ladies *l*   Dear Sir or Madam *dS*

Ladies and Gentlemen *ly*

Punctuation Symbols

Write *!* to indicate an exclamation mark:

What happy news we have for you! *l hpe nz e v f u !*

Write *=* to indicate a hyphen:

Will you recommend a well-known book? *l u rcm · l = nnbc ×*

Write *=* to indicate a dash:

We do not know the reason—do you? *e du n no r rzn = du u ×*

To indicate solid capitalization, double the curved line underneath the last letter of the *Speedwriting* word.

MONEY MANAGEMENT, mun-e manage-ment *me ym*

To indicate an underlined title, draw a solid line under the *Speedwriting* word.

Newsweek, n-z-w-k *nz̲c̲*

PRINCIPLES SUMMARY

1. Write *O* for the sound of *ow* (ou): allow, a-l-ow *alo* .
2. Write a printed capital *S* (joined) for the word beginnings *cer*, *cir*, *ser*, *sur (sir)*: certain, cer-t-n *Sen* .

Reading and Writing Exercises

(shorthand exercises -1-, -2-, -3-)

· nu aM f hr. ll
e no f u v.
m l gv hr. ul

-4-

dS r u pa hr rM
+ yl v v lll l so
f. Ph u d lc l
o u o h yl cn
s l sv enf
me f don pam,
f so e c hlp u.
e r no ofr. nu
h pam pln
C l alo u l
pls. lo don pam
o u nu h. e
Aso v. byl pln
f hos pams. f
u lc ol. ln f
s no u c scyl

u pams ne a
u s, gv s.
ml v u +
e l so u. eze
pam pln f u
hoshld. cu

-5-

f e r rel cpe
An e bl f u
fr. s s
An l n prM.
n dz prM
cpes r m clr, e
v d me cls n
SC v. aM hu
Svss u Ans.
nn c gl pls
e nd f rprs,
e hp u c ofr s
. An C gvs

-6-

Key

1

Dear Sue:

Can you tell me when you will finish your report on savings certificates? Bill Brown told me you are[1] making a survey. If we can, we would like to use the information in your survey in our own report.

Very[2] truly yours, (42)

2

Gentlemen:

We are hoping to hold a company luncheon in your hotel soon. Can you give us information[1] on your policy for renting luncheon rooms? What services do you offer, and how many people will your rooms[2] hold? Also, what is your minimum rental fee? How much time do you allow for reserving the room?

We hope to[3] make our final plans very soon.

Sincerely yours, (69)

3

Dear Joe:

I have written a letter to Gail Brown telling her we are canceling her policy. We are certain[1] to hear from her the minute she receives the letter. Perhaps we can recommend a new agent for her. Let me[2] know if you have a name to give her.

Yours truly, (49)

4

Dear Sir or Madam:

Are you paying high rent and yet have very little to show for it? Perhaps you would like to[1] own your own home, yet cannot seem to save enough money for the down payment.

If so, we can help you. We are now[2] offering a new home payment plan which will allow you to place a low down payment on your new home. We also[3] have a budget plan for house payments. If you take out a loan from us now, you can schedule your payments any way[4] you wish.

Give us a minute of your time, and we will show you an easy payment plan for your household.

Cordially[5] yours, (101)

5

Gentlemen:

We are returning the copying machine we bought from your firm. Sometimes the machine will not print. When[1] it does print, the copies are not clear.

We have made many calls in search of an agent who services your machines.[2] None can get the parts we need for repairs.

We hope you can offer us a machine which gives better service. Will you[3] let us know what you plan to do?

Sincerely yours, (69)

6

Dear Sir:

Now is the time to visit our shop. We have a new truckload of home furnishings which we are offering[1] at big, big savings to you.

Don't delay! Visit us now and choose from many fine items shown on each floor. Don't forget[2] —visit our shop now and save.

Yours very truly, (50)

LESSON 6

1. To form the past tense of any regular verb, write a hyphen after the *Speedwriting* word (pronounced *duh* or *ed*).

used, u-z-duh	*uz-*	received, re-s-v-duh	*rsv-*
copied, k-p-e-duh	*cpe-*	finished, f-n-ish-duh	*fns-*
helped, h-l-p-duh	*hlp-*	limited, l-m-t-ed	*lmt-*

Writing Numbers. Write figures to indicate cardinal numbers.

someone	*s 1*	12 pairs	*12 prs*
anyone	*ne 1*	two girls	*2 grls*

Abbreviations

north	*N*	west	*W*
south	*S*	corporation	*corp*
east	*E*	enclose, enclosure	*enc*

Abbreviated Word Development

northern	*Nrn*	eastern	*Ern*
*southern	*Srn*	western	*Wrn*

*Note: Word beginnings and endings may be added to brief forms and abbreviations to form derivatives, even though the pronunciation of the derivative may differ from the root word.

Brief Forms

be, but, been, buy, by	*b*	accept	*ac*
during	*du*	after	*af*
necessary	*nes*	appropriate	*apo*
why	*y*	determine	*dt*

PRINCIPLES SUMMARY

1. To form the past tense of any regular verb, write a hyphen after the *Speedwriting* word: used, u-z-duh *uz-* .

Reading and Writing Exercises

-1-

d dvd f u r l l
~ bc E + ac r
fb v pln ~yr ı
l b nes f u l sn
r enc- agrem.
af u rel r agrem
e c dt ~n u
dtes l bgn, ı hp
u l dsd l b·mbr
v r corp. s

-2-

dS f. l~t- L
e l afr ı ~cs
fre vzt l r clys.
b r se. y u ac ı
l n b nes f u l
pa ne f u r ~ +
~ls, du u vzt
e l so u mu +
uz- ~dt clys
~c u ~a b o r
eze pam pln b

-3-

-4-

-5-

u ll s no yf e
c uz / x ru

-6-

dS ι d lc l b · cpe
v u nu bc ho l
ncrs rll sls, af
rd · rsN rvu v
⌐ bc ι blv, l
hlp n · cly crs
n ⌐ C ι v nrl-

bcz clss v bgn ι
nd ⌐ bc no, cd
u rs · cpe l ⌐
h adrs gvn n
⌐ abv Lhd x, ι
v alC-· Cc l
cvr ⌐ prs v ⌐ bc
+ ⌐ l fes, ι l b
egr l v u rpli,
su

Key

1

Dear David:

If you are willing to move back East and accept the job of plant manager, it will be necessary[1] for you to sign the enclosed agreement. After you return the agreement, we can determine when your duties[2] will begin.

I hope you will decide to be a member of our corporation.

Sincerely, (57)

2

Dear Sir:

For a limited time, we will offer one week's free visit to our Cottages by the Sea. If you[1] accept, it will not be necessary for you to pay anything for your room and meals.

During your visit we will[2] show you new and used model cottages which you may buy on our easy payment plan, but don't delay. Why not call[3] now and determine a time for your free week?

We would like to show you how happy life can be at Cottages by[4] the Sea.

Sincerely yours, (84)

3

Dear Sir:

We cash checks for residents of our town. After you have filled out the appropriate forms, you will receive[1] a check-cashing card which allows you to cash checks here at any time. We hope to serve you soon.

Very truly yours,[2] (40)

4

Dear Ed:

Enclosed is a copy of the letter you wanted to see. The letter tells why it will be necessary[1] to increase our mailing fees and also how we determined the increases. After you have read the letter,[2] return it to the appropriate file.

Sincerely, (49)

5

Dear Sir:

Having read your article on selling houses, I would like to ask you for a favor. Would you allow[1] us to reprint your article in our company bulletin?

We are certain what you say is true—the market[2] will get better when we see an increase in loan money. We are telling our agents to be patient, and your[3] article will help.

Will you let us know if we can use it?

Respectfully yours, (74)

6

Dear Sir:

I would like to buy a copy of your new book, *How to Increase Retail Sales*. After reading a recent[1] review of the book, I believe it will help in a college course in which I have enrolled. Because classes have begun,[2] I need the book now. Could you rush a copy to my home address given in the above letter-head?

I have[3] attached a check to cover the price of the book and mailing fees. I will be eager to have your reply.

Sincerely[4] yours, (81)

LESSON 7

RECAP AND REVIEW

You now know enough *Speedwriting* to write most of the words used in business correspondence. Before going on, let's review the principles you've studied so far. No new principles will be introduced in this lesson. Instead, use this opportunity to check your progress.

1. The following words illustrate principles you studied in Lessons 1-6:

view, v-u	*vu*	package, p-k-j	*pcj*
build, b-l-d	*bld*	much, m-chay	*mc*
easy, e-z-e	*eze*	while, w-l	*l*
billing, b-l-ing	*bl*	jobs, j-b-s	*jbs*
billings, b-l-ings	*bl*	Ted's, t-d-s	*lds*
something, s-m-thing	*s*	helps, h-l-p-s	*hlps*
member, mem-b-r	*mbr*	she, ish-e	*Ae*
money, mun-e	*me*	wish, w-ish	*A*
remind, re-mind	*rm*	advice, ad-v-s	*avs*
settlement, s-t-l-ment	*sllm*	also, al-s-o	*aso*
patient, p-ish-nt	*pAn*	certain, cer-t-n	*Sln*
engineers, en-j-n-r-s	*njnrs*	surplus, sur-p-l-s	*Spls*
house, h-ow-s	*hos*	copied, k-p-e-duh	*cpe-*

2. Following are the brief forms you have studied. How quickly can you write the *Speedwriting* brief form for each of these words?

are	of	is
at	very	for
a	too	in
the	not	us
will	his	full
can	it	have
our	well	to
an	we	from
during	firm	your
part	perhaps	own
letter	port	on
market	would	manage
be	after	buy
why	but	determine
by	appropriate	been
accept	necessary	

3. Can you write the brief form derivatives for these words that are developed from some of the above brief forms?

haven't	yours	cancel
welfare	manager	formal
report	forgotten	cannot
forgive	informing	letters

4. The following words represent the abbreviations you have studied. How quickly can you read them?

Reading and Writing Exercises

-1-

-2-

-3-

bs- o · old ～ r
Sva ～ d b r VP,
ι hp u l fgv r
dla ᴨ gl~ r ιnf
ι u, e cd ᴨ gl
r b r ι~ u ～N-
r bcz v r cpe
～sn, r P v r fr
sN r ～sn ol
f rprs r s ～
～ c e rsv- u L,
e v · co plse
～ C dz ᴨ alo s
ι lc fl ι～s ol
v r ofs, cu

no l crss u
～ l lc, r enc-
cal sd b v hlp,
u ～ a b Sln r
scls u lrn hr l
b apo f ne ofs,
y u Cʒ r ～dcl
or nyᴨr flds u
lrn l Sv u l,
du fl fre l asc
s f Avs r ne
ι～, e r hpe l
b · pl v u flr,
su

drCrd no , r
ι～ l pln r
s ～ r sl, me
rll ～yrs hld
lry sls du dfrN

d fl e r gld l
rpl u v b ac-f
clss bgn ᴨ r fl,
e rcm u pln

ᒪ᠆ᛋ v r yr. y
dM e lu s ‿
nu + dl . ᒪ f
ı bq ‿r evN.
e c lrn r nlr
sp sMr nl .
‿yr sd c sl,
ı d lc l se r
sl rn f . f ‿c.
Ph e cd cp r sps
opn af rglr clz,
ᒪ᠆s, y u agre
ı l lc l ‿
‿rCMs + ll u
no ‿l , dsd‿,
ul

cpe v . nu pln
ofr‿ b . sv + ln
co n lon. af rd
r brsr ı fll Sln
u d ‿M l se ı.
Ph e cd uz r
pam pln ofr‿,
v crs ı no e l
nd ‿C ınf l
dl yf r pln, apo
f r co. l u ll
‿e no yf u lc
r pln, ı l b
gld l sl . ᒪ᠆ f
r ‿yr + s l lc.
vlu

-6-

d hord alC‿, .

Key

Brief Forms

Brief Form Development

Abbreviations

company	corporation	president
enclose, enclosure	and	vice president
information	return	east
west	north	south
Mr.	Mrs.	Miss
Ms.	catalog	

1

Gentlemen:

  We are happy you have decided to buy your new company cars from us.

  Why don't you visit us[1] sometime during the week and determine which models you wish to buy? We have many cars which would be appropriate[2] for your corporation.

  Our service people are very well trained and will keep your cars in top shape. At our firm,[3] we take pride in our service, and we want you to be happy. We are ready to help in any way we can.[4]

Sincerely, (81)

2

Dear Sir:

Perhaps you have forgotten your payment is due. Would you take a minute to mail us a check?

We have been[1] patient, but we do not know if you have received our letters reminding you to make your payment on time. Won't you[2] call us? It is not necessary to pay your bill in full. If you cannot manage to pay the entire bill, we[3] will accept part of it.

If the current plan is too much for your budget, why not visit our loan office? Our agent[4] may be of help to you.

Yours very truly, (89)

3

Dear Ed:

Enclosed is the information you wanted. It is a report based on an old market survey made by[1] our vice president. I hope you will forgive the delay in getting the information to you. We could not get[2] it by the time you wanted it because of our copy machine. The president of our firm sent the machine out[3] for repairs the same week we received your letter. We have a company policy which does not allow us to[4] take file items out of the office.

Cordially yours, (89)

4

Dear Jill:

We are glad to report you have been accepted for classes beginning in the fall. We recommend you[1] plan now what courses you wish to take. The enclosed catalog should be of help.

You may be certain the skills you learn[2] here will be appropriate for any office. If you choose the medical or engineering fields, your training[3] will serve you well.

Do feel free to ask us for advice at any time. We are happy to be a part of your[4] future.

Sincerely yours, (84)

5

Dear Richard:

Now is the time to plan our summer sale. Many retail managers hold large sales during different[1] times of the year. Why don't we try something new and determine a time for one big summer event? We can turn the[2] entire shopping center into a major sidewalk sale.

I would like to see the sale run for a full week. Perhaps[3] we could keep the shops open after regular closing times.

If you agree, I will talk to the merchants and let[4] you know what is decided.

Yours truly, (87)

6

Dear Howard:

Attached is a copy of a new plan offered by a savings and loan company in town. After[1] reading the brochure, I felt certain you would want to see it. Perhaps we could use the payment plan offered.

Of course,[2] I know we will need much information to determine if the plan is appropriate for our company. Will[3] you let me know if you like the plan? I will be glad to set a time for the manager and us to talk.

Very[4] truly yours, (82)

Cplr 2 *

WHAT WILL SPEEDWRITING DO FOR ME?

Now that you are studying *Speedwriting*, you are developing a skill you can be proud of. Your new skill will do much toward bringing you success in your career.

Speedwriting will give you an advantage in the marketplace. Why? *Speedwriting gives you an added skill and makes you a more versatile employee.* Your employer will also know that you had the ambition and ability to learn this skill.

Here are some facts about *Speedwriting* and what it can do for you:

Speedwriting enables you to begin at higher levels in the business world, which in turn leads to advancement in other areas. The future of office work is rapidly changing to adjust to the needs and ambitions of today's workers. You will find that *Speedwriting* is helpful at any level—either for recording dictation or

*Chapter Two

giving dictation. Your *Speedwriting* can help you get a good job. Advancement from there will depend on your ambition, career goals, and performance.

You can use Speedwriting in many ways at any job level. Reporters find *Speedwriting* helpful in taking notes for a news story. Executives may make notes in *Speedwriting* while listening to a presentation, talking on the phone, or sitting in a meeting. Anyone who does research—administrative assistant, student, teacher, or writer—will find *Speedwriting* invaluable in recording notes. Using *Speedwriting* saves time and reduces fatigue.

You can learn Speedwriting quickly. Speedwriting is an alphabetic system of writing that can be learned quickly and easily. With more experience on the job, your speed and accuracy will continue to improve.

LESSON 8

1. Write   *L*   for the sound of *ith* or *th*.

them, ith-m   *L*

then, ith-n   *Ln*

growth, guh-r-ith   *grl*

health, h-l-ith   *hll*

methods, m-ith-d-s   *Lds*

although, al-ith-o   *Alo*

2. Write   *l*   for the word ending *ly* or *ily* (pronounced *lee* or *uh-lee*).

family, f-m-ly   *fl*

yearly, y-r-ly   *yrl*

certainly, cer-t-n-ly   *Stnl*

easily, e-z-ly   *ezl*

recently, re-s-nt-ly   *rsNl*

rapidly, r-p-d-ly   *rpdl*

3. Write a capital   *D*   for the word beginning *dis*.

discuss, dis-k-s   *Dcs*

display, dis-p-l-a   *Dpla*

dismay, dis-m-a   *Da*

disturb, dis-t-r-b   *Dtrb*

dislike, dis-l-k   *Dlc*

distant, dis-t-nt   *DtN*

4. Write a capital   *M*   for the word beginning *mis*.

mistake, mis-t-k   *Mtc*

mislead, mis-l-d   *Mld*

misplaced, mis-p-l-s-duh   *Mpls-*

mislay, mis-l-a   *Mla*

misfit, mis-f-t   *Mfl*

misgivings, mis-guh-v-ings   *Mgv*

Word beginnings, word endings, and sound blends that can also be individual words may be used to express those words.

add   *a*

all   *a*

missing   *M*

*men   *m*

*Remember that *man* is written   *m* .

Practice writing these additional words:

discover, dis-k-v-r	*Dcvr*	either, e-ith-r	*elr*
evidently, e-v-d-nt-ly	*evdNl*	these, ith-z	*lz*
really, r-l-ly	*rll*	this, ith-s	*ls*
nearly, n-r-ly	*nrl*	there, their, ith-r	*lr*
gladly, guh-l-d-ly	*gldl*	misprint, mis-p-r-nt	*MprN*

Brief Form Development.   Use the principles you've learned in this lesson to develop new *Speedwriting* words from brief forms.

necessarily	*nesl*	reportedly	*rpt-l*
appropriately	*apol*	willingly	*ll*
partly	*pll*	firmly	*frl*

Your Business Vocabulary	When you begin your career, you will learn many words that are commonly used in business offices. Some you may already know. Others will become familiar as you use them. The following words will appear in the reading and writing exercises in this lesson. Make these words part of your business vocabulary.

marketing	⌒ᴨ	Those activities involved in getting a product from the producer to the consumer, such as advertising, promoting, and selling.
yearly report	*yrl rpt*	A summation of the activities of a department, division, or entire corporation over a 12-month period.

PRINCIPLES SUMMARY

1. Write   _ℓ_   for the sound of _ith_ or _th_: them, ith-m   _↳_   ;
   growth, guh-r-ith   _grℓ_ .
2. Write   _ℓ_   for the word ending _ly_ (lee) or _ily_ (uh-lee): family,
   f-m-ly   _fmℓ_ .
3. Write a capital   _𝒟_   for the word beginning _dis_: discuss,
   dis-k-s   _𝒟cs_ .
4. Write a capital   _m_   for the word beginning _mis_: mistake,
   mis-t-k   _mtc_ .
5. Word beginnings, word endings, and sound blends that can also be
   individual words may be used to express those words.

Reading and Writing Exercises

-1-

(shorthand outlines)

-2-

(shorthand outlines)

-3-

(shorthand outlines)

-4-

-5-

pln_ l sl hu gls	d r bron e r hpe
f sls ls yr +	l sa e r enc .
nd as l hlp	Cc f r me e o u .
s acr L . Ph	e dd ndd Dcvr
u cd gv s rzlls	. Mlc n u hll bl
v u rsN r	+ r gld l rel u
rSC n C u	me . e d lc u
asc- dlrs f lr	l ac r enc- gfl .
vus o fCr sls .	Slfcl f . fre vzl
/ a b nes l	l r hll . e hp
dl . nu plse l	l hr f u sn .
b uz-n r co . y	n c u lrvl
so u rpl d Slnl	plns b Sln l
b v hlp .	gv s . cl . su

Key

1

MEMO TO: Bob Smith

It is nearly time for our family camp to begin. We have not heard from all the families.[1] Will you call and remind them to fill out their health forms? The forms can be mailed to us. We really need the forms before[2] camp opens. (43)

2

MEMO TO: All Company Managers

Attached are the names of missing files. Apparently the files have been[1] misplaced. Would each of you look through your papers to see if the missing files could have been mislaid on your desk?

Many of[2] our folders are old and have misleading titles. Thus, mistakes can easily be made. (55)

3

Dear Mrs. Wilson:

I want to tell you how much I like the new health food displays you have in your pharmacy. It[1] is encouraging to see the growth in health foods in this city. I thought you would like to see the enclosed article[2] which discusses some reasons we are seeing such a rapid change in the health food market. Perhaps it will[3] encourage you to keep adding to your display.

Sincerely, (70)

4

Dear Sir:

Recently I bought two lovely chairs from your company. Although the chairs have been used for a floor display,[1] neither showed any damage at the time. When the chairs arrived at my home, I felt very disturbed. To my dismay,[2] I discovered a rather large rip in the fabric. Either I did not see the rip when I bought the chairs, or it[3] happened during the trip to my house. In either case, the chairs will have to be returned.

Sincerely, (77)

5

MEMO TO: All Marketing Heads

In your yearly report, will you discuss some new methods of marketing our new[1] engines? We are planning to set high goals for sales this year and need ways to help us achieve them. Perhaps you could give[2] us the results of your recent market research in which you asked dealers for their views on future sales. It may be[3] necessary to determine a new policy to be used in our company. If so, your report would[4] certainly be of help. (84)

6

Dear Mr. Brown:

We are happy to say we are enclosing a check for the money we owe you. We did indeed[1] discover a mistake in your hotel bill and are glad to return your money. We would like you to accept the[2] enclosed gift certificate for a free visit to our hotel. We hope to hear from you soon. When making your[3] travel plans, be certain to give us a call.

Sincerely yours, (70)

LESSON 9

1. Retain beginning or ending vowels when building compound words. When you combine two words to make one word, you are building a compound word. If one of these words begins or ends in a vowel, keep the vowel in the *Speedwriting* word: payroll = pay + roll *parl* .

headache, h-d + a-k *hdac*   teenage, t-n + a-j *lnaj*

seaside, s-e + s-d *sesd*   highway, h-i + w-a *hia*

2. Retain the initial and final root-word vowel when adding prefixes and suffixes. When a prefix contains a long vowel followed by a root-word vowel, omit the prefix vowel.

disappear, dis-a-p-r *Dapr*   misuse, mis-u-z *Muz*

payment, p-a-ment *pam*   disallow, dis-a-l-ow *Dalo*

reapply, re-a-p-l-i *rapli*   readmit, re-ad-m-t *rad*

3. Write ordinal numbers as follows:

42nd *42 d*   53rd *53 d*

85th *85 l*

Abbreviations

credit *Cr*   number *No*

total *lol*   percent *%*

amount *a l*   attention *all*

Brief Forms

as, was	*ʒ*	great, grate	*gr*
hospital	*hsp*	were, with	*⌣*
general	*jn*	that	*la*
arrange	*ar*		

Brief Form Development. Use your new brief forms to develop other *Speed-writing* words.

within	*⌣n*	generally	*jnl*
greatly	*grl*	without	*⌣ol*
arrangements	*arms*		

Your Business Vocabulary	reassess *rass*	To re-evaluate, or to determine a new value of property as a basis for taxation.
	minimum payment *mm pam*	The minimum amount of money required at specific dates on a credit purchase.

PRINCIPLES SUMMARY

1. Retain beginning and ending vowels when building compound words: payroll = pay + roll *parl* .
2. Retain the initial and final root-word vowel when adding prefixes and suffixes: reopen, re-o-p-n *ropn* ; payment, p-a-ment *pam* .
3. Write ordinal numbers as follows: 42nd, *42 d* 53rd, *53d* 85th, *85 l* .

Reading and Writing Exercises

SERIES A	SERIES B

(handwritten shorthand exercises, numbered 1–5 in each series)

SERIES C

1. Alo e v no jbs opn, ls h e Avz u l raplc n r nu hsp opns, e l c arms l Dcs u L, la h.

f lr jbs e rasn h l nu dles, c blv la e l rasn · gr No ls yr.

2. e l A. lol v 20 nu m l r parl, e l nd la me l hlp bld r nu hca.

3. z · rlr r co dz n la of ppl, rlr ln rls m + m

4. n jn r co ofrs blr bnfls ln ne lry fr n lon, c v b l ls corp f 11 yrs no + c no la ls, lru.

5. e l b hpe l rAl u n r clss, u l rsv f cr f r crss u lc erlr.

-1-

mo l A clvs
yrs z hd v ls
corp i z v hpe
l lrn A . gr jb
u r A du . No v
ppl v rtn l sa
la h clvs gvn
v fn all . ol .
dol A v u dzrv
cr f u pl n gv ls
co . gr n .

-2-

dS pa bls c m
hdac af hdac .
la , y e r ofr .
nu cr pln .
ls pln u pa i lol
a l . ln e uz la
a l l pa A v r
bls u o , y u bls

r lc l C cs
f u byl ll s
ar . eze pln f u .
n . yr u bls l
b pd + u hdac
l b gn . su

-3-

y e rsv- u L nf
s la r sesd cy l
b rass- o r 14l .
r L N o l sa
la r vlu v ls
hos ncrs- grl=
b 25 %= n r nu
h a z bll , e r
sre b u v d .
Mlc , r h a
C rns nr r
bC hos , n nu .
y ne r , old +

-4-

-5-

b m̄ ` ι hp u   lgl dcms r b̄
c Āvz ⌣e o ho   cpl n r lgl ofs.
l gl . cpe ` ul   ⌣n u nd . d⌣

_____   . fl̲ clrc l b gld
-6-   l gl / f u ` ls
d m hnre alc- r   ⌣ld ṡd rds
⌢ cpes u nd.   fl̲ mlcs + Aso
bcz r fls v grn   alo u l gl inf
so lry + r uz-   rpdl ` e hp /
b so me ppl /   Svo u l f⌢ no
; nes l uz . dfrm o ` c
fl̲ ⌣ld. crml a

Key

SERIES A

1. We will admit you to the hospital as soon as we can arrange it.
2. We are increasing the amount of your credit. The new total of your loan is shown below.
3. We are offering this chair at 20 percent less than the regular price.
4. Did you know that a great number of teenage drivers are insured with our firm?
5. In general, the training class went well even though there was a great deal of disagreement.

SERIES B

1. The total amount was due by the 12th. Your attention to this matter would be a great help.
2. There were as many men as there were women in the total number of people on the payroll.
3. You will receive your new credit card without delay.
4. As soon as the matter was brought to my attention, I asked that new arrangements be made.
5. We were happy to learn that sales are generally doing very well in the East.

SERIES C

1. Although we have no jobs open at this time, we advise you to reapply when the new hospital opens. We will make arrangements to discuss your letter at that time.
2. We will add a total of 20 new men to the payroll. We will need that many to help build the new highway.
3. As a rule, our company does not lay off people. Rather than release men and women from their jobs, we reassign them to new duties. I believe that we will reassign a great number this year.
4. In general, our company offers better benefits than any large firm in town. I have been with this corporation for 11 years now, and I know that this is true.
5. We will be happy to readmit you in our classes. You will receive full credit for the courses you took earlier.

1

MEMO TO: All Claims Managers

As head of this corporation, I was very happy to learn what a great job[1] you are all doing. A number of people have written to say that their claims were given very fine attention.[2] Without a doubt, all of you deserve credit for your part in giving this company a great name. (57)

2

Dear Sir:

Paying bills can mean headache after headache. That is why we are offering a new credit plan. With this[1] plan, you pay one total amount. Then we use that amount to pay all of the bills you owe.

If your bills are taking[2] too much cash from your budget, let us arrange an easy plan for you. Within a year, your bills will be paid and your[3] headache will be gone.

Sincerely yours, (66)

3

Gentlemen:

We received your letter informing us that our seaside cottage will be reassessed on the 14th.[1] The letter went on to say that the value of this house increased greatly—by 25 percent—when the[2] new highway was built.

We are sorry, but you have made a mistake. The highway which runs near our beach house is not new.[3] If anything, it is old and badly in need of repair. The highway was built a few years after we bought our[4] beach house. To our knowledge, the road was never repaired after it was built.

We hope that your office will take a better[5] look at that highway. If our house is reassessed, we would like to see appropriate repairs made on the road.[6]

Very truly yours, (124)

4

Dear Mr. Miller:

We did check to see if you will receive your cars on schedule. We called the trucking firm to[1] determine when the cars would arrive in New Haven, and the manager said the cars left early this morning. Although[2] some of the trucks are being delayed, yours should arrive on time this week. The manager assured us you will get a[3] call if there is anything new to report. We are happy to have been of help.

Very truly yours, (78)

5

Dear Lou:

I received a letter from the Brown and Ames trucking firm asking for a copy of our yearly agreement.[1] I have looked in all of the file cabinets, but I have not seen the agreement. Could it have been misplaced? There are[2] two files which should have a copy of the agreement. Each copy seems to be missing. I hope you can advise[3] me on how to get a copy.

Yours truly, (68)

6

Dear Miss Henry:

Attached are the copies you need. Because our files have grown so large and are used by so many[1] people, it is necessary to use a different filing method. Currently, all legal documents are[2] being kept in our legal office. When you need an item, a filing clerk will be glad to get it for you. This[3] method should reduce filing mistakes and also allow you to get information rapidly. We hope it serves you[4] well from now on.

Cordially, (85)

LESSON 10

1. Write a capital *P* (disjoined from other letters) for the word beginnings *per* and *pur*.

person, per-s-n *Psn*

per *P*

personnel, per-s-n-l *Psnl*

purchase, pur-chay-s *PCs*

permit, per-m-t *PΛ*

purpose, pur-p-s *Pps*

Write a capital *P* also for the word beginnings *pre*, *pro*, and *pro (prah)*.

preview, pre-v-u *Pvu*

produce, pro-d-s *Pds*

prefer, pre-f-r *Pfr*

proposal, pro-p-z-l *Ppzl*

prevent, pre-v-nt *PvN*

problem, prah-b-l-m *Pbl*

provide, pro-v-d *Pvd*

proper, prah-p-r *Ppr*

2. Write *q* for the word ending *gram*.

program, pro-gram *Pq*

telegram, t-l-gram *Uq*

Your Business Vocabulary		
proposal *Ppzl*		A plan of action, usually presented in writing.
out-patients *ot = psNs*		Patients receiving treatment at a hospital without being admitted for overnight stays.
building permit *bld PΛ*		A legal document authorizing an organization or individual to begin construction of a building.

PRINCIPLES SUMMARY

1. Write a disjoined capital P for the word beginnings *per*, *pur*, *pre*, *pro*, and *pro (prah)*: person, per-s-n *Psn* ; prepare, pre-p-r *Ppr* ; produce, pro-d-s *Pds* ; problem, prah-b-l-m *Pbl* .

2. Write q *Pq* for the word ending *gram:* program, pro-gram .

Reading and Writing Exercises

-1-

[shorthand]

-2-

[shorthand]

-3-

-4-

-5-

-6-

z l z r psNs, l   se ls dr fnll
dl. nd f ls unl.   rsv r all r nds.
Sva z rd lcl   z mbrs v r hsp
rzdNs. v r lol   brd u l no dol s
Sva- 80% n   l rsv. f rpl o
fvr v ls unl. l   ls nu pln. vlu
fl hpe + prod l

Key

1

MEMO TO: Manager of Purchasing

What is our current policy on purchasing office supplies? Which[1] companies have allowed us credit? Do we need a credit card to make a purchase, or can we provide our office[2] number?

Also, what is the name of the person who assigns credit cards? I hope you can provide me with this[3] information. It will be a great help to learn the proper purchasing methods. (74)

2

MEMO TO: All Personnel

Enclosed is a copy of the new proposal. As you can see, it provides many[1] needed changes. With this plan, each person will receive death benefits without paying for the increased coverage.[2] Personally, I believe this plan is what we have needed for many years. I see no problems with it at all.[3]

We are also revising our policy for training new personnel. Susan Jones is preparing a memo[4] which will provide all the details. I believe that these new policies will solve many problems in the company.[5] (100)

3

MEMO TO: Mr. Robert Temple

In my proposal for the new hospital, I plan to provide a design[1] for the building as well as general information needed to get a building permit. Why don't you prepare[2] a news release giving details of the proposal? Residents of this city should know that our hospital will[3] offer many new programs which will benefit out-patients as well as in-patients.

We have received much attention[4] from the newspaper recently due to increased hospital fees. This would seem to be an appropriate time[5] to let people know our plans to increase services. (109)

4

MEMO TO: James Brown

What is your advice on the attached health care program? With this program, the company would[1] provide a place, as well as a time, for running or swimming. It was proposed that we use the south side of the building[2] for this purpose. This plan was proposed by the president, who believes that people should be allowed to get proper[3] health care while on their jobs. Do you see any problems with such an arrangement? (74)

5

Gentlemen:

The purpose of this letter is to determine why we have not received the cards we purchased from your[1] company. When we decided to buy the cards, you were certain that we would have them ahead of time. As I[2] recall, we asked that the cards be rushed. Your agent assured us that there would be no problem during this time of the[3] year. We have been patient, but three weeks have gone by and we have not received the cards.

We hope that it will not be[4] necessary to cancel, but after this week we will not accept the cards. From now on, it would be appropriate[5] for you to inform us of delays by telegram.

Yours truly, (110)

6

Gentlemen:

As the head of this hospital, I was happy to hear that a new children's unit is being proposed.[1] As part of this proposal, parents will be allowed to remain here in the hospital with their children.[2] Generally, such an arrangement provides a great benefit to the parents as well as the patients.

To determine[3] a need for this unit, a survey was made with local residents. Of the total surveyed, 80 percent were[4] in favor of this unit. I feel happy and proud to see this matter finally receiving the attention[5] it needs. As members of the hospital board, you will no doubt wish to receive a full report on this new plan.[6]

Very truly yours, (124)

LESSON 11

1. Write *y* for the sound of *oi* (oy). Always write this sound in a *Speedwriting* word.

boy, b-oi	*by*	loyal, l-oi-l	*lyl*
choice, chay-oi-s	*Cys*	voice, v-oi-s	*vys*
join, j-oi-n	*jyn*	annoy, a-n-oi	*any*

Write the months of the year this way:

January	*Ja*	July	*Jl*
February	*Fb*	August	*Ag*
March	*Mr*	September	*Sp*
April	*Ap*	October	*Oc*
May	*Ma*	November	*Nv*
June	*Jn*	December	*Dc*

Abbreviations

department	*dpt*	insurance	*ins*
envelope	*env*	regard	*re*
invoice	*inv*		

Brief Forms

between *bln*

ship *A*

situate *sil*

those *loz*

operate *op*

point *py*

participate *pp*

property *prp*

refer *rf*

respond, response *rsp*

suggest *sug*

Brief Form Development

leadership *ldrs*

operator *opr*

appointment *apym*

situated *sil-*

shipment *Am*

disappoint *Dapy*

PRINCIPLES SUMMARY

1. Write *y* for the sound of *oi* (oy): boy, b-oi *by* .

Vocabulary Builder. Practice writing these frequently used words:

enjoyed, en-j-oi-duh *njy-*

joining, j-oi-n-ing *jyn_*

oil, oi-l *yl*

avoid, a-v-oi-d *avyd*

choice, chay-oi-s *Cys*

boys, b-oi-s *bys*

membership,
    mem-b-r-ship *mbrA*

cooperate, k-operate *cop*

Reading and Writing Exercises

SERIES A

1. *r nu ofss l b sut- o ⌐ prp bln r ⌐m plN + ⌐ old ofs bld.*

2. *r plN l n op bln Ja 28 + Fb 15. l l uz loz ⌐cs l sut frns n ⌐ nu bld. A v r ppl l pp n ⌐ ⌐v.*

3. *du loz ⌐cs e sug la A sms b rf- l r ⌐m plN. A invs sd b rf- l r s dpl.*

4. *n re l u rsN mo r ⌐v l b cvr- b ins. cpe v r plse, enc-n ⌐ alC- env.*

5. *c u sug Cnys n ls scgl. ⌐n ⌐a l v u rsp l ly plns.*

SERIES B

1. *nsr lnay drvrs c b. gr hdac. ndd s ⌐ prNs v cl- ⌐ hu a rbre. f u r pq l ⌐C l nsr u lnay drvrs ll jn lf. hlp. jn lf c nsr u lnayr f 10% ls ln ne lry co n lon.*

2. *[shorthand outline]*

3. *[shorthand outline]*

4. *[shorthand outline]*

5. *[shorthand outline]*

-1-

j n u L v Ap 13 u
rf- L · dla n r Ja
sm v ofs splis,
e r sre f ne Pblns
cz- b r dla b r cpe
v r inv sos la u
splis ⌣ s- z sn
z pam z rsv-.
a e sug ls ld
f gl u sm v envs
o h , u c avyd
dla b l u Cc b
Ma 30, u envs l
b s- o Jn z or r
flo c, yf u flo
ls pln f fCr PCss
e c Pvd u blr
Svs, su

-2-

d jsn u rsN apym

z VP z gr nz, co
Stnl d· z Cys,
z hd v r s dpl u
Pvd- me yrs v lyl
Svs, , rasr l
se r co rsp b gv
u Ppr cr, u ldrs
A dpls l no op
efsNl, i hp u l
cl o e l hlp n
ne a i c, z sn
z u v s fre l
y dN e gl lglr f
lnC, vlu

-3-

dS dd u no la u
a b pa bln 15 +
20% l c f u ins,
dd u Aso no la
loz plses a n

cvr ⌐ crN vlu
v u h⌐ + Psnl
prp.x., no ⌐ c h⌐
l ⌐c Sln la u
bnfls r Q la u sd
v, bln Mr 15 + Qp1
r aʃN l cl o u, y
n ⌐c ⌐, . py l v
u plses rde f rvu.
cu

-4-

mo l VP folr n
re l u mo v Sp 5
⌐ prN ⌐Ans l b
sil- n r plN b ⌐
bgn v Dc, z u no
e ⌐N- l v h⌐ rde
erl n Qc b cd n
ar l v h⌐ A-⌐ la
h⌐, e v asc-. lol

v 30 ⌐An oprs l
pp n . lrn Pq du
Nv b e v n rsv-
rsps f Q v h⌐,
Ph e sd pln l hr
mu ppl l op⌐ ⌐Ans.
l du u suq.

-5-

mo l frd gra ⌐ c
no gv u r mu plse
f nsr ⌐Ans A- b
lrc, l u nf⌐ Q pp-
dlrs la bgn Jl e
l n rpls ⌐Ans
dy- o ⌐ dlrs prp.
yf ⌐ dlrs A l Dcs
ls ⌐dr rf h⌐ l ⌐
chrs dpl, e asc
la ne dy b An o
⌐ lnv ⌐ py v

arvl, e d lc ~
dlrs l b Uld v ~
Cnys no. ~n. fu
~cs Ls l b ~l-
gv f dlls v ~ nu
plse.

-6-

mo l ~yr v bys ~r
e l ofr sv v bln
20 + 30 % o a bc =l=
scl nds = cll z l z
spls. a cll sd b
~rc- don 20%. a

scl spls l b Dpla-
bln ~ bys + grls dpls,
e l ac pam n ~f
v c+ cr crds + Psnl
Ccs. loz Psns +l
c+ parl Ccs sd b
sM l ~ cr ofs. a
Psnl Ccs sd b sn
b ~ dpl ~yr, e
sug u clrcs rm a
sprs la cll ch~s
~a b rel- ~n 1
~c flo ~ PCs.

Key

SERIES A

1. Our new offices will be situated on the property between our main plant and the old office building.
2. Our plant will not operate between January 28 and February 15. We will use those weeks to situate furnishings in the new building. All of our people will participate in the move.
3. During those weeks, we suggest that all shipments be referred to our main plant. All invoices should be referred to our shipping department.
4. In regard to your recent memo, our move will be covered by insurance. A copy of our policy is enclosed in the attached envelope.
5. Can you suggest changes in this schedule? When may I have your response to these plans?

SERIES B

1. Insuring teenage drivers can be a great headache. Indeed, some parents have called it highway robbery. If you are paying too much to insure your teenage drivers, let GENERAL LIFE help. GENERAL LIFE can insure your teenager for 10 percent less than any large company in town.
2. Here is great news for the head of the family. Our health benefits now pay as much as 90 percent of the total hospital bill. When can we arrange to show you this policy?
3. Attention Policyholders: We are now offering the new dental coverage you have been asking for. You, as well as your family, will benefit greatly from this policy.
4. In response to the increased need, we are opening a central claims department to serve the entire company. Beginning January 2, all claims should be referred to the central claims department. This change will provide an efficient means of processing all claims.
5. My files show that it is now time to review your homeowner's insurance policy. May we get together soon? I will call this week for an appointment.

1

Gentlemen:

In your letter of April 13, you referred to a delay in our January shipment of[1] office supplies. We are sorry for any problems caused by the delay, but our copy of the invoice shows that[2] your supplies were shipped as soon as payment was received. May we suggest this method for getting your shipment of[3] envelopes on time? You can avoid delay by mailing your check by May 30. Your envelopes will be shipped on[4] June 7 or the following week.

If you follow this plan for future purchases, we can provide you with better[5] service.

Sincerely yours, (104)

2

Dear Jason:

Your recent appointment as vice president was great news. The company certainly made a wise choice.[1] As head of the shipping department, you provided many years of loyal service. It is reassuring to[2] see the company respond by giving you proper credit.

With your leadership, all departments will now operate[3] efficiently. I hope you will call on me to help in any way I can. As soon as you have some free time,[4] why don't we get together for lunch?

Very truly yours, (90)

3

Dear Sir:

Did you know that you may be paying between 15 and 20 percent too much for your insurance? Did[1] you also know that those policies may not cover the current value of your home and personal property?[2]

Now is the time to make certain that your benefits are all that you should have. Between March 15 and April 1,[3] our agent will call on you. Why not make it a point to have your policies ready for review?

Cordially yours,[4] (80)

4

MEMO TO: Vice President Fowler

In regard to your memo of September 5, the printing machines will be[1] situated in our plant by the beginning of December. As you know, we wanted to have them ready[2] early in October but could not arrange to have them shipped at that time. We have asked a total of 30 machine[3] operators to participate in a training program during November, but we have not received responses[4] from all of them.

Perhaps we should plan to hire new people to operate the machines. What do you suggest?[5] (100)

5

MEMO TO: Fred Gray

I can now give you our new policy for insuring machines shipped by truck. Will you inform[1] all participating dealers that beginning July 1 we will not replace machines damaged on the dealer's[2] property? If the dealers wish to discuss this matter, refer them to the claims department.

We ask that any[3] damage be shown on the invoice at the point of arrival.

We would like the dealers to be told of the changes[4] now. Within a few weeks, letters will be mailed giving full details of the new policy. (96)

6

MEMO TO: Manager of Boy's Wear

We will offer savings of between 20 and 30 percent on all[1] back-to-school needs—clothing, as well as supplies. All clothing should be marked down 20 percent. All school supplies will be[2] displayed between the boy's and girl's departments.

We will accept payment in the form of cash, credit cards, and personal[3] checks. Those persons wishing to cash payroll checks should be sent to the credit office. All personal checks should be[4] seen by the department manager.

We suggest your clerks remind all shoppers that clothing items may be returned[5] within one week following the purchase. (107)

LESSON 12

1. For words ending in a long vowel + *t* (*ate, ete, ite, ote, ute/oot*), omit the *t* and write the vowel.

rate, r-ate *ra*

right, write, r-ite *ru*

late, l-ate *la*

might, m-ite *~u*

greet, guh-r-ete *gre*

wrote, r-ote *ro*

cheat, chay-ete *Ce*

boat, b-ote *bo*

cute, k-ute *cu*

suit, s-oot *su*

Write these additional words that are used in the reading and writing exercises in this lesson.

locate, l-k-ate *lca*

delighted, d-l-ite-ed *dli-*

hesitate, h-z-t-ate *hzla*

white, w-ite *~u*

receipt, re-s-ete *rse*

fight, f-ite *fu*

defeated, d-f-ete-ed *dfe-*

vote, v-ote *vo*

invite, in-v-ite *nvu*

promoted, pro-m-ote-ed *P~o-*

Reviewing Proper Names.   You have already learned how to write proper names. As a brief review exercise, read and write the following names. Each name is written according to the principles you have learned.

Janet, j-n-t *jnl*

William, w-l-y-m *ly~*

Pamela, p-m-l-a *p~la*

David, d-v-d *dvd*

Elizabeth, e-l-z-b-ith *elzbl*

Ronald, r-n-l-d *rnld*

Claire, k-l-r *clr*

Martin, m-r-t-n *~rln*

Shelley, ish-l-e *sle*

Jim, j-m *j~*

PRINCIPLES SUMMARY

1. For words ending in a long vowel + *t*, omit the *t* and write the vowel: rate, r-ate *ra* .

Reading and Writing Exercises

-1-

[shorthand text]

-2-

[shorthand text]

-3-

-4-

yr l b hpe l pln
· re b · s

c · Ph ⁄ ⟩ n l la
l Cny ⟩ m o ls dr ·

-5-

mo l VP rbrls e
⌣ a Sprz- l lrn
la P ↄ rzn- ⟩
ofs af r brd e ·
z u no ⟩ Ppzl z
dfe- b · vo v 8 l 4 ·
evdNl r brds vo
z · dp Psnl Dapym ⟩
e a fl sre la r P
flt ⁄ nes l rzn ·
⌣ c v ls coo grl
z rla- l ⟩ ldrs · e
hp r P l dsd l
rm ⌣ ls corp ·
⁄ ⌣ ↄ hlp yf u d
ru · L asc P ↄ
l re ⌣ r brd ls

-6-

d snlr rln z u
mo s mbrs v r
grp v b nvlv- n ·
fu l PvN ncrss n
yl + gsln ras · e
nvr u l hlp b vo l
dfe ls gsln bl ⟩ ls
bl d alo coo l dl
lr o ras · ⁄ d Aso
Pvd nu plses f lca
yl o prps nr r se ·
loz nu plses cd
b v dry l · gr No
v ppl n me as · e
hp la u l jyn r cz ·
hlp s n ls fu · ul

Key

1

Dear David:

I was delighted to hear that you were promoted to department manager. Fred certainly chose[1] the right person for the job.

Now that you are part of the management team, I will enjoy seeing you regularly[2] at meetings. I know that this will be a busy year for you. If you have problems locating information,[3] I hope you will call on me. We all operate as a team here. Don't hesitate to ask for help.

Cordially yours,[4] (80)

2

Gentlemen:

I have a problem. A shipment of white paint is due at my local dealer's by February 15.[1] I want very much to get this paint and begin decorating my new offices.

Your letter tells me that[2] a receipt for the paint was enclosed. The receipt was not in the letter. What shall I do?

Will I need the receipt[3] when I get the paint? If so, will you mail me a copy right away?

Call me if there is anything I need to[4] do.

Yours very truly, (84)

3

Dear Editor Burns:

We were delighted with the great coverage you gave our fall carnival. We could not have hoped[1] for a better response than we received.

We are now inviting you to participate in an event we have[2] been planning for two years. This event will be called the Village Boat Show. The boats will be displayed in our village shopping[3] center. Right now it looks as though we may have some rather large boats here. If necessary, those boats will be located[4] in the east parking lot.

We are planning to have between 20 and 30 boats on display for one week[5] in April.

Will you plan to write an article to run during the week of the show? We also suggest running[6] an article sometime late in March. I feel certain that I could arrange a preview of the boats if that would help.[7]

Why don't we meet for lunch to discuss ways of promoting the show?

Sincerely, (154)

4

Dear Sir:

Enclosed is your June billing. If you pay the total amount by the date shown on the bill, you will save money.[1] Following that date, a 5 percent fee will be added to your bill.

It would be wise to avoid late payments.[2] If your due date is a problem, you might wish to discuss new billing dates with our credit manager. If you call[3] for an appointment, the manager will be happy to plan a meeting time.

Sincerely, (76)

5

MEMO TO: Vice President Roberts

We were all surprised to learn that President White resigned his office after[1] the board meeting. As you know, his proposal was defeated by a vote of 8 to 4. Evidently, the board's[2] vote was a deep personal disappointment.

We all feel sorry that the president felt it necessary to[3] resign. Much of this company's growth was related to his leadership. We hope the president will decide to[4] remain with this corporation. It might help if you would write a letter asking President White to meet with the[5] board this week. Perhaps it is not too late to change his mind on this matter. (113)

6

Dear Senator Martin:

As you know, some members of our group have been involved in a fight to prevent increases[1] in oil and gasoline rates. We invite you to help by voting to defeat this gasoline bill.

This bill would[2] allow companies to determine their own rates. It would also provide new policies for locating oil on[3] properties near the sea. Those new policies could be very damaging to a great number of people in many[4] ways. We hope that you will join our cause. Help us win this fight.

Yours truly, (92)

LESSON 13

1. Write *a* for the word beginning *an*.

answer, an-s-r *asr*

anticipate, an-t-s-p-ate *alspa*

antique, an-t-k *alc*

analyze, an-l-z *alz*

2. Write *g* for the medial or final sound of any vowel + *nk* (*ank, enk, ink, onk, unk*).

bank, b-ank *bg*

length, l-enk-ith *lgl*

blank, b-l-ank *blg*

rank, r-ank *rg*

thank, ith-ank *lg*

link, l-ink *lg*

Abbreviations

junior *jr*

second, secretary *sec*

senior *sr*

Brief Forms

am, more ⌒

go, good *g*

charge *G*

he, had, him *h*

doctor, direct *dr*

they *ly*

Phrasing. We use some word combinations, such as *we are* and *to be,* so often that we usually say them and read them as a group. In *Speedwriting,* we take advantage of this natural association by joining words together. We call this practice *phrasing.*

we are *er*

to be *Ub*

The pronouns *I*, *we*, and *you* followed by a verb and the word *to* followed by a verb can be easily written and recognized as phrases.

I am	⌐	you are	*ur*
I can	*ıc*	you can	*uc*
we are	*er*	to be	*Ub*
we can	*ec*	to go	*Lg*

With experience in recording dictation, phrases will occur to you naturally as you write. The context, or meaning, of the sentence will help you read the phrase correctly when you see it in your notes.

The following phrases will be used in the reading and writing exercises in this and following lessons.

I am	⌐	you are	*ur*
I can	*ıc*	you can	*uc*
I had	*ıh*	you have	*uv*
I have	*ıv*	you know	*uno*
I will	*ıl*	you will	*ul*
I will be	*ılb*	you would	*ud*

we are	*er*	to be	*Ub*
we can	*ec*	to go	*Lg*
we have	*ev*	to have	*Lv*
we hope	*ehp*	to have you	*Lvu*
we would	*ed*	to have your	*Lvu*
we would be	*edb*	to know	*Lno*
		to pay	*Lpa*

Writing Contractions.   When writing contractions that might be read back as a phrase, use an apostrophe to avoid confusion.

I will	*ul*	I'll	*u'l*
you will	*ul*	you'll	*u'l*
we are	*er*	we're	*e'r*

Words Omitted in High-Frequency Phrases.   A few word combinations occur together so frequently that certain words within the combinations may be omitted from your *Speedwriting* notes. Three such high-frequency phrases are *thank you for, thank you for your,* and *thank you for your letter.*

*thank *you* for   *lqf*   thank *you* for *your*   *lqf*

thank *you* for *your* letter   *lqfL*

*Italicized words have been omitted in the *Speedwriting* phrases.

PRINCIPLES SUMMARY

1. Write   *a*   for the word beginning *an*: answer, an-s-r   *asr* .

2. Write   *bq*   for the medial or final sound of any vowel + *nk*: bank, b-ank   *bq* .

Reading and Writing Exercises

Watch for phrases beginning with the words *I, we, you,* and *to.*

SERIES A

1. ᷄ dr gᵥ h · q rpl + sⁿ h h ᷄.   ⟩ cr + ar · ln ſ ᷄ ſ a ᷄ᵈ.

2. h ᷄ Ms lq a ᷄ a ſ · srl h᷄.   2. ls ℒ ⟩ l nſ u la u pam ₃ du o ᷄ 30 l. ⟩f lr, s᷄ rzn y u cn pa ᷄ lol a ᷄ᵈ ll s no. e l dl · nu mm pam bo- o ᷄ a ᷄ᵈ u c pa.

3. e h · dla n ᷄ dr flᵢ ſ᷄ dnvᵣ̣ l sⁿ frnssco̠,

4. ᷄ pl n̲ l G ᷄ ln h G̅o.

3. e ſnl ᷄ᵈ r bℓ̲ o ᷄ 15 l. ⟩f u rel u pam ᷄ n ⟩ ᷄ c u l b cr- ᷄· sv̲ u sv l a ᷄ᵈ l 2 % v ᷄ lol bl.

5. h ⟩ no sr VP v ᷄ bq̲.

1. al C- ⟩ · ℒ ſ᷄ bℓ s ᷄ᵈ asc̲ l raplᵢ ſ · ln̆ ᷄ c e rass

4. r bq l grⁿ ᷄ sec

5.

-1-

-2-

-3-

-5-

-4-

· ns alc dsc f u
sec. u'l lv ⌒ lc
oc fn+. ι lg ⁄ d
b ⌒ apo f u ⌒a
r⌒ ln f u ofs. e
⌒ι v ι Pbl⌒. ⌐
sp ⌒ yr, G⌐ · gr
dl ⌒ ln u ⌒a +
lpa. Ph ec gl h l
lc ls. ll ⌒e no
⌒n ιc +o u lz fn
alcs. su

-6-

d⌒s jcsn lgf asr
l ⌒ι L. ⌐ bclls u

sM l grl hlp ⌒e
m du‿ · rSC ppr
du ls ln, ι alspa
fn+ ⌐ ppr m 2 ⌒cs.
⌐ ol Pbl iv h ,
obln‿ dla f⌒ cos
lca- ol v lon. ol v
· lol v 7 uv hrd
f⌒ ol 4. ⌒ no
⌒a f rsps f⌒ ⌐
r⌒m‿ 3 bf alz‿ ⌐
fnl rzllo, ul Stnl
rsv · cpe v ⌒ι
fn+- rpl. ul

Key

SERIES A

1. The doctor gave him a good report and sent him home.
2. He wants to go away for a short time.
3. We had a delay in the direct flight from Denver to San Francisco.
4. I am planning to charge more than he charges.
5. He is now senior vice president of the bank.

SERIES B

1. Attached is a letter from Bill Smith asking to reapply for a loan. Can we reassess his credit and arrange a loan for the full amount?
2. This letter is to inform you that your payment was due on the 30th. If there is some reason why you cannot pay the total amount, let us know. We will determine a new minimum payment based on the amount you can pay.
3. We generally mail our billings on the 15th. If you return your payment within one week, you will be credited with a savings. Your savings will amount to 2 percent of the total bill.
4. Our bank will grant the second mortgage that you applied for. We will certainly try to finalize the loan and have the money ready for you between the dates of August 30 and September 6. In the meantime, someone from our firm will visit the property to make an assessment of the current value.
5. From this point on, your charges will be processed by a new manager assigned to give you the personal attention that you need. If you wish to discuss a billing procedure, you may call that person directly. He or she will respond without delay.

1

Dear Mr. Smith:

We are having a great number of problems with our Magic Teller bank machines. Evidently[1] they were not programmed to accept charge cards from this city. Will we have to replace the machines? We are hoping that[2] you can help us avoid doing that. New machines sell for a high price, while our used machines are worth little more than junk.[3]

Our marketing manager is planning to be in San Francisco very soon. Could you meet with him?

Cordially[4] yours, (81)

2

Dear Miss Anderson:

Thank you for your letter regarding jobs for high school seniors. Your grades do indeed rank you at[1] the top of your class. We would be glad to have you apply. I am enclosing a company bulletin which will[2] supply many of the answers you need.

Although generally we need secretaries on a full-time basis,[3] we sometimes have a few part-time openings for high school juniors and seniors.

Bill Gray is a senior who is[4] finishing his second year with our firm. I suggest that you talk with him. You can also get more information from[5] our personnel manager, Mark Lee. If you cannot see him personally, his secretary will give you the[6] appropriate forms to fill out.

Very truly yours, (129)

3

Dear Ms. Miller:

I am returning the blank check you sent us by mistake. We hope that you will mail us a second[1] check without delay. Because you have a good credit rating, you will not be charged a late fee.

We would like to[2] suggest that you use our printed envelopes for mailing your payments. Those envelopes are addressed to the credit[3] department, and your payments will be sent directly to the proper office.

Thank you for giving this matter your[4] attention.

Yours truly, (84)

4

Dear Bob:

Thank you for your advice on the Frank Nelson case. Frank will be glad to know that a senior member of the[1] firm is willing to go to bat for him. Frank and I have had enough time to discuss his problem at length. Although[2] he does not anticipate receiving his old rank, Frank believes that a great number of people will benefit[3] if he wins this case. I think he is right, and we're hoping the judge thinks so too.

I'll certainly let you know if you[4] can help.

Cordially yours, (84)

5

Dear Dr. Ames:

I want you to know that I am looking for more antique furnishings for your office. I have[1] located a desk and chair which I think you will like, but I am afraid that the length of the desk is not right for your[2] office. What would be a good time for you to look at it?

I also know of a nice antique desk for your[3] secretary. You'll love the light oak finish. I think it would be more appropriate for your waiting room than for your[4] office. We might have one problem. The shop manager is charging a great deal more than you may wish to pay. Perhaps we[5] can get him to take less. Let me know when I can show you these fine antiques.

Sincerely yours, (116)

6

Dear Ms. Jackson:

Thank you for your answer to my letter. The booklets you sent will greatly help me in doing a[1] research paper due this term.

I anticipate finishing the paper in two weeks. The only problem I've had[2] is obtaining data from companies located out of town. Out of a total of seven, I have heard from[3] only four. I am now waiting for responses from the remaining three before analyzing the final[4] results.

You will certainly receive a copy of my finished report.

Yours truly, (94)

LESSON 14

RECAP AND REVIEW

You have earned another rest. No principles will be introduced in Lesson 14. Use this review to pinpoint any principles or words you need to practice.

1. Here are the word beginnings you studied in Lessons 8-13:

dis   *D*   mis   *M*

per, pur   *P*   an   *a*

pre, pro, pro *(prah)*   *P*

2. The following word endings were also presented:

long vowel + t   ly   *l*

ate   *a*   gram   *q*

ete   *e*

ite   *i*

ote   *o*

ute/*oot*   *u*

3. The following words illustrate all of the principles you studied in Lessons 8-13:

dismay, dis-m-a *Ɔ↷a*   person, per-s-n *Psn*

mistake, mis-t-k *Mtc*   purpose, pur-p-s *Pps*

recently, re-s-nt-ly *rsNe*   prevent, pre-v-nt *PvN*

rate, r-ate *ra*   program, pro-gram *Pg*

health, h-l-ith *hll*   loyal, l-oi-l *lyl*

reapply, re-a-p-l-i *rapli*   payroll, p-a-r-l *parl*

answer, an-s-r *asr*   bank, b-ank *bq*

4. Months of the year are written this way:

January *Ja*   July *Jl*

February *Fb*   August *Ag*

March *Mr*   September *Sp*

April *Ap*   October *Oc*

May *Ma*   November *Nv*

June *Jn*   December *Dc*

5. Can you automatically write these brief forms? If you are unsure of any brief form, practice the word until you can write it without hesitation.

that	arrange	were
participate	between	ship
response	great	as
was	with	hospital
those	situate	general
refer	property	operate
respond	suggest	am
more	direct	doctor
charge	go	he
good	had	they
him	point	

6. How do you write these brief form derivatives?

arrangement	generally	operators
within	without	wasn't
greatly	referred	shipping

7. How quickly can you read the following abbreviations?

cr	*no*	*ins*
re	*all*	*a-t*
%	*env*	*dpl*
inv	*lol*	*jr*
sr	*sec*	

Vocabulary Builder.   Practice writing these frequently used words:

banking, b-ank-ing	*bg‿*	later, l-ate-r	*lar*
anxious, a-ank-ish-s	*agts*	proceed, pro-s-d	*Psd*
answers, an-s-r-s	*asrs*	duplicate, d-p-l-k-ate	*dplca*
date, d-ate	*da*	sheets, ish-ete-s	*ses*
meeting, m-ete-ing	*‿e‿*	profit, prah-f-t	*Pft*
united, u-n-ite-ed	*uni‿*	treatment, t-r-ete-ment	*trem*
early, e-r-ly	*erl*	related, re-l-ate-ed	*rla‿*
prepare, pre-p-r	*Ppr*	permanent, per-mun-nt	*PmN*
freight, f-r-ate	*fra*	light, l-ite	*li*
separate, s-p-r-ate	*spra*	weight, w-ate	*‿a*
currently, k-r-nt-ly	*crNl*	heating, h-ete-ing	*he‿*

Reading and Writing Exercises

-1-

d~r bron , dlus
~e l nf~ u la r
cr dpl agre- l ~
lol a~l v u ln.
ec Aso ar f . don
pam v bln 12 +
15 % , u ln z rf-
l ~ cr ~yr + ,
rsv- cls all . z
u ~a no er v
Pbl~s gl prp lns
lru . ~ z . hlp la u
prp , lca- nr ~ nu
hsp . la As . gr dl l
~ vlu v u prp , d
u rel ~ enc-
agrem n ~ env
Pvd- , e l nd u
rsp b Fb 10 . su

-2-

mo l A Psnl hr ,
gr nz f loz v u hu
lc- r old hll pln .
ul lv r nu l , bgn
Ag 15 e l ofr . nu
plse ~C l Pvd me
v ~ bnfls uv b asc
f , ~l pa z ~C z
80 % v ~ lol hsp
bl . ~ Aso pas ~dcl
fes + Pvds dMl cvrj
z l , ~ ls pln uc
ar f ~ ins co lpa u
~dcl bls f u . lr l
b no nd f u l ru .
Cc v u o , ls Svs l
sv L + me f u ,
loz v u ~ l l lrn
~ dlls v ls pln l

-4-

b nvr- l Dcs / n
. ⌐e / r ofs.

_____

-3-

d szn e l sn b op_
⌣ nu ldrs. rsNl
/ brd vo- l apy .
nu P. . No v n⌐s
⌣ sug-. . ofrz ⌐d
ru a a b / Psn
Czn dd n ac⌐ / ls
L uc sa la e nvr-
. v fn Psn l ac r
ofr + se rsp- l l
∠. hr n⌐ l b gvn
/ / brd ⌐e o Oc 4.
ehp la A brd mbrs
l b lr l pp. l u ⌐c
arms f s⌐ . Ub lr
f ⌐ eC v r dpls. ul

d⌐r evns ls , n
rsp l u L Ul s y
e dd n rsv / Ja
sm. w Dcs- /
Pbl ⌣ ⌐u ppl +
c no Ul u l hpn-,
e dd v s⌐ o dle /
/ L / sm arv-
b / sm z n brl l
/ ru pls, n / fCr
d u nf⌐ u brc fr
la A sms sd arv
/ / rsv_ dc o r E
sd v r bld_, e l
b Sln lv. Psn lr /
A Ls l sn / inv
+ ac / sm. vlu

-5-

d bl ch . q ⌐e⌣

dr j s, h lqs e
sd Pcs ⌐ dl
580 unl, Pvds
· dr lq bln ⌐ opr
+ ⌐ sNrl mre
bq, ls , · nu Pq
 ⌐ c b ofr- / ·
mm G, dr j s,
fls la · sec unl
d alo s l op evn
 efsNl, il b gld
lvu Avs, du u alspa
q l ⌐ e n ls vqs,
ilb ls if u gl · dr
flu f dnvz, vlu

3d b z rsv- o ⌐ 9h,
r Jn + Jl sms arv-
nrl 2 cs la, ls
Pbl a v b cz- b
r rsN v, r L
v Ap 2 asc- u l
dla ⌐ Ma sm l
e gl sul- n ⌐
nu bld, Ph e dd
n sa n l rz
4 ⌐ ⌐ rglr da,
uv r apljes f ⌐
Mld sj, e no
4 l rel l ⌐ old
sgl, ul

-6-

d rs gbsn r sms
v b arv- af- du da,
r Ma pq z du o ⌐

Key

Brief Forms

Brief Form Derivatives

Abbreviations

credit	number	insurance
regard	attention	amount
percent	envelope	department
invoice	total	junior
senior	second, secretary	

1

Dear Mr. Brown:

It delights me to inform you that our credit department agreed to the total amount of[1] your loan. We can also arrange for a down payment of between 12 and 15 percent.

Your loan was referred to[2] the credit manager, and it received close attention. As you may know, we are having problems getting property[3] loans through. It was a help that your property is located near the new hospital. That adds a great deal to[4] the value of your property.

Would you return the enclosed agreement in the envelope provided? We will[5] need your response by February 10.

                         Sincerely yours, (110)

2

MEMO TO: All Personnel

Here is great news for those of you who liked our old health plan. You will love our new one.[1]

Beginning August 15, we will offer a new policy which will provide many of the benefits you have[2] been asking for. It will pay as much as 80 percent of the total hospital bill. It also pays medical[3] fees and provides dental coverage as well.

With this plan, you can arrange for the insurance company to[4] pay your medical bills for you. There will be no need for you to write a check of your own. This service will save time[5] and money for you.

Those of you wishing to learn the details of this plan will be invited to discuss it in[6] a meeting at our office. (124)

3

Dear Susan:

We will soon be operating with new leadership. Recently the board voted to appoint a new[1] president. A number of names were suggested. An offer was made right away, but the person chosen did not[2] accept.

At this time I can say that we invited a very fine person to accept our offer, and she[3] responded well to it. Her name will be given at the board meeting on October 4. We hope that all board[4] members will be there to participate. Will you make arrangements for someone to be there from each of our departments?[5]

Yours truly, (102)

4

Dear Mr. Evans:

This is in response to your letter telling us why we did not receive the January[1] shipment. I have discussed the problem with my people and can now tell you what happened.

We did have someone on duty[2] at the time the shipment arrived, but the shipment was not brought to the right place.

In the future, would you inform[3] your trucking firm that all shipments should arrive at the receiving dock on the east side of our building? We will be[4] certain to have a person there at all times to sign the invoice and accept the shipment.

Very truly yours,[5] (100)

5

Dear Bill:

I had a good meeting with Dr. James. He thinks we should purchase the model S80 unit. It[1] provides a direct link between the operator and the central memory bank. This is a new program which can[2] be offered at a minimum charge.

Dr. James feels that a second unit would allow us to operate even[3] more efficiently. I'll be glad to have your advice.

Do you anticipate going to the meetings in Las[4] Vegas? I will be there if I can get a direct flight from Denver.

Very truly yours, (96)

6

Dear Mrs. Gibson:

Our shipments have been arriving after the due date. Our May package was due on the 3rd but[1] was received on the 9th. Our June and July shipments arrived nearly two weeks late.

This problem may have been caused by[2] our recent move. Our letter of April 2 asked you to delay the May shipment while we were getting situated[3] in the new building. Perhaps we did not say when to resume shipping at the regular date. You have our[4] apologies for the misleading message.

We now wish to return to the old schedule.

Yours truly, (98)

Cplr 3 ✳

WHAT IS MEANT BY DICTATION AND TRANSCRIPTION?

Speedwriting involves a two-part process: **recording dictation** and **transcribing**. Since both are equally important to your success, let's take a look at the skills you'll need for each.

Recording Dictation.   The ability to write *Speedwriting* is a skill that comes with study and practice. As you move forward in this text, your speed and confidence will increase. Later, when you are on the job and recording notes regularly, your writing efficiency will increase even more. You will become familiar with the words used most often in your office. You will learn to write common phrases and terms as quickly as you hear them.

There are many techniques and habits that you should develop *now*—before on-the-job training begins. These techniques and habits, or dictation aids, will help you take notes in a way that is efficient for you.

*Chapter Three

Transcribing Notes. Transcription is the process of converting *Speedwriting* notes into acceptable form. The equipment you use may be as simple as a typewriter or as sophisticated as a computer. Whatever the equipment, you'll need the ability to type or keyboard accurately; spell correctly (plan to keep a dictionary nearby); and punctuate as needed (no misplaced commas, please).

All transcribed documents have one thing in common—they should be absolutely free of errors.

Because transcription skills are so important, this text will present **Transcription Aids.** Beginning in Lesson 16, spelling words will be highlighted in each lesson. Those selected for practice are among the most commonly misspelled words in business correspondence.

Beginning in Lesson 22, basic rules for punctuation will be presented. The rules will be simple, but very important. They are the most commonly used punctuation rules in business correspondence.

If spelling and punctuation are not among your favorite subjects, don't despair. You are not alone! You will, however, need these skills to be successful.

LESSON 15

1. Write a printed capital S (disjoined) for the word beginning *super.*

supervise, super-v-z   *Svz*

superman, super-m-n   *S⌐m*

supermarket,
   super-market   *S⌐r*

supersonic, super-s-n-k   *Ssnc*

superpower,
   super-p-ow-r   *Spor*

supervisor, super-v-z-r   *Svzr*

2. Write a printed capital S (disjoined) also for the word endings *scribe* and *script*, and for the sound of *scrip.*

describe, d-scribe   *dS*

inscribe, in-scribe   *nS*

described, d-scribe-duh   *dS-*

script   *S*

prescribe, pre-scribe   *PS*

*manuscripts,
   m-n-script-s   *⌐nSs*

*A disjoined word ending is disjoined from the letters that precede it, not from those that follow it.

3. Write *el* for the word beginning *electr.*

electric, electr-k   *elc*

electrical, electr-k-l   *elcl*

electronic, electr-n-k   *elnc*

electronically,
   electr-n-k-ly   *elncl*

More About Phrases.   In Lesson 13, you learned to write phrases beginning with *I, we, you,* and *to.* You can also write other very common word groups as phrases. The following phrases are among those that appear in the reading and writing exercises in this and following lessons.

I could	*icd*	will be	*ll*	
I hope	*ihp*	would be	*db*	
to see	*lse*	it is	*/*	
for the	*f*	it's	*'/p*	(contraction)
of the	*v*	its	*/p*	(possessive)
that you	*lau*	that your	*lau*	

Your Business Vocabulary	supermarket chain *S~n Cn*	A group of large grocery stores owned by the same individual or corporation.
	programming *Pg-*	Providing a computer with programs, which are sets of coded instructions.

PRINCIPLES SUMMARY

1. Write a printed capital   *S*   (disjoined) for the word beginning *super*: supervise, super-v-z   *S vz*   .
2. Write a printed capital   *S*   (disjoined) for the sound of *scrip* and the word endings *scribe* and *script*: describe, d-scribe   *dS*   ; manuscripts, m-n-script-s   *~n Ss.*
3. Write   *el*   for the word beginning *electr*: electric, electr-k   *elc*   .

Reading and Writing Exercises

-1-

-2-

-3-

-4-

-5-

Key

1

Dear Mrs. Brown:

Are you looking for a new electronic typewriter? We have a new model we call the[1] SUPERSONIC. It is a new type of electronic memory typewriter which will change your office routine.[2] This great little machine does big jobs. You name it. Our machine does it.

You and your secretary can operate it[3] easily. How? By pressing a few keys, you can produce a letter in seconds or an entire report in minutes.[4] You are the supervisor. The machine does all the hard jobs. Describing this unit as merely an electronic[5] typewriter would be a mistake. It is far more than that.

To show you what we mean, we are enclosing a brochure[6] describing how our machine operates. We are proud to say that the brochure was produced on this electronic[7] unit.

Let us show you more. Pay us a visit and try the SUPERSONIC. We think you'll love it.

Sincerely,[8] (160)

2

Dear Fred:

I am delighted that your chain of supermarkets will be joining our corporation. I hope it is[1] evident how happy we are to have you on board. You are now part of the family. We hope to see you[2] often.

In your letter accepting our offer, you used many generous words to describe my role. I am very[3] glad to have played a part in these happenings.

As a team, we are certain to achieve many changes in this firm.[4] It's good to know that you will be supervising the chain.

Yours very truly, (94)

3

Dear Dr. Evans:

Dr. Green advised me that he will not be teaching for us this fall. As you know, Dr. Green[1] is an electrical engineer and head of the engineering department here. He is leaving our school to[2] join a local firm. As vice president, he will supervise electronic programming for the entire corporation.[3]

We are happy for Dr. Green, but sorry to see him go. He will not be easy to replace, but[4] corporations can pay electrical engineers more than we can.

Dr. Green is offering to write an ad[5] describing his job. I suggest that we place it in the engineering journals and see what happens.

Yours truly,[6] (120)

4

Dear David:

I am afraid I will have to be away from the office for a week or so. During my trip out[1] West, I injured my back in a bad fall. The doctor prescribed medicine and a week in bed. I am hoping that[2] his advice will solve the problem. If it does not, the doctor may have to operate. It would then be necessary[3] for me to take a medical leave of three to four weeks.

I will let you know more as soon as I can. In the[4] meantime, I plan to keep writing at home. I am nearly finished with the report and feel certain that I can[5] supervise the research by phone as easily as I could in the office.

Sincerely, (116)

5

Dear Evelyn:

What information do you have on electronic games? We are thinking of adding two new[1] models to our catalog. MR. AND MRS. SUPERMAN is a game appropriate for people between the[2] ages of seven and fifteen. We are also looking at a model called SUPERSONIC SPACESHIP. The point of this[3] game is to prevent a war between two superpowers. People of all ages like this game.

The market for[4] electronic games is changing rapidly. How are we to know which games to offer? We really need the benefit[5] of your knowledge. Won't you respond as soon as you can?

Cordially yours, (112)

LESSON 16

1. Write *ur* for the word ending *ward.*

backward, b-k-ward *bcw*

downward, d-ow-n-ward *donw*

forward, for-ward *fw*

toward, to-ward *tw*

rewarding, re-ward-ing *rw*

awards, a-ward-s *aws*

2. Write *h* for the word ending *hood.*

boyhood, b-oi-hood *byh*

neighborhood, n-b-r-hood *nbrh*

girlhood, guh-r-l-hood *grlh*

likelihood, l-k-ly-hood *lclh*

childhood, chay-l-d-hood *cldh*

parenthood, p-r-nt-hood *prnh*

Abbreviations

avenue *ave*

hour *hr*

boulevard *blvd*

record *rec*

day *d*

example, executive *ex*

month *~o*

Brief Forms

appreciate *ap*

distribute *D*

please, up *p*

present *P*

specific, specify *sp*

correspond, correspondence *cor*

Brief Form and Abbreviated Word Development

upon	*po*	pleasing	*p_*
today	*td*	specifically	*spl*
daily	*dl*	monthly	*mol*

Phrases.   Look for the following phrases in the reading and writing exercises that follow.

I would	*id*	you can be	*ucb*
I would appreciate	*idap*	you would like	*udlc*
I would be	*idb*	and the	*+*
we should	*esd*	at the	*s*
we will	*el*	that we	*lae*
we would appreciate	*edap*		

Your Business Vocabulary

likelihood	*lclh*	The probability that something will happen.
specify	*sp*	To state explicitly.
company records	*co recs*	Items kept on file (letters, reports, contracts, receipts, and so on).

TRANSCRIPTION AID Learn to spell correctly.

Correct spelling is so important to business correspondence that even one error can spoil a letter. Spelling errors not only embarrass the typist, they also reflect poorly upon the executive and detract from the company's image.

To build spelling skills, learn to rely upon the dictionary. Look up any word you are not sure about; read the definition and the correct spelling for that particular usage.

Some words are so commonly misspelled that it is difficult to detect an error in them. As your transcription skills grow, you will learn to identify these problem words. This text will highlight some of these problem words in the lessons.

Commonly Misspelled Words	The following words will be used in your reading exercises. They have similar sounds but totally different meanings, depending upon how they are spelled and used. Notice how their meanings differ in each of the sentences below.

their	*ん*	(shows possessive for more than one): Please tell the *Smiths* that *their* payment is overdue.
there	*ん*	(used to designate a place): We will be *there* on Friday.
there	*ん*	(used in place of the subject): *There* will be six vice presidents at the meeting.

PRINCIPLES SUMMARY

1. Write *ur* for the word ending *ward*: backward, b-k-ward *bcur* .
2. Write *h* for the word ending *hood*: boyhood, b-oi-hood *byh* .

Vocabulary Builder. Practice writing these frequently used words:

forwarded, for-ward-ed	*fur-*	days, day-s	*ds*
forwarding, for-ward-ing	*fur*	holiday, h-l-day	*hld*
awarding, a-ward-ing	*aur*	months, month-s	*oo*
neighborhoods, n-b-r-hood-s	*nbrhs*	rewards, re-ward-s	*rurs*

Reading and Writing Exercises

SERIES A

1. _idap ⌐ if ud sp ⌐ ⌐ʋ u ⌐ + lse._   v u ave or blvd f ⌐ r recs.

2. _p ll ⌐e no if ucb P ⌐ ⌐e._   2. du ls ⌐o er asc eC Psn l rec ⌐ hr la h or ₊e arvs eC d.

3. _e pln l D loz ⌐sns l sp dlrs m ls lon._   3. ⌐r sno) · ex ⌐ r fr.

4. _ll ⌐e no ⌐n ⌐u ⌐, p._   4. il ₊so u· ex v cor er lc f.

5. _hu l P ⌐ Pg f s. ×_   5. ho ofn du u cor ⌐ h. ×

SERIES B

1. _p g⌐ ⌐e ⌐ m_

-1-

-2-

, fre v errs. h or
se Aso nds lt .
Psn hu rlas l l A
lps v ppl , i lc fw
l e u t Dco lz
isus n grr dll- su

suq lau l nlss
l ppl u cor o .
rglr bss. edb hpe
l spli u apo
fro. cu

-3-

dvs grn lqfl
nf s lau l
adrs lb Cny sn.
el c Cny n r
recs z sn z e
rsv enc- f.
p gv s sp inf f
fw u cor. prN or
lp u hos No t f
m v u ave or blvd.
b Sln l sp o
t du l bgn rsv
l u nu adrs, e

-4-

dmbrs lpc v ls
os e lb "grlh
drs." e lb hld
n old scl bld o N
sr blvd. Ph ec A
sr Cldh mres l
er lr, p nls la n
e, b v-p l.
nu hr. z Aso
suq-lae Cny r rglr
e d. p b Ppr-l
Dco lr esd w
p lw bgn v
o, il D cpes v

-5-

Key

SERIES A
1. I would appreciate it if you would specify the items you wish to see.
2. Please let me know if you can be present at the meeting.
3. We plan to distribute those machines to specific dealers in this town.
4. Let me know when my time is up.
5. Who will present the program for us?

SERIES B
1. Please give me the name of your avenue or boulevard for our records.
2. During this month, we are asking each person to record the hour that he or she arrives each day.
3. Mr. Snow is an executive with our firm.
4. I will show you an example of the correspondence we are looking for.
5. How often do you correspond with him?

1

Dear Mr. Jones:

Our senior class was pleased to learn that you lived in our town during your childhood. As an executive[1] in a large corporation, you are a good example of someone from our own neighborhood who moved up to[2] the top of his field. We have voted you an award and are inviting you to be present at our awards night[3] on March 1.

During the program, we will present a look at the future, and we would appreciate having your[4] views on office careers. For example, what are some specific skills that executives and secretaries need?[5] We have heard that many companies are hiring now. What is the likelihood that we will get good jobs?

Any advice[6] you would like to give us will help us plan our futures. I will make copies of your response and distribute them[7] to the entire class.

Very truly yours, (148)

2

Dear Howard:

Your letter brought back pleasant boyhood memories from the days when I was growing up on College[1] Avenue. Tell your class I would be pleased to accept their award in person. Let me know what hours you would like me to[2] be present.

It is rewarding to know that you are looking ahead. There are many issues facing executives[3] today, but the chief problem is locating good people to keep the office running efficiently.

Any[4] good executive relies upon the help of a skilled secretary. Secretaries need a wide range of skills,[5] from managing company records to producing correspondence that is free of errors. He or she also[6] needs to be a person who relates well to all types of people.

I look forward to meeting you and discussing[7] these issues in greater detail.

Sincerely yours, (149)

3

Dear Mrs. Green:

Thank you for your letter informing us that your mailing address will be changing soon. We will make[1] the change in our records as soon as we receive the enclosed form. Please give us specific information for[2] forwarding your correspondence. Print or type your house number and the full name of your avenue or boulevard. Be[3] certain to specify the month and day you wish to begin receiving mail at your new address.

We suggest that[4] you mail notices to people you correspond with on a regular basis. We would be happy to supply[5] you with the appropriate forms.

Cordially yours, (109)

4

Dear Members:

The topic of this month's meeting will be "Girlhood Dreams." The meeting will be held in the old school[1] building on North Shore Boulevard. Perhaps we can all share childhood memories while we are there.

Please notice that our[2] meeting is being moved up to a new hour. It was also suggested that we change our regular meeting day.[3] Please be prepared to discuss whether we should move it up toward the beginning of the month.

I will distribute[4] copies of our recent survey in which we asked you to specify goals for the new year. Your answers were very[5] rewarding, and I look forward to sharing them with you. I hope you will all be present.

Very truly yours,[6] (120)

5

Dear Henry:

Thank you for forwarding a set of your designs for the new electric engine. Now that we have had[1] some time to look at them, we are delighted to say that we think you have given us a fine example for the[2] future, as well as the present.

We have decided to distribute copies to our field engineers, and we have[3] asked them to respond in 30 days. In all likelihood we will hear from them even before then. I am sure[4] you will be as eager as I am to see their reports, so I will forward them as soon as I can.

We appreciate[5] the efficient service you have given us.

Sincerely yours, (111)

LESSON 17

1. Write *1* for the word ending *tion* (pronounced *shun, zhun,* or *chun*: sion, cian, shion, cean, cion) or for a vowel + *tion* (a-tion, e-tion, i-tion or ish-un, o-tion, u-tion).

vacation, v-k-tion	*vcy*	physician, f-z-cian	*fzy*
position, p-z-tion	*pzy*	ocean, o-cean	*oy*
nation, n-tion	*ny*	fashion, f-shion	*fy*
supervision, super-v-sion	*Svy*	session, s-sion	*sy*

These additional words will appear in your reading and writing exercises.

application, a-p-l-k-tion	*aplcy*	situation, situate-tion	*suy*
addition, a-d-tion	*ady*	operation, operate-tion	*opy*
decision, d-s-sion	*dsy*	suggestion, suggest-tion	*sugy*
solution, s-l-tion	*sly*	distribution, distribute-tion	*Dy*
national, n-tion-l	*nyl*		

Phrases

I believe	*iblv*	for your	*fu*
you do	*udu*	in the	*n*
you should	*usd*	of you	*vu*
to keep	*lcp*	of your	*vu*
could be	*cdb*	will you	*lu*
for you	*fu*	will your	*lu*

Commonly Misspelled Words	Look for these words in your reading and writing exercises.
	here *hr* (to designate a place) Someone will be *here* at noon.
	hear *hr* (to perceive a sound) If you *hear* the telephone, please answer it.

Your Business Vocabulary	marketing division *~r dvy*	Those departments of a business concerned with the sales, promotion, and distribution of a product.

PRINCIPLES SUMMARY

1. Write   *1*   for the word ending *tion* or for a vowel + *tion*: vacation, v-k-tion   *vcy*   .

Vocabulary Builder.   Practice writing these frequently used words:

action, a-k-tion	*acy*	portion, p-r-tion	*pry*
emotional, e-m-tion-l	*eyl*	obligation, o-b-l-guh-tion	*oblgy*
production, pro-d-k-tion	*Pdcy*	provisions, pro-v-sion-s	*Pvyo*
section, s-k-tion	*scy*	regulations, r-guh-l-tion-s	*rglyo*
division, d-v-sion	*dvy*	inspection, in-s-p-k-tion	*nspcy*
invitation, in-v-t-tion	*nvly*	legislation, l-j-s-l-tion	*lysly*
professional, pro-f-sion-l	*Pfyl*	discussion, dis-k-sion	*Dcy*
protection, pro-t-k-tion	*Plcy*	cancellation, can-s-l-tion	*csly*
mentioned, men-tion-duh	*my-*	selection, s-l-k-tion	*slcy*
edition, e-d-tion	*edy*	recommendations, r-k-mend-tion-s	*rcmyo*
location, l-k-tion	*lcy*	relationship, re-l-tion-ship	*rlys*

Reading and Writing Exercises

-1-

-2-

-3-

-4-

cor l ~ a a.,
ι dM v · sly l ~
byl ιsu. 's. Y Pbl~,
il ll uno z sn z ι
hr s~ frlr. w
~mt~ p rf A cls
drl l r prs sec,
du uno ~r l lca
sp inf o ~ lcl lbr
sily f ~e. ιdap u
hlp. ul

-5-

d j~ A du u lg √
enc- artcl rln b
szn~ ly~s. × ι sos
ho e cd ncrs ol=
p∧N Svss z · ~a

v rds~ hsp fes. dr
ly~s sz la ~
Ppr Svy ~ p∧Ns
cdb rls- o ~ d af
· opj. n me css ~
Psn cd q h~ o ~
s~ d, ιblv esd
lc nl A dr ly~s
, sq~ se , Pvd~ ·
gr Svo b gv~ s l z
sugjs. yf u agre
il D cpes l A exs.
Ph ec uz ~ artcl
l dl nu plses hr.
uvl

Key

1

MEMO TO: Members of the Board

I am recommending Dr. Albert Brown for a position on our Board of[1] Directors. Dr. Brown was a physician here for more than 20 years. Some of you may remember the firm[2] leadership he provided for our neighborhood schools. For example, it was Dr. Brown who urged a decision in[3] favor of building South Junior High. He also raised revenue to purchase the property for an addition[4] to that building.

I believe Dr. Brown will agree to head our drive for better educational programs. He[5] takes charge of tough situations and is not afraid to go on record for what he thinks is right. This man ranks highly[6] as a leader in our city. (126)

2

Dear Ms. Smith:

Thank you for your letter of application. At the present time we have no openings in the[1] department of fashion design. I am forwarding your letter to our marketing division with the suggestion[2] that the manager correspond directly with you.

We are producing a new fashion line which will be ready[3] for distribution between July 15 and July 30. We may decide to market these items on a[4] national basis. If so, it will be necessary to add more personnel. Your education and training[5] would seem to be appropriate for such a position.

If you do not hear from the manager within a few[6] days, perhaps you should give him a call. In the meantime, I will be happy to keep a copy of your letter[7] in our records. If our situation does change, we will let you know.

Cordially yours, (155)

3

Dear Mr. and Mrs. Gray:

Remember when the two of you hoped to enjoy the vacation of your dreams aboard[1] an ocean liner? Year after year you wanted to go, but didn't. Could the problem have been money?

If your[2] answer is yes, we have a solution for you. Our ship will sail on the morning of May 10 to seven different[3] ports on the Atlantic Ocean. What a vacation that will be! If you have had a relationship with our bank[4] for three years or more, you will receive a reduced rate. In addition, senior citizens may participate in[5] a credit plan with low monthly payments.

We can accept applications no later than April 1, so please don't[6] delay. It's a boat you can't afford to miss.

Cordially yours, (131)

4

Dear Shelley:

The news from our nation's capital is not good these days. It appears that neither the House nor the[1] Senate will accept the President's budget during this session. Because of the delays here, I will be returning[2] to my office a few days later than I had planned. Will you please answer all correspondence while I am away?[3]

I don't have a solution to the budget issue. It's a tough problem. I will let you know as soon as I hear[4] something further. In the meantime, please refer all calls directly to our press secretary.

Do you know where to[5] locate specific information on the local labor situation for me? I would appreciate your[6] help.

Yours truly, (123)

5

Dear Jim:

What do you think of the enclosed article written by Susan Williams? It shows how we could increase[1] out-patient services as a way of reducing hospital fees. Dr. Williams says that with proper supervision,[2] more patients could be released on the day after an operation. In many cases, the person could go[3] home on the same day.

I believe we should look into what Dr. Williams is saying. She is providing a great[4] service by giving us these suggestions. If you agree, I will distribute copies to all executives.[5] Perhaps we can use the article to determine new policies here.

Yours very truly, (116)

LESSON 18

1. Write amounts of money in the following way:

$29.95 29^{95} $6,500,000 $6 M 5 H T$$

$300 $3 H$$ $2,000,000,000 $2 B$$

Abbreviations

cent, cents   ¢   hundred H

dollar, dollars $ thousand T

pound   *lb*   million M

inch   *in*   billion B

ounce   *oz*

Brief Forms

about   *ab*   over O

has   *hs*   under U

order   *od*   customer K

include   *I*

Brief Form and Abbreviated Word Development

customers   *Ks*   orders   *ods*

overall   *Oa*   holidays   *hlds*

included   *I-*   inclusion   *Ig*

Phrases

we do	*edu*	have been	*vb*
we feel	*efl*	of our	*vr*
you need	*und*	to you	*lu*
to make	*Lc*	to your	*lu*

Commonly Misspelled Words		
cancellation	*csly*	
recommend	*rcm*	

Your Business Vocabulary	word processing unit *rd Pss unt*	Computerized typewriting equipment having many automatic features, including text editing and high-speed printing.

PRINCIPLES SUMMARY

1. Amounts of money.

Reading and Writing Exercises

-1-

[Shorthand outlines]

-2-

[Shorthand outlines]

ajM ho rcm- lae
ncrs ꞁ sNrl mre
bg b a̱ fCrs l ⁄ ,
efl la ꞁ a- fCrs ɖd
vb ɖ- U ꞁ lr⁀s
vr orjnl agrem .
le b G— ꞁ f aꞁꞁd
f Cnjs er fo- lrc ͯ͞
e nd · dsj sn +
lc fw lu Avo o
ls ⁀lr ˎ su

-3-

d⁀rs prcr jyn s
+ uʒ ꞁ nu Cc̱ Svs ˎ
ʼͦ v eze ͦ ꞁd dʒ ꞁ
bg ofꞁ u ͯ ev me
Cc̱ plns l ⁀e u
nds ˎ f ex fu cp
· mm v 2H$ ꞁ
bg lr lb no Svo

G ˎ fu dM ⁀⁀ɫ
lcp · mm aꞁꞁd uc
pa · ⁀ol fe v 4⁵⁰ ,
u ⁀a Pfꞁ lpa f eC
Cc u ru ⁄ 10¢ P Cc ͦ
lr ͦ no lⁿl o ꞁ
No v Cco u ⁀a
ru ˎ fu od no ul
rsv 2 H Cco fre
v G ˎ drp b u lcl
brnC ofꞁ o srḻn̥
ave + ll s U u ⁀
ab ꞁ Cc̱ + sv̱ plns ˎ
ꞁ bg̱ Svos ꞁ dʒn—
lrc efɫM me ⁀jm
eze f ꞁ Ko ˎ cu

-4-

d mbrs ꞁ brd
alC— ͦ · cpe vꞁ nu
op̱ lyl ˎ ʒ uc se ꞁ

lol a d , · lll U
2 M $, ls , · ncrs
v nrl 2 2 5 T $ O r
old byl, pl ✓ ncrs
, du l r plns l PCs
prp b 2 Ppz- plNs,
evn ⌣ r prp PCss
r byl s s l hu, lrf
⌣ apy- grp v exs
l rvu lz fgrs +
rcm sp cls, chp
la s ⌣ vu l pp n
la rvu, id Aso
ap hr u sugjs r
brd ⌢e o fn 2, p
pln Ub P o la d, su

-5-

d rs crlsn e rgrl

l nf u la ⌒ blu
fbrc u od-, n ⌢d
m · 54 = in ⌣dl, cd
u uz / m · 45 = in
⌣dl, Also edu n
crNl v r 45 = in fbrc
m r sp edb hpe l
od , fu, sC ods
lc ab 2 l 3 ⌣co l
arv , r r m ths
u sp- ⌣ 4- ld, r
lol a d vu od ,
79 96 , v crs la a d
dz n l r prs ✓ blu
fbrc or s 4 Cjs, r
4 ⌣a ✓ 45 = in
fbrc , 7 lbs 6 ozs ,
e lc fw l Sr u n
fCr, ul

Key

1

Dear Mrs. Smith:

There is truth in the saying, "You are what you eat." Think about the billions of meals that are[1] prepared yearly.

To be a great cook, you need cookbooks you can rely upon. Why not join our cookbook club for great[2] dining enjoyment? As a member of our cookbook club, you can learn to prepare great daily meals. You will also[3] save money at the supermarket. There is more good news—your membership fee is included in the purchase[4] of three or more books.

Enclosed is a brochure which describes a new cookbook we are offering. It has won five[5] national awards. Why not try it for two weeks with no obligation to buy? If you decide to keep your copy,[6] mail us a check or money order for $15.95. This book would make a great gift for the[7] holidays.

Please use the enclosed form to specify the number of copies you wish to order. You may charge your[8] purchases, or we will bill you directly. We can accept cancellations up to ten days following the date[9] your order is received.

Yours very truly, (188)

2

Dear Mr. May:

As you know, we have had some problems with the word processing unit we purchased from your firm.[1] Overall, the machine operates well, but it does not do all of the tasks we believed it would do. Your agent has[2] recommended that we increase the central memory bank by adding features to it. We feel that the added[3] features should have been included under the terms of our original agreement. Will we be charged the full[4] amount for the changes we are forced to make?

We need a decision soon and look forward to your advice on this[5] matter.

Sincerely yours, (104)

3

Dear Mrs. Parker:

Join us and use our new checking service. It's very easy.

What does our bank offer you? We[1] have many checking plans to meet your needs. For example, if you keep a minimum of $200 in[2] the bank, there will be no service charge. If you don't wish to keep a minimum amount, you can pay a monthly fee[3] of $4.50. You may prefer to pay for each check you write at 10¢ per check.

There is no limit[4] on the number of checks you may write. If you order now, you will receive 200 checks free of charge. Drop by[5] your local branch office on Shoreline Avenue and let us tell you more about our checking and savings plans. Our[6] banking services are designed to make efficient money management easy for our customers.

Cordially[7] yours, (141)

4

Dear Members of the Board:

Attached is a copy of our new operating budget. As you can see, the total[1] amount is a little under $2,000,000. This is an increase of nearly $225,000[2] over the old budget. Part of the increase is due to our plans to purchase property for two proposed[3] plants. Even with the property purchases, the budget seems too high.

Therefore, I am appointing a group of[4] executives to review these figures and recommend specific cuts. I hope that some of you will participate[5] in that review. I would also appreciate hearing your suggestions at the board meeting on June 2. Please[6] plan to be present on that day.

Sincerely yours, (129)

5

Dear Mrs. Carlson:

   We regret to inform you that the blue fabric you ordered is not made in a 54-inch[1] width. Could you use it in a 45-inch width? Although we do not currently have the 45-inch fabric[2] in our shop, we would be happy to order it for you. Such orders take about two to three weeks to arrive.[3]

   The remaining items you specified were shipped today. The total amount of your order is[4] $79.96. Of course, that amount does not include the price of the blue fabric or its shipping[5] charges. The shipping weight of the 45-inch fabric is 7 pounds 6 ounces.

   We look forward to serving[6] you in the future.

                                        Yours truly, (125)

LESSON 19

1. Write *a* for the initial and final sound of *aw*.

law, l-aw *la*　　　　saw, s-aw *sa*

audit, aw-d-t *adl*

authorized,
  aw-ith-r-z-duh *alrz-*

auto, aw-t-o *alo*　　　drawings, d-r-aw-ings *dra*

2. Write *q* for the sound of *kw* (qu).

quite, q-ite *qi*　　　　equipment, e-q-p-ment *eqpm*

quickly, q-k-ly *qcl*　　adequate, ad-q-t *aql*

quote, q-ote *qo*　　　　frequent, f-r-q-nt *frqN*

Phrases

we appreciate *eap*　　　to use *luz*

we had *eh*　　　　　　have had *vh*

we were *e*　　　　　　on the *o*

you were *u*

Commonly Misspelled Words	personnel *Psnl*	(employees) We will employ more *personnel* in the new office.
	personal *Psnl*	(private) Jane is away on *personal* business today.

Your Business Vocabulary	resumé *rz⁀a*	A document summarizing a job applicant's education, skills, and employment history.
	authorized *alrz-*	Having the right to make decisions and take specific action.

PRINCIPLES SUMMARY

1. Write *a* for the sound of *aw*: saw, s-aw *sa* .
2. Write *q* for the sound of *kw*: quite, q-ite *qi* .

Reading and Writing Exercises

-1-

[shorthand text]

-2-

[shorthand text]

gts bttr —ly ln ne
nu —dl crNl ö
—r, du— —o v
Fb er atrz— l sl ls
cr / · v lo prs, blv
/ or n la prs l I
u Cys v eqpm. N
u drv br r sor— +
se ls gr vlu., l u'r
hr sn p f r fre dra—
· lvl nu cr lb aw—
l · lce rzdN vr
ste, la —nr cdb
u, ul

-3-

d—s le lqfL re—
pzj —r fr, enc—
,, brsr dS r plse
ö ejcj ul nd, z uc
se e jnl asc la A

—ym lrnes v · clj
dgre, n · fu css ev
ofr— pzjs l ppl hu vh
s— clj=lvl crss +
rla— jb scls evn
if ly dd n v · dgre,
f frlr inf p cl or ru
r Psnl dvj lca—/
412 el— blvd, e
rcm lau —l s ·
cpe vu rz—a aco—
b · L v aplcj, n u
L b Sln l my ne
adjl scls or lrn
u —a v rsv— olsd
clj crss, su

-4-

j lqfL v Ma 12,
u— qi ru, — lol
a—l v bl sd vb

bs- ʃ go e gv u.
fu ⌐os aq. er ⌐c
⌐ Cny n r recs ⊬
u env l so ⌐ nu
a⌐l, u G-ʃ prs
bcz eh n nf⌐- r
ayN v agrem eh
⌐d ⌐ u. ʃ no
o el se l / la A
ples n op U ⌐s
agrem. eap u od
⊬ l v ⌐ eqpm ʌ-
lu b ⌐ da u sp-,
⌐ gld u brl ls
⌐lr l ⌐ Psnl
all ⊬ lc fw l Sv
u n fCr. uvl

-5-

d⌐q e ⌐ qu Sprz-

b ⌐ rsp l ⌐ opn
vr nu sp. Alo e
alspa- v bln 3H
⊬ 4H ppl ⌐ ln
6H Ko ⌐ P ʃ
evN, ⌐ lol a⌐l
v slo ʒ l O 15 T$.
r jn ⌐yr fls la ls
lry brnol ʒ ⌐rzll
v. S P ⌐y efl. se
hs asc- ⌐e l lq
eC mbr v l.
la ⌐ls u, u gv s
me fn sugjs. n
adj u pla-. ⌐yr
rl n Ose ⌐ evN
⊬ b sl p ⌐ fre
dra ⊬ aw przs,
u efls r ap-⌐ ul

Key

1

Dear Mr. Wilson:

Our office building is quite old. Recently we were told that our lighting is not adequate[1] to meet current laws. We are faced with a decision. Can we solve the problem by equipping all desks with electric[2] lamps, or should we call in a company such as yours to replace our overhead lights with new units?

Our[3] electrical engineer has said that new overhead lights would provide better lighting. He also added that the[4] total amount for such a purchase could run about $2,000 or more. We are hesitant to allow[5] the price to go over $2,000 because many of our people have suggested that they would be[6] equally happy with electric lamps.

Would you be willing to give us your suggestions on how to solve our problems?[7] I would appreciate your response as quickly as you can give it to us.

Cordially yours, (156)

2

Dear Customer:

Could your family use a second car? If so, we have the auto for you. This model is great[1] for frequent trips about town, but it's equally good for highway driving. Either way you plan to use it, this auto[2] will save money on gasoline. It gets better mileage than any new model currently on the market.[3]

During the month of February, we are authorized to sell this car at a very low price. Believe it or[4] not, that price will include your choice of equipment. Won't you drive by our showroom and see this great value?

While you're here,[5] sign up for our free drawing. A lovely new car will be awarded to a lucky resident of our city.[6] That winner could be you.

Yours truly, (126)

3

Dear Ms. Lee:

Thank you for your letter regarding a position with our firm. Enclosed is a brochure describing[1] our policy on the education you will need. As you can see, we generally ask that all management[2] trainees have a college degree. In a few cases we have offered positions to people who have had some college-[3] level courses and related job skills, even if they did not have a degree.

For further information,[4] please call or write our personnel division located at 412 Elm Boulevard. We recommend that you mail[5] us a copy of your resumé accompanied by a letter of application. In your letter, be certain[6] to mention any additional skills or training you may have received outside college courses.

Sincerely[7] yours, (141)

4

Gentlemen:

Thank you for your letter of May 12. You were quite right. The total amount of the bill should have been based[1] on the quote we gave you a few months ago. We are making the change in our records, and your invoice will show the[2] new amount.

You were charged full price because we had not informed our agent of the agreement we had made with you.[3] From now on, we will see to it that all parties are operating under the same agreement. We appreciate[4] your order and will have the equipment shipped to you by the date you specified.

I am glad you brought this matter[5] to my personal attention and look forward to serving you in the future.

Yours very truly, (119)

5

Dear Meg:

We were quite surprised by the response to the opening of our new shop. Although we anticipated[1] having between 300 and 400 people, more than 600 customers were present for the event.[2]

The total amount of sales was well over $15,000. Our general manager feels that this large[3] turnout was the result of a super promotion effort. She has asked me to thank each member of the team. That[4] includes you.

You gave us many fine suggestions. In addition, you played a major role in overseeing the[5] event and by setting up the free drawings and awarding prizes.

Your efforts are appreciated.

Yours truly,[6] (120)

LESSON 20

1. Write a capital $\mathcal{N}$ for the sound of *end*, *nd* (pronounced *end*).

friend, f-r-nd *(shorthand)*

sending, s-nd-ing *(shorthand)*

handling, h-nd-l-ing *(shorthand)*

indicate, nd-k-ate *(shorthand)*

found, f-ow-nd *(shorthand)*

foundation,
   f-ow-nd-tion *(shorthand)*

Abbreviations

feet *(shorthand)*

square *(shorthand)*

yard *(shorthand)*

agriculture *(shorthand)*

economic, economy *(shorthand)*

Brief Forms

advantage *(shorthand)*

again, against *(shorthand)*

business *(shorthand)*

several *(shorthand)*

Write the following additional words that will be used in your reading and writing exercises:

land, l-nd *(shorthand)*

fund, f-nd *(shorthand)*

bonds, b-nd-s *(shorthand)*

dividends, d-v-d-nd-s *(shorthand)*

find, f-nd *(shorthand)*

window, w-nd-o *(shorthand)*

ground, guh-r-ow-nd *(shorthand)*

economical, economic-l *(shorthand)*

Phrases

I know	*ino*	to get	*lgl*
we are not	*ern*	to hear	*Uhr*
we will be	*elb*	to send	*lsN*
you will be	*ulb*	can be	*cb*

Commonly Misspelled Words

customer *K*

occurred *ocr-*

Your Business Vocabulary

dividends *dvdNs* Profits received from shares of ownership in a corporation.

purchasing department That department responsible for buying equipment and supplies for the entire company.

PCs dpl

PRINCIPLES SUMMARY

1. Write a capital *n* for the sound of *end, nd*: friend, f-r-nd

   frn

Vocabulary Builder.   Practice writing these frequently used words:

kind, k-nd	*cN*	attend, a-t-nd	*alN*
end, nd	*N*	around, a-r-ow-nd	*aroN*
sound, s-ow-nd	*soN*	friendship, f-r-nd-ship	*frNs*
intended, in-t-nd-ed	*nlN-*	behind, b-h-nd	*bhN*
refund, re-f-nd	*rfN*	background, b-k-guh-r-ow-nd	*bcgroN*

Reading and Writing Exercises

-1-

d hord ulb p- Uhr
la ∽ ∼c Pgrs б
Pfl + ls rpl u ∽M-
uAd v ∕ b ∽ ↳ u
grp ∼es aq, ι qι
agre la eAd ∼c
s∽ Cnγs n r ∼γm
v cpll, ↳∽c loz
dsγs eAd lc · q lc
∫ nγl eco, w rd
sv arlclo suq la
ls , n · apo ↳ l
b or sl bNo so lr
db lll Aνγ l c+
n r dvdNo no,
n γn ιd Aso rcm
aq b lN ƒ 2 rγno ⹀
prp νluιs ν hι +
∼rgγ me , hrd l
obln, ∪blv eAd lc

nl b̲ fn∼ lM, ∽
sec ∨ aqr hs Ppγ-
lγslγ ∽C d P∼l nu
fn∼ oro lgl lno ∕
· 9oγ ra l U ∽ P
∼r ra, uνl

-2-

mo l elγbl bron
drr ∨ PCo̲ er pln̲
lsM ab 2T Lo ƒ r
ƒM drν, d-∼ eC
L lb · rel env, d
∕ b ∼ ecol ƒ s luγ
∽ No envo er
no uγ n r ofo, Ph
eAd od rglr bo
envo, ιno la rglr
envo cb PCo- ƒ ls
me b ed ∨ lpa Gs

-3-

-4-

s cr crd K ulb nvi- l Cz ne cN v crpl u s. f ex loz rglrl prs-/ 14⁹⁹ P sq yd lb ofr-/ 11⁹⁶ P sq yd. A. ecol a l A nu lf lu h !, ehp ul lc Avy v ls gr ofr. elb hpe lpa u. Psnl vzl l dl cNo v sq yds ul nd. ls , s a v sa lqf bs. su

-5-

d crs l rsv- u cpes v nu lN ls agrems. ly apr lb n od b

ern yl Sln Ir or n ec gl P l drl. z uno nu lysly cd PvN s f drl o Sln cNs v agrl lN. no lcs z yf loz las l n apli l cos drl ls ln 9H fl nl r groN sn gr clr Ir la aplis l nCrl gs or yf s fA- l yf ls, r P hs rln l snlr bron lgl inf b afrd el n v. dfnl asr f sv cs. ab A ec du no s n psN. ul

Key

1

Dear Howard:

You will be pleased to hear that I am making progress on the profit and loss report you wanted. You[1] should have it by the time your group meets again.

I quite agree that we should make some changes in our management of[2] capital. To make those decisions, we should take a good look at the national economy. I have read[3] several articles suggesting that this is not an appropriate time to buy or sell bonds, so there would be little[4] advantage to cashing in our dividends now.

In general, I would also recommend against buying land[5] for two reasons— property values are high and mortgage money is hard to obtain. I believe we should look into[6] buying farm land. The Secretary of Agriculture has proposed legislation which would permit new farm[7] owners to get loans at a percentage rate well under the present market rate.

Yours very truly, (158)

2

MEMO TO: Elizabeth Brown, Director of Purchasing

We are planning to send about 2,000 letters[1] for our fund drive. Included with each letter will be a return envelope. Would it be more economical[2] for us to use the window envelopes we are now using in our office? Perhaps we should order regular[3] business envelopes. I know that regular envelopes can be purchased for less money, but we would have to pay[4] charges for having our address added to each envelope.

If we decide to order envelopes, we should do[5] so right away to make certain that they can be shipped without delay. I am inclined to order more window[6] envelopes.

If it would save time for you, we would be happy to place our own order and have the invoice mailed directly[7] to the purchasing department. (146)

3

Dear Mary:

Enclosed is a copy of the invoice from Roadway Truck Lines saying that they have not been paid for the[1] handling charges on the recent shipment we received. I have checked the receipt and found that we paid a total of[2] $638.59—which is more than the amount of our regular shipments.

Can[3] you find out where the problem is? If the handling charges were not included in our regular payment, we paid[4] too much for the shipment. If they were included, we should send that information to the trucking lines.

A similar[5] situation occurred several months ago, and we found that the trucking firm had made a mistake. It would[6] be to our advantage to check the matter closely.

Very truly yours, (133)

4

Dear Friend:

To show you how much we appreciate your business, we are planning a sales event. During the month of[1] April, we will mark 20 percent off all carpeting. As our credit card customer, you will be invited[2] to choose any kind of carpet you wish. For example, those regularly priced at $14.99[3] per square yard will be offered at $11.96 per square yard. What an economical way[4] to add new life to your home!

We hope you will take advantage of this great offer. We will be happy to pay you[5] a personal visit to determine the number of square yards you will need. This is our way of saying thank you[6] for your business.

Sincerely yours, (126)

5

Dear Chris:

I received your copies of the new land leasing agreements. They appear to be in order, but we are[1] not yet certain whether or not we can get permission to drill. As you know, new legislation could prevent us[2] from drilling on certain kinds of agricultural land. It now looks as if those laws will not apply to companies[3] drilling less than 900 feet into the ground. It is not quite clear whether the law applies to natural[4] gas or if it is limited to oil wells.

Our president has written to Senator Brown to get more information,[5] but I am afraid we will not have a definite answer for several weeks. About all we can do[6] now is remain patient.

Yours truly, (126)

LESSON 21

RECAP AND REVIEW

You have completed one-half of the principles lessons in this text. Let's take a look at the principles, brief forms, and abbreviations you studied in Lessons 15 through 20.

1. The following word beginnings were presented:

super   *S*   electr   *el*

2. These word endings were presented:

ward   *ur*   hood   *h*

tion   *1*   scribe, script   *S*

3. The following *Speedwriting* words represent all of the principles you studied in Lessons 15–20:

manuscripts, m-n-script-s	*mSs*	prescribe, pre-scribe	*PS*
vacation, v-k-tion	*vcy*	supermarket, super-market	*S—r*
auto, aw-t-o	*alo*	backward, b-k-ward	*bcw*
electrical, electr-k-l	*elcl*	quite, q-ite	*ql*
childhood, chay-l-d-hood	*Cldh*	friend, f-r-nd	*frn*
neighborhood, n-b-r-hood	*nbrh*	electrician, electr-cian	*ely*
toward, to-ward	*lw*	law, l-aw	*la*

4. You learned to write money amounts this way:

$29.95 29^{95} $2,000,000 $2M\$$

$300,000 $3HT\$$

5. What words do these abbreviations represent?

6. Write the *Speedwriting* words for these brief forms:

appreciate	present	about
over	advantage	under
correspondence	distribute	please
specify	has	again
order	against	specific
several	up	business
customer	correspond	include

Reading and Writing Exercises

-1-

[The following is handwritten shorthand notation.]

59 ^{95}

30 =

-2-

-3-

-4-

lc_ f . Psn l rpls | √ Pbl o f o_ r eco.
r cor sec hu , b_ | l z qi p- ⌣ u sugg o
P o- l . dfrN pzy, | f lca_ nu rzrvs v
n alC_ . cpe √ fb | yf f ex. u sly s o
dSy, yf u ⌣ l aplu | Ub , la no , els ho
f lo sp pzy p ru . | Uv , l agre ntrl
L Nca_ n ud b | ⌣ u vrus o olda- ls_
fre l bgn + lvl | agrems + fre us v
v slre u dzr. p | agrl lN, s qi clr
rmbr l l . cpe vu | la A ples d bnfl
rz a ⌣ l L, ehp | fo Cny_ lz las, l
l C z fnl cddls | ⌣ u l n fn± ls
n . fu ds so ed | bc + l gldl hlp yf
lc lv u L no lar | r nd arz o. cu
ln Fb , uvl |

-5-

-6-

ddr sn i njy- | d ro bl r njo
rd_ u nS o y_ | bgo hNl Bo v $
r nCrl nvrnm, | eC yr f Mo v Ko
u Slnl ofr . clr vu | b lr , no K r s
| bq h e vlu ⌣

Key

Abbreviations

avenue	pound	day
billion	inch	record
square	hundred	agriculture
month	boulevard	thousand
hour	ounce	feet
million	dollar, dollars	economic, economy
example, executive	cent, cents	yard

Brief Forms

ap	*p*	*ab*
O	*avɣ*	*U*
cor	*D*	*p*
sp	*hs*	*aq*
od	*aq*	*sp*
sv	*p*	*bs*
K	*cor*	*ɪ*

1

Dear Mr. Wilson:

Enclosed is the bill for repairing your television set. As you can see, the charges total[1] $59.95. This price includes a 30-day guarantee on parts and service. If you[2] have more problems, be certain to call our customer service department while the repairs are under warranty.[3] We will visit your home and make the repairs at no additional charge to you.

Your set is in good shape generally[4] and should provide you with many years of good service, but why not think about adding a second set to your[5] home? We have several models which you could easily move from room to room. If you buy now, we will include[6] a fine rolling cart free of charge with your purchase. We hope you'll take advantage of our offer.

Sincerely yours,[7] (140)

2

Dear Jason:

As I was preparing the program for our meeting, I discovered that we have several items[1] of new business to cover. Now I am afraid that our meeting will run over the time we have allowed. Can you[2] meet with me in order to go over some of these items? Perhaps some of them can be handled at a future[3] meeting.

Also, do you plan to present your findings on the marketing survey? If so, please let me know how much[4] time you will need. Our building manager has taken a position against purchasing certain kinds of electrical[5] equipment. He anticipates taking about ten minutes to discuss specific examples.

I have asked[6] each department manager to be present for this meeting. So far I have received one cancellation. Ms.[7] Wilson called to say that she will be on vacation that week and has asked Dr. Evans to take her place.

Yours[8] truly, (161)

3

Gentlemen:

I am quite surprised that we have not heard from you regarding the marketing books we ordered.

When we[1] placed the order, we were assured that the books would be shipped directly from your plant by the day specified. When the[2] books did not arrive on time, my secretary called the supervisor of your shipping department. The supervisor[3] found that the order placed by our business education department had been overlooked. He promised to send[4] the shipment right away.

More than a week has gone by, and we have no books. We plan to distribute them during[5] the opening class session on August 19. Please let us know what you plan to do about this matter. We would[6] appreciate hearing from you very soon.

Very truly yours, (131)

4

Dear Miss Collins:

This is in response to your letter of application. It so happens that we are looking for[1] a person to replace our correspondence secretary, who is being promoted to a different[2] position.

I am attaching a copy of the job description. If you wish to apply for this specific[3] position, please write a letter indicating when you would be free to begin and the level of salary you[4] desire. Please remember to include a copy of your resumé with the letter.

We hope to choose final[5] candidates within a few days, so we would like to have your letter no later than February 1.

Yours very[6] truly, (121)

5

Dear Dr. Mason:

I enjoyed reading your manuscript on managing our natural environment. You[1] certainly offer a clear view of the problems facing our economy. I was quite pleased with your suggestions for[2] locating new reserves of oil, for example. Your solution seems to be one that no one else has thought of.

I[3] agree entirely with your views on outdated leasing agreements and free use of agricultural land.[4] It is quite clear that all parties would benefit from changing these laws.

I wish you well in finishing this book and will[5] gladly help if the need arises.

Cordially yours, (109)

6

Dear Mrs. Billings:

Our nation's banks handle billions of dollars each year for millions of customers, but there is[1] no customer at our bank whom we value more than you. Enclosed is your bank receipt for the money you have asked[2] us to manage for you.

According to our agreement, we will make all your monthly payments while you are out of[3] town. When you return, we will provide you with a report indicating which bills we have paid. The report will also[4] show any earnings on your deposit here at our bank.

If you make arrangements to lease your apartment while[5] traveling, please be sure to send us a copy of the lease agreement. Please include the name of your attorney.[6] We want to be certain we have all the information we may need to manage your money well.

Yours truly,[7] (140)

Cplr 4 *

INPUT: TAKING DICTATION

When your supervisor asks, "Will you please come in for dictation?," a special teamwork begins. It's an interesting time, one set aside for a most important duty. Approach this activity with poise and involvement. Be alert, be enthusiastic, and be prepared.

Preparing for Dictation

Remember, your objective is to record dictation completely, quickly, and accurately. By following a few systematic procedures, you will be able to record all information and special details in a poised, organized manner without interrupting the thoughts of the person dictating. Practice these step-by-step procedures:

*Chapter Four

4. Write continuously.
   a. If you miss a word, wait[...] finished. Then ask, "Exc[...] May I read the sentence[...]
   b. Should your supervisor [...] the time to read your n[...] punctuation, write inst[...] that need clarification. }
   c. Flag rush items—with a[...]

Before Returning to Your Des[...]

Make sure you have all the inf[...] tions, ask them. If you are [...] addresses, or certain enclosure[...]

Before Transcribing

As soon as you return to your [...] details and instructions. Tran[...] ning with priority dictation.

As a member of this team[...] executives set aside a certain ti[...] rupted by phone calls, appoi[...] times each day, depending upo[...] you will always be ready to re[...] bility makes you a valuable p[...]

LESSON 22

[...]ial sound of *em* or *im* (pronounced *m*).

impress, im-p-r-s

impatient, im-p-ish-nt

impose, im-p-z

prompt, prah-m-t

promptly, prah-m-t-ly

especially

et cetera

university

character, characteristic

industry

[...]rd Development

whatever

another

quarterly

industries

Phrases

I have been	*wb*	we believe	*eblv*
I should	*isd*	we know	*eno*
I was	*iz*	as well as	*zlz*

TRANSCRIPTION AID Learn to punctuate correctly.

We punctuate our writing for one reason: to add clarity. When we speak, we use voice tones and pauses to punctuate. We use an uplifted tone to ask a question. We pause between words and phrases to give order and meaning to the thought we are expressing. Without changes in voice tone and natural pauses, our words would run together and much of the meaning would be lost.

On the printed page, however, we do not have the benefit of voice tones or natural pauses. We use punctuation marks instead.

The comma is an important mark of punctuation. We use a comma to separate a word or phrase from the rest of the sentence. The comma forces us to pause as we read. To help you understand when and where to use commas, we will present examples in future lessons. You will probably find that your supervisor will expect you to provide all of the punctuation needed in the material you transcribe.

USE COMMAS BETWEEN THREE OR MORE WORDS IN A SERIES.

The last word in a series will be preceded by either of these two words: *and, or.* In this text, we will always place a comma before *and* and *or* in a series. Some offices, however, may prefer that this comma be omitted. Use the style preferred in your office.

Letters arrived for Mary, Todd, Steven, and James.

Please ask someone to answer the phone, sort the mail, and file all correspondence.

There are three subjects I especially enjoy—accounting, typewriting, and history.

In the reading and writing exercises, commas in a series will be circled. The word **Series** will be highlighted.

| Your Business Vocabulary | merchandising *~dse* | The planning of sales programs directed toward creating a market demand for a product. |
| | market analysis *~r anlss* | Research concerned with all factors that affect the sales of goods and services. |

PRINCIPLES SUMMARY

1. Write ⌒ for the initial sound of *em* or *im*: emphasize, em-f-s-z *~fsz* .
2. Omit *p* in the sound of *mpt*: prompt, prah-m-t *P~l* .

Reading and Writing Exercises

-1-

(shorthand outlines)

hsp. ι ⌒N– u lno
Psnll la ⁄ ol psNs
+ ι ap–⁄﹐ su

-2-

⁊ lqf qs re‗ r ⩳ +
D⁊ plses﹐ e ofr sv
plns﹐ me l⁊ bss
lc Av⁊ ✓ flo‗ b⁊l
pln﹐ ⁊ u od · mm
v 12T$ n ⌒dse P
yr ul rsv · rds–
ra ⌒C cⱱ pd n
ι aⱱ yrl or 4 aⱱs
qlrl · ⸱ E ad⁊l ѕm
ul pa ol 10% vu
rglr ⩳ fe﹐ aol pln
e suq ﹐ · arm ofn
uz– ⱱ sⱱ rll bss﹐
u pls ods ₃ und
L﹢ + ɾ bl–⸱ eⒸ od﹒

⁊ u lol ѕms ⸱ ne
gvn yr aⱱ ι ⌒
ln 7T2H$ ul rsv
· sv‗ ⌒C llb cr– lw
u PⒸss ⸜ flo‗ yr﹐ ellb
hpe ι Dcs ol plns
L⌒e u nds﹐ p ⸱l fre
ι cl o s ⁄ ne L⌒﹐ ul

-3-

dS w sv qs ab u
U﹐ d u p sN ⌒e ·
cpe vu cal⸝·aplⱼ
⸱ ₍Series 9₎ + ol ⁊n mnf re‗
nrlm plses﹒ ⌒
enc‗ cpes v ⌒ι
acdⱼc recs ⌒C
⸝hp ul ⸱M sal﹐ r
lɾ ol crss ιsd lc
ι nѕɾ la ⌒ι aplⱼ
llb ac–﹐ ιd Aso lc

Series

Series   Series

-4-

-5-

Key

1

Dear Dr. Davidson:

Recently, I was a patient under the care of your efficient personnel. I[1] especially appreciated the efforts of your nurse, Ellen Jeffries. It is not easy to find people who[2] perform over and above the call of duty, but Ms. Jeffries is one of those rare persons. I was impressed by[3] her kind manner, her dedication, and the prompt attention she gave to every patient under her care.

She was[4] never too busy to listen to our problems and often did so on her own time. I believe her character[5] was encouraging to the other personnel as well as to the patients.

It was very satisfying to[6] see the high level of professional care throughout your hospital. I wanted you to know personally that[7] the other patients and I appreciated it.

Sincerely yours, (152)

2

Gentlemen:

Thank you for your questions regarding our shipping and distribution policies. We offer several[1] plans. Many large businesses take advantage of the following budget plan.

If you order a minimum[2] of $12,000 in merchandise per year, you will receive a reduced rate which can be paid in one amount[3] yearly or four amounts quarterly. For every additional shipment, you will pay only 10 percent of your[4] regular shipping fee.

Another plan we suggest is an arrangement often used by small retail businesses.[5] You place orders as you need them and are billed for each order. If your total shipments for any given year[6] amount to more than $7,200, you will receive a savings which will be credited toward[7] your purchases the following year.

We will be happy to discuss other plans to meet your needs. Please feel free to[8] call on us at any time.

Yours truly, (167)

3

Dear Sir:

I have several questions about your university. Would you please send me a copy of your[1] catalog, an application form, and other general information regarding enrollment policies? I[2] am enclosing copies of my academic records, which I hope you will find satisfactory. Are there other[3] courses I should take to ensure that my application will be accepted?

I would also like specific[4] details about your School of Business. Currently I am thinking of majoring in marketing, with an emphasis[5] in merchandising and marketing analysis. I hope you can advise me on other fields such as[6] personnel management, sales management, economics, etc.

I have been told that you place seniors in jobs[7] related to their chosen fields for one full quarter during the final year. Is this the case for every senior?[8] I would also appreciate receiving whatever information you have about job markets in business[9] and industry.

Yours very truly, (186)

4

Dear Mr. and Mrs. Ames:

We want this holiday season to be especially happy for you and your[1] family. That's why we designed a holiday budget plan—to make your shopping easier and your holidays[2] happier.

Our budget plan provides the cash you need and an easy payment schedule. Here's how we can help you.[3] Visit our loan department and talk with our credit officer. When you have determined the amount of cash you need,[4] you can choose a payment plan designed to fit your monthly budget. If you wish, you may delay making payments up[5] to 90 days following the loan.

You will find our service prompt and our officers eager to help. By serving[6] customers like you, we have learned how to make the holidays an easier time for many people, and we take[7] pride in doing so.

While you are here, ask for information on our full line of banking services. We think[8] you will be impressed with the wide range we offer. At General Savings and Loan, when we add a new customer,[9] we know we have made a new friend.

Very truly yours, (189)

5

Dear Dr. Sharp:

Thank you for your correspondence asking about our plans for publishing your book, *Guide to Word[1] Processing.* I think I can now answer those questions to your satisfaction.

We anticipate having the books on[2] the market by the end of February or the beginning of March. I am very pleased to report that we[3] had the manuscript reviewed by several people in the industry and received very good responses. They[4] were especially impressed with the final chapter in which you discuss other uses for electronic[5] equipment in the office.

Because your manuscript is so timely, we wish to prepare it for future use as[6] quickly as we can. We believe your book is a very good example of what our readers want. I will make every[7] attempt to keep you up to date on what's happening.

Yours very truly, (153)

LESSON 23

1. Write *k* for the sounds of *com, con, coun (ow), count.*

common, com-n *kn* council, coun-s-l *ksl*

accommodate, a-com-d-ate *akda* account, a-count *ak*

concern, con-s-r-n *ksrn* county, count-e *ke*

2. Write *s* for the sound of *st* (pronounced *est*).

still, st-l *sl* trust, t-r-st *trs*

state, st-ate *sa* most, m-st *s*

instead, in-st-d *nsd* fastest, f-st-st *fss*

Write these additional words:

discount, dis-count *Dk* constant, con-st-nt *ksn*

commission, com-sion *kj* cost, k-st *cs*

postage, p-st-j *psj* finest, f-n-st *fns*

confirm, con-firm *kfr* storage, st-r-j *srj*

condition, con-d-tion *kdj* concerning, con-s-r-n-ing *ksrn_*

Phrases

I would like *idlc* you could *ucd*

we are pleased *erp-* to receive *trsv*

you cannot *ucn* to say *lsa*

Commonly Misspelled Words	accommodate *akda*
	almost *a—s*

Your Business Vocabulary	real estate *rl esa*	A term that refers to land and the buildings or permanent structures on the land.
	commerce *krs*	The buying and selling of goods and services; usually on a widespread basis, such as national commerce.

PRINCIPLES SUMMARY

1. Write *k* / count-e *ke*   for the sounds of *com, con, coun (ow), count*: county,
2. Write *s*   for the sound of *st*: still, st-l *sl*

Reading and Writing Exercises

-1-

[Shorthand writing exercises, two columns]

-2-

-3-

os v gn b + ev n
rsv- u Cc ., , lr s
rzn ucn sN evn
r mm pam ., , lr ,
Sl L Lc u ak
crN + mln u q
cr SN . p cl r ofs
ld + c arms l
sll ls lr , elb
gld l hlp n ne a.
uf e USN u Pbl Ph
ec ar . pam scyl
l akda u nds . ul

-4-

dn ly s Pfsr
bron lls e la uv
rln sv arlcls ab
r kpur N . w fS fns-
. Sde o uz kpurs n
ejcy + idlc l sr

e fN u . enc-
rpl , bs- o e
rSC . d u lc . lc ,
, + ll e uf u lqr
rpl cdb pbls- z .
bc ., A S A v rpl
ksrns nu uss f
kpurs n clsr . ,
P l8 r lds
n e o clsr +
c arms lr L
l8- els r . r rsps
f lCrs vb v q ,
idlc l P rpl l
. pblsr + d ap ne
sugjs uv ab ru_
dll- Ppzl . ihp uc
fN L n u bze
scyl l gv e u
kNs . id grl vlu
u Avs + Ppr- lpa

-5-

Key

1

Gentlemen:

It was most satisfying to read your article concerning air traffic. When the airport was built,[1] the runway size was more than adequate. During the last several years, conditions have greatly changed. We now have[2] a much larger number of aircraft using our airport on a daily basis.

I agree that the cost of[3] increased services should not be paid by the city alone. It would be more economical for everyone[4] if the county were to pay a greater share of the costs. Personally, I would like to see a proposal placed before[5] the county council asking for an increase in funding.

Do you know if anyone has investigated[6] using other revenue? I would be willing to help start a fund drive in order to raise money from private[7] sources such as business, industry, and foundations. Perhaps you could address this topic in a front-page story.[8]

The need for increased services is a major issue today. I hope you will keep giving it the coverage[9] it deserves.

Sincerely yours, (185)

2

Dear Mr. and Mrs. Smith:

I was delighted to receive your call asking me to be your real estate agent.[1]

I believe that your asking price is right. You have a fine home in a very good location. There is every reason[2] to believe that your home will be sold in a very short time. As I mentioned earlier, your house will be listed[3] in the newspaper as well as in our real estate bulletin. The bulletin is published on a weekly[4] basis and distributed all over the county in stores and office buildings. It is well read and often gives[5] the best results of all sources used.

We will show your home as frequently as we can. To make those visits more pleasant[6] for you, I will call at least one hour ahead of time to make an appointment. The decision whether or not[7] to remain at home during those visits is entirely up to you.

I look forward to serving as your agent.[8]

Very truly yours, (164)

3

Dear Ms. Miller:

We have sent several notices informing you that your account is past due, and still we have[1] not heard from you. Almost three months have gone by, and we have not received your check. Is there some reason you cannot send[2] even the minimum payment?

There is still time to make your account current and maintain your good credit standing.[3] Please call our office today and make arrangements to settle this matter.

We will be glad to help in any way.[4] If we understand your problem, perhaps we can arrange a payment schedule to accommodate your needs.

Yours truly,[5] (100)

4

Dear Ms. Williams:

Professor Brown tells me that you have written several articles about the computer[1] industry. I have just finished a study on using computers in education, and I would like to share my[2] findings with you. The enclosed report is based on my research. Would you take a look at it and tell me if you think[3] the report could be published as a book?

Almost all of the report concerns new uses for computers in the[4] classroom. At present, I am testing the methods in my own classroom and making arrangements to have them tested[5] elsewhere. The responses from teachers have been very good.

I would like to present my report to a publisher[6] and would appreciate any suggestions you have about writing a detailed proposal. I hope you can find[7] time in your busy schedule to give me your comments. I would greatly value your advice and am prepared to pay[8] a fee for this service.

Please let me know if you can help.

Cordially yours, (173)

5

Dear Lisa:

Thank you for your comments on our proposed shopping center. We are pleased to say we will present our plans[1] to the city planning commission on January 11.

I especially appreciate your[2] advice in regard to providing necessary information. The report you included with your letter[3] provided a fine example to follow. I believe our request for a zoning change will be granted. A[4] location west of town is the best choice for a large center like ours.

Our shopping center will contain several large[5] businesses—three discount stores, five department stores, and two supermarkets. It will accommodate up to[6] 100 other businesses.

The center should draw customers from several counties. Thus, it will increase commerce[7] for the entire city. For that reason, we anticipate a great deal of support for our plan.

Yours very truly,[8] (160)

LESSON 24

1. Write the days of the week as follows:

Sunday *Sn*   Thursday *Th*

Monday *Mn*   Friday *Fr*

Tuesday *Tu*   Saturday *Sl*

Wednesday *Wd*

Abbreviations

federal *fed*   street *S*

government *gvt*   okay *ok*

represent, representative *rep*   incorporate,
                                    incorporated *inc*

Brief Forms

continue *ku*   accomplish *ak*

deliver *dl*   complete *kp*

opportunity *opt*   contribute *kb*

come, came, committee *k*   convenient, convenience *kv*
cont

Brief Form Development

continued *ku-*   accomplishments *akms*

completed *kp-*   contributions *kbjs*

opportunities *opts*   income *nk*

Phrases

I feel   *yfl*

you would be   *udb*

*as *soon* as   *zz .zfz*

as we   *ze*

*Omit the italicized word in the *Speedwriting* phrase.

USE COMMAS AFTER INTRODUCTORY DEPENDENT CLAUSES.

An introductory dependent clause is a group of words containing a subject and a verb that occurs at the beginning of a sentence. However, this clause is not a complete thought and cannot stand alone. It requires a main (independent) clause to make the sentence complete.

Introductory dependent clauses usually begin with recognizable words. The most common words are *when, as,* and *if.* Other common examples are *although, though, unless, since, while, until, before, after, whether,* and *because.*

When Dr. Ellis arrives, please have her call my office.

As I may have mentioned earlier, that contract has already expired.

If you prefer, we will have the order shipped directly to you.

Beginning with this lesson, introductory dependent clauses that start with *when, as,* and *if* will be highlighted in your reading and writing exercises. The abbreviation **Intro DC** will be highlighted.

Your Business Vocabulary

capital investment   Funds spent for additions or improvements in plant, equipment, or personnel.

cpll nvdm

PRINCIPLES SUMMARY

1. Days of the week.

Reading and Writing Exercises

-1-

[shorthand]

-2-

[shorthand]

Intro DC

Series

-3-

-4-

Intro DC

Intro DC

Intro DC

413 W

kpl sal- ⌣ hr ₃
· spcr ⌐ su

-5-

mo l Pfsr edws
⌐ P hs apy- · k l
rvu r plse o ⌣su
fed lns l SdNs.
d u b fre l rep ⌐
scl v eycy o la k.⌐
⌐ k l alz r crN
⌐lds v Pss aplcys
+ nvSga nu ⌐lds
la ⌐ rzll n · ⌐

efsN ss ⌐ w ·
fl kln bcgroN inf
⌐ l hlp u ⌐ ⌐ ds
· cpe v gvl rglys
+ · Sam v U plse
ic Aso Pvd cpes
v fro Ub kp- b
aplcNs, if s kv
fuip pln l Sp b
⌐ ofs o Ju os
Wd ⌐ lg uil fN ls
asnm Ub v Clny
+ rw ⌐

Intro DC
⑨

Key

1

Gentlemen:

We have good news for you. Your shipment of office furnishings came in last Friday. Will it be okay[1] to deliver it this week?

If you have a specific day in mind, please call our shipping department and make the[2] arrangements directly with them. Otherwise, someone will be in touch with you. It would also be wise to confirm[3] your street address.

As soon as you accept delivery, please check each item with care. When you are satisfied that[4] the shipment is complete and contains no damaged goods, return one copy of the invoice with your full payment.

Thank[5] you for allowing Movers, Inc., to handle these shipping arrangements for you. Please call on us[6] again. We are a brief phone call away from serving you.

Sincerely yours, (132)

2

Dear Frank:

A question came up Thursday concerning our lease agreement on the old federal building. This morning[1] a government representative called to ask if we still wish to purchase the property. A firm called Investors,[2] Inc., has made an offer and is waiting for a reply. What do you think about this opportunity?[3]

The building has about 10,000 square feet of floor space, and we are using about 60 percent of it.[4]

We have often discussed whether we should buy the building, continue renting, or move to a new location.[5] Now the time has come to make a decision about this capital investment.

Very truly yours, (119)

3

MEMO TO: All Sales Personnel

You should be especially pleased with your accomplishments this year. We not only[1] met our sales goals, we surpassed them.

This year's record sales offer a fine opportunity to point out the[2] contributions made by sales representatives. The growth of our corporation is directly related to your[3] outstanding efforts.

As we look ahead to the coming year, let's set our goals for continued growth in the marketplace.[4] I feel confident that the new year will yield the best results ever. When we meet again at the regional[5] convention, we will discuss how to achieve those results.

Please accept the enclosed bonus check with our compliments.[6] It is our way of showing our appreciation for a job well done. (133)

4

Dear Mrs. Davis:

Thank you for your invitation to address the National Life Insurance convention. I[1] would very much like to accept, but my present schedule will not permit me to attend. Perhaps I can suggest[2] someone else.

When I was in New Orleans last year, I had the opportunity to hear a fine speaker, Janet[3] Chase. Her background and accomplishments are impressive.

You can reach Ms. Chase at her home at 413 West Elm Street.[4] I think you would be completely satisfied with her as a speaker.

Sincerely yours, (95)

5

MEMO TO: Professor Edwards

The president has appointed a committee to review our policy on[1] issuing federal loans to students. Would you be free to represent the School of Education on that[2] committee?

The committee will analyze our current methods of processing applications and investigate[3] new methods that might result in a more efficient system. I have a file containing background information[4] which will help you. It includes a copy of government regulations and a statement of university[5] policy. I can also provide copies of forms to be completed by applicants.

If it is convenient[6] for you, please plan to stop by my office on Tuesday or Wednesday. I think you'll find this assignment to be very[7] challenging and rewarding. (145)

LESSON 25

1. Write *q* for the word ending *quire*.

require, re-quire *rq*

inquiry, in-quire-e *nqe*

requirements,
   re-quire-ment-s *rqms*

acquire, a-quire *aq*

inquire, in-quire *nq*

required, re-quire-duh *rq-*

2. Write *3* for the sound of *zh*.

pleasure, p-l-z-r *plzr*

treasure, t-r-z-r *trzr*

measure, m-z-r *mzr*

leisure, l-z-r *lzr*

Writing State and City Names

The United States Post Office requests that two-letter state initials be used on all business envelopes. To indicate states in your *Speedwriting* notes, write the same two-letter state initials that the Post Office uses.

Alabama = AL   *AL*

California = CA   *CA*

City names are written according to rule. Listed below are examples of how to write city and state names. For a list of all the states, see the appendix at the back of this book.

Boston, MA   *bsn MA*

Columbus, OH   *clbs OH*

Tulsa, OK   *Ulsa OK*

Las Vegas, NV   *ls vgs NV*

Madison, WI   *dsn WI*

Buffalo, NY   *bflo NY*

The *Speedwriting* capitalization mark is used when writing the city name by itself, but not when both the city and the state are used. Note that the state is set off by commas in transcription.

Boston   *bsn*

Boston, MA   *bsn MA*

Phrases

I look *ulc*

we could *ecd*

we have been *evb*

we would like *edlc*

to do *Ldu*

to give *lgv*

to visit *Lvzl*

Commonly Misspelled Words	representative *rep*
	convenient *kv*

Your Business Vocabulary	test market *ls ~r*	A geographical area selected for sales of goods or services during a trial period to determine the marketability of a product.

PRINCIPLES SUMMARY

1. Write *q* for the word ending *quire*: require, re-quire *rq*

2. Write *3* for the sound of *zh*: pleasure, p-l-z-r *plzr*

Vocabulary Builder. Practice writing these frequently used words:

requirement, re-quire-ment *rqm*

requires, re-quire-s *rqs*

treasury, t-r-z-r-e *lrzre*

inquiries, in-quire-e-s *nqes*

measuring, m-z-r-ing *~zr*

measurement, m-z-r-ment *~zrm*

inquiring, in-quire-ing *nq_*

acquire, a-quire *aq*

Reading and Writing Exercises

-1-

-2-

Series

Series

Series

Intro DC

-3-

· Cny ⟨Intro DC⟩ e sM nqes
l hlls + kvny
sMrs n sv ⟨yr
sles, e Cz ch bs
OH bcz ⟨ kdys ls
⟨l r rqms,
ch bs Aso ofr-
⟨ bs kvny ras f
r gss, z · mbr v
arms k ⟨ ⟨c
· Sva, du Pfr l
hld ⟨ kvny nr s⟨
sle eC yr or d u
Pfr lvzl dfrM
sles, p gv ⟨ e u
sugjs nr sps
⟨rc-"kNs" o
rzrvy f⟨, eap u
ku- spl f r ⟨e
ilc fw lse u aq
ls yr, vlu

mo l ed prcr ⟨
S p- ⟨ r plns f
hld No Oplas,
⟨n r k z f- ⟨Intro DC⟩ e asc-
· rep v eC dpl l
kb sugjs, ⟨ z rw
lse ⟨ No + rny v
sugjs e rsv-, if
r plns r ok ⟨ u ⟨Intro DC⟩
el inc nu lys ⟨
lrdyl i ⟨ v ps,
f ex e lca- s ⟨ ss
alc lys l P aq,
bcgroM v ⟨drn
pM edlc l aq,
ss ⟨ v lis + soMs
lgv A- fss, ecd
Sl uz r pM- lMscps
if e gv ⟨ · nu lc,
e ⟨ lri ar elnc
gns + lys aq ⟨ old

-4-

-5-

[Shorthand content]

Key

1

Dear Mr. and Mrs. Gray:

The minute you see our guide to managing money, you'll know we designed it for you.[1] Our authors talked with people like you across the country. Their purpose was to learn ways to help people on set[2] incomes live more economically. The result is a book called *Money—How to Make the Most of It.*

Money[3] gives you a complete guide to managing your income. It shows you how to make, save, budget, and spend your earnings to your[4] best advantage. *Money* is easy to read and convenient to use. It provides everything our advisers[5] wanted and more. Planning a trip? *Money* tells you how to do it and save. Shopping for food? *Money* can reduce your food[6] bills by 40 percent.

You must see this guide to appreciate what it will do for you. Order your copy by[7] returning the enclosed form in our postage-free envelope. Send your check today and put *Money* in your home[8] planning.

Yours truly, (164)

2

Dear Miss Brown:

It gives me great pleasure to invite you to this year's national convention. If you plan to attend,[1] please complete the enclosed reservation form and return it by October 2.

This year's location represents[2] our response to the results of a questionnaire sent to our members. When the membership requested a change, we[3] sent inquiries to hotels and convention centers in several major cities. We chose Columbus, Ohio,[4] because the conditions there met our requirements. Columbus also offered the best convention rates for our[5] guests.

As a member of the arrangements committee, I am making a survey. Would you prefer to hold the[6] convention in the same city each year, or would you prefer to visit different cities? Please give me your suggestions[7] in the space marked "comments" on the reservation form.

We appreciate your continued support for[8] our meetings. I look forward to seeing you again this year.

Very truly yours, (174)

3

MEMO TO: Ed Parker

I am most pleased with our plans for holiday window displays. When our committee was formed,[1] we asked a representative of each department to contribute suggestions. It was rewarding to see the[2] number and range of suggestions we received.

If our plans are okay with you, we will incorporate new toys with[3] traditional items of the past. For example, we located some rare antique toys to present against a[4] background of modern paintings. We would like to acquire a system of lights and sounds to give added emphasis.

We[5] could still use our painted landscapes if we give them a new look. We might try arranging electronic games and toys[6] against the old background. As soon as you have the opportunity, won't you meet with me to discuss these suggestions?[7] (140)

4

Dear Mrs. Moore:

Thank you for your letter concerning the use of our floor cleaner. We are delighted to hear that[1] the machine performed so well. We have been pleasantly surprised by the large demand for this machine. So many[2] people requested it that we have a waiting list.

In order to serve more customers, we are acquiring[3] another machine. As soon as this machine is ready for use, you may call in your reservation directly to[4] our store on Second Street. We hope the new system provides more efficient service for everyone.

We appreciate[5] your comments. I hope you will visit us often.

Very truly yours, (112)

5

MEMO TO: Manager of Marketing and Sales

When the Board of Directors met last Monday, they voted to start[1] a new division to produce paper goods. This represents a major change and offers opportunities in[2] a new market.

We will distribute the paper goods through our food division. This system appears to be the most[3] economical and convenient method of handling the new merchandise.

Sales representatives who call on[4] supermarkets will increase their calls to include discount stores, drug stores, and other retail outlets which carry our[5] goods.

We anticipate using Denver, Colorado, as a test market for the new line. We will measure the[6] results of a six-month test to form future marketing plans. If we accomplish our goals in the test market, we[7] will turn our attention to national sales. (148)

LESSON 26

1. Write ____ for the word ending *ness*.

kindness, k-nd-ness _cn′_

witnesses, w-t-nesses _ι″_

illness, i-l-ness _il′_

carelessness, k-r-l-s-ness _crls′_

*happiness, h-p-e-ness _hpe′_

helplessness,
h-l-p-l-s-ness _hlpls′_

*Always write long vowels before marks of punctuation.

Brief Forms

both _bo_

individual _nv_

public _pb_

important, importance _⌐pl_

Brief Form Development

publicly _pbl_

publication _pbj_

willingness _l′_

individually _nvl_

Phrases

to come _tk_

to determine _tdt_

to offer _tofr_

MORE INTRODUCTORY DEPENDENT CLAUSES

In addition to *when*, *as*, and *if*, introductory dependent clauses beginning with such words as *although*, *before*, and *because* will be highlighted.

Although two months have passed, we still have not heard from you.

Before you order supplies, please contact our purchasing department.

Because you are a valued customer, you will receive a discount.

| Your Business Vocabulary | homeowner's policy *h—ors plse* | An insurance policy covering the cost of the policyholder's home and personal belongings in case of damage or loss. |
| | suggested retail price *sug-rll prs* | The ultimate sale price (sometimes referred to as *list price*) recommended by the manufacturer. |

PRINCIPLES SUMMARY

1. Write ╱ for the word ending *ness*: kindness, k-nd-ness *cn´*.

Vocabulary Builder. Practice writing these frequently used words:

fitness, f-t-ness *fl´*

fairness, f-r-ness *fr´*

illnesses, i-l-nesses *il˝*

kindnesses, k-nd-nesses *cn˝*

witness, w-t-ness *l´*

eagerness, e-guh-r-ness *egr´*

weakness, w-k-ness *c´*

slowness, s-l-o-ness *slo´*

Reading and Writing Exercises

-1-

[Shorthand outlines]

Intro DC

Intro DC

Intro DC

-2-

[Shorthand outlines]

Intro DC

(shorthand notation)

Intro DC

-3-

Intro DC

Series

Series

-4-

-5-

z u ms co e M | a√M l hlp lca
l rel u lu h gcl. | plz√M + kv akdjs.
r mh p alo r | cu

Key

1

Dear Mr. and Mrs. Cramer:

I am delighted to inform you that I have been assigned to handle your[1] policy. As you learned from his letter, your former agent was promoted to vice president. I would like to add[2] that the promotion came in recognition of his outstanding contributions to our company.

Although[3] assuming his duties will be very challenging, I plan to continue the prompt and thorough service characteristic[4] of Mr. Johnson. As a first step, I would like to meet you personally and review your policy[5] to determine that the coverage meets your current needs.

Because it is important for both of you to be[6] present during our conversation, I will call on Wednesday, May 27, to find a time convenient for[7] everyone. It will be a pleasure visiting with you. I am new to your city, and I look forward to making[8] new friends.

Sincerely yours, (164)

2

Dear Mr. Wilson:

It is with great pleasure that we welcome you to our consumer club. The enclosed membership[1] card allows you to shop during regular store hours from Monday through Saturday.

Because our store is reserved[2] for the use of members only, we ask that you not invite visitors on regular shopping days. However,[3] on the first Sunday of each month, we hold an open house in which club members invite guests to learn about our club[4] and the many benefits it offers.

We now have 250 members. As our membership continues[5] to grow, we will offer even greater discounts on merchandise. At the present time, we are selling brand-name[6] items at 20 percent below the suggested retail price. You can help our membership grow by telling people[7] in your neighborhood about our program. Visit our Sunday open house and ask a friend to come with you.

Sincerely[8] yours, (161)

3

Dear Melvin:

Although I have given much thought to your suggestion that I run for a seat in the House of Representatives,[1] I have decided against doing so at this time. My wife is recovering from a recent illness,[2] and her continued return to good health is our most important concern.

However, I would like to offer my[3] support to another individual who would make an outstanding representative. Sue Martin has[4] served as manager of public relations, director of consumer affairs, and assistant to the Secretary[5] of State. I feel confident she would be received well by the public.

Both my wife and I wish to thank you[6] for your kindness and encouragement. Under different conditions, I would have gladly accepted. I hope the[7] opportunity comes again in the future.

Yours very truly, (152)

4

Dear Mr. and Mrs. Smith:

It gives us great pleasure to invite you to attend the private opening of our[1] new store at 301 North State Street.

Our shop will carry a full line of men's and women's clothing, from sporting goods[2] to formal wear. We have taken great care to choose your favorite brands and designs. Just as important, we are[3] providing a wide range of prices from which to choose.

Our store opens to the public on November 6. On the[4] evening before, we would like you to be our guest for a private showing in which our models will be wearing[5] original designs from New York. Following the show, we invite you to have refreshments, visit, and browse.

Please join[6] us for what promises to be an evening of fun, fashion, and surprises on Friday, November 5.

Very[7] truly yours, (142)

5

Dear Mr. Stevens:

Thank you for your promptness in reporting the damages to your home.

We understand that the[1] fire damage makes it necessary for you to find other living quarters while repairs are being made. We have[2] forwarded your claim to a local agent who will help you make those arrangements.

Because your homeowner's policy[3] provides complete coverage, all repairs will be made at no cost to you. This coverage includes whatever[4] living arrangements you choose. Before we can process your claim, we will need a complete list of the individual[5] items damaged or lost. Please mail or deliver that list to your agent's office at 2100 Main[6] Street.

As your insurance company, we want to return you to your home quickly. In the meantime, please allow our[7] agent to help locate pleasant and convenient accommodations.

Cordially yours, (155)

LESSON 27

1. When using salutations and closings in context, write them according to the rule.

gentlemen, j-nt-l-men   *jnlm*   sincerely, s-n-s-r-ly   *snsrl*

cordially, k-r-j-l-ly   *cryll*

Abbreviations

advertise   *av*   Christmas   *X⌇s*

Brief Forms

always   *a*   prove   *pv*

consider   *ks*   note   *nl*

ordinary   *ord*

Brief Form Development

consideration   *ksj*   improvement   *⌇pvm*

noted   *nl-*   approval   *apvl*

ordinarily   *ordl*

Commonly Misspelled Words	opportunity *opl* preferred *Pfr-*

Your Business Vocabulary	corporate stocks *crprl scs* search and screen committee *SC + scrn k*	Shares in the ownership of a corporation. Committee appointed to evaluate the credentials of job applicants and recommend candidates for the position. Often used in educational institutions.

PRINCIPLES SUMMARY

1. In context, write salutations and closings according to the rule: gentlemen, j-nt-l-men 〰 .

Reading and Writing Exercises

-1-

[This section contains handwritten shorthand notation that cannot be accurately transcribed as standard text.]

-2-

[This section contains handwritten shorthand notation that cannot be accurately transcribed as standard text.]

hs rep- r cly o sv
ks n sle + ke gvl,
bcz v dvds pl l
r cly idb sre lse h
lv. ι Aso no la
ddca- Nws S w
o l nu gls n od l
sal ls o nd f grl,
if uv ol gs re dr
lsn Intro DC ⑨ ilb gld l asr
L. uvl

-3-

dK Ap 15, gcl
aprC + e S rds
r nlr Sc v nu +
uz- crs. la ms gr
sv f z sprs. ls
yr el ofr blr Dks
ln E bf, bgn Fb 3
el rn f= pq nzppr

Avms ll r pb ab r
lo prss b er gv u.
opl lgl ahd v rs.
er nvr lyl Ks lc
u l lc Avq v lz gr
sv o Fb 2. ul fN.
d rny v cs Series ⑨
dls Series ⑨ + prss f
C l Cz, ul Aso
v E ksq n c ord
cr arms. r Cf cr
ofsr lb o hN du
sl hrs l apv u cr,
rmbr erl sprs
A v r bS Cyss.
ehp lse u ls. ul

-4-

d prN r scl dNl
hll Pq, ab lgl
ll a, z pl v ls Pq

u Cld l v r opl l
pp n . dNl clnc
fre v G . eC Cld
lb gvn . fre Ubrs
+ sn ho luz , Pprl ,
bcz v ~ pl v q h
cr dy ls Pq e asc
A prNs l hlp s b
Svz ls Cldrns brs
hbts bo n ~ vn +
n evn , p nl la ls
Pq dz n rpls rglr
dNl cr . Alo u Cld
~ a b rsv rglr
dNl trems _{Intro DC} h or se
c Sl bnfl f pp n
clsr clnc , ls Pq
ho b apv- b r ke
dNl ksl . yf u ~ su
Cld l pp _{Intro DC} p sn r f
blo gv u ksN rel

/ lu Clds lCr
b Oc 5 , su

-5-

dr evns z r vlu-
K uno la r Sr lcs
prd n hNl ol r
bl n Nlms ~ r . ls
plse ho pv- Ub r
~ S pl rzn Nvo
lc u ku l sp hr , ls
yr ev . Sprz fu . l
so r apf f spl uv
gvn r bs el ofr . bf=
Xs sl f Pfr- Ks , f
so r slsppl ls L +
ul rsv 20% of r
rglr prss = I r
nlr ln v sus _{Series} coo _{Series}
srls _{Series} + spls r , ls ,
. Cnf f ps yrs

~n prss ~ rds.
af X~s, b sp_erl
uc ak 2 ~pl gls =
i fu + ol f jNlm
o u sp_ ls, e cryll

nvr u l alN ls
sl + njy Cz_ f~r
f Sc. / d gv s gr
plzr l Sv u aq, cu

Key

1

Dear Executive:

You are one of the few people chosen to receive three free issues of *Business Review.*

Why?[1] Because we mail inquiries only to the individuals who meet our requirements. *Business Review* is[2] directed at informed individuals like you who have shown a concern for major problems and opportunities[3] facing our nation.

To help you decide that our magazine is right for you, we are sending you the first three[4] issues free of charge. Then you may choose to receive the six following issues at half price.

Included in those nine[5] issues will be major news stories. One issue will investigate the purchasing of corporate stocks. Other[6] articles will discuss health care, banking services, and programs for retirement.

Please watch for *Business Review* in[7] your mail.

Yours very truly, (145)

2

Dear Dr. Brown:

I am pleased to recommend Dr. David Wilson for the position of vice president of[1] your university. Having known David both personally and professionally for the past five years, I[2] feel that I can comment on his character, educational leadership, and accomplishments.

David relates[3] well to people. He has provided an especially important link between industry and academic[4] affairs. David has represented our college on several committees in city and county government.[5]

Because of David's importance to our college, I would be sorry to see him leave. I also know that dedicated[6] individuals must move on to new goals in order to satisfy their own need for growth.

If you have other[7] questions regarding Dr. Wilson, I will be glad to answer them.

Yours very truly, (157)

3

Dear Customer:

April 15 is quickly approaching, and we must reduce our entire stock of new and used cars.[1] That means great savings for wise shoppers. This year we will offer better discounts than ever before.

Beginning[2] February 3, we will run full-page newspaper advertisements telling the public about our low prices, but[3] we are giving you an opportunity to get ahead of the rush. We are inviting loyal customers[4] like you to take advantage of these great savings on February 2. You will find a wide range of makes, models,[5] and prices from which to choose.

You will also have every consideration in making ordinary credit[6] arrangements. Our chief credit officer will be on hand during sale hours to approve your credit.

Remember,[7] early shoppers always have the best choices. We hope to see you there.

Yours truly, (154)

4

Dear Parent:

Our school dental health program is about to get underway.

As part of this program, your child will have[1] the opportunity to participate in a dental clinic free of charge. Each child will be given a free[2] toothbrush and shown how to use it properly.

Because of the importance of good home care during this program, we[3] ask all parents to help us by supervising their children's brushing habits both in the mornings and in the evenings.[4]

Please note that this program does not replace regular dental care. Although your child may be receiving regular[5] dental treatments, he or she can still benefit from participating in the classroom clinic.

This program[6] has been approved by the county dental council. If you wish your child to participate, please sign the form below[7] giving your consent. Return it to your child's teacher by October 5.

Sincerely yours, (156)

5

Dear Mr. Evans:

As our valued customer, you know that our store takes pride in handling only the best in[1] gentlemen's wear. This policy has proved to be the most important reason individuals like you continue[2] to shop here.

This year we have a surprise for you. To show our appreciation for the support you have given[3] our business, we will offer a before-Christmas sale for preferred customers.

Just show our salespeople this letter,[4] and you will receive 20 percent off our regular prices—including our entire line of suits, coats,[5] shirts, and sportswear.

This is a change from past years when prices were reduced after Christmas. By shopping early, you can[6] accomplish two important goals—one for you and the other for the gentlemen on your shopping list.

We[7] cordially invite you to attend this sale and enjoy choosing from our full stock. It would give us great pleasure to serve[8] you again.

Cordially yours, (165)

LESSON 28

RECAP AND REVIEW

You have learned several additional ways of increasing your *Speedwriting* speed and efficiency since Lesson 21. These various aspects of your skill development are reviewed here.

1. Since your last review, you have learned to write the following word beginnings:

em, im ⌒

2. The following word endings were also presented:

quire *q*   ness *'*

3. The words listed below illustrate all of the new principles you learned in Lessons 22 through 27.

emphasize, em-f-s-z	*fsz*	account, a-count	*ak*
impress, im-p-r-s	*prs*	common, com-n	*kn*
image, im-j	*y*	concern, con-s-r-n	*ksrn*
attempt, a-t-m-t	*atd*	still, st-l	*Sl*
promptly, prah-m-t-ly	*Pdl*	estate, e-st-ate	*eSa*
temptation, t-m-t-tion	*Ldy*	most, m-st	*s*
requirement, re-quire-ment	*rqm*	pleasure, p-l-z-r	*plzr*
inquiry, in-quire-e	*nqe*	measure, m-z-r	*zr*
acquire, a-quire	*aq*	treasure, t-r-z-r	*brzr*
kindness, k-nd-ness	*cn'*	illness, i-l-ness	*il'*

4. You learned to write salutations and closings in context this way:

sincerely, s-n-s-r-ly *snsrl*   cordially, k-r-j-l-ly *cryll*

gentlemen, j-nt-l-men *jntlm*

5. Days of the week are written this way:

Sunday *Sn*   Thursday *Th*

Monday *Mn*   Friday *Fr*

Tuesday *Tu*   Saturday *St*

Wednesday *Wd*

6. The names of cities and their state abbreviations are written as follows:

Boston, MA *bsn MA*   Tulsa, OK *tlsa OK*

Las Vegas, NV *ls vgs NV*   Dallas, TX *dls TX*

7. Do you recall the following abbreviations?

dse   *etc*   *fed*
$ *q*   *esp*
gvt   *ok*   *ql*
U   *rep*   *inc*
av   *Xs*

8. How quickly can you write the brief forms for these words?

committee	come	industry
ever	satisfy	continue
other	character	deliver
both	public	satisfactory
individual	important	complete
came	characteristic	every
importance	contribute	opportunity
convenient	convenience	always
note	prove	consider
accomplish	ordinary	

Reading and Writing Exercises

-1-

-2-

eC ~o, r Avo, lau
~c 2 pams ~n
1 ~o. y uc du ls u ^(Intro DC)
pam db at ~lcl
rsv- bf o du da
eC ~o, chp ls
sug hlps. p fl
fre l cl ~nE uv
go. cu

-3-

d dvd iz p-l lrn
vu rsN apym z
VP v Wrn U. ino
(SC + scrn k ks-
me lp exs bf ~c
. fnl dsp, z dn vr
cly u ~d me ~pl
kbjs l r nSly.
bcz vu akms hr
ev sn ncrss n

nrlm ^(Series) ~pvms n
UC ~lds ^(Series) + Srl
v me nd- Pgo, e
~+ l nvr u + u
fl Ur r gls /.
bngl Ur gvn b r
Sf ^(Series) fclle ^(Series) + SdN
ksl. ls, r a v
lq u f Pgrs aCv-
U u dry, nr fCr el
cp u nf-o l er
du hr. chp ul du
(s ~ f o. bl so
n u nu pzy. vlu

-4-

mo l frd ~u ~a
l Ppz. nu ~ld f
rec cho n r sNrl
dla Pss unl x l sug
la cho reps uz. Sp

Intro DC

Intro DC

-5-

-6-

v ls L, ⌐ alC-
brsr gvs ⌐ inf u
rqs- ab r rz bso
+ ol plNs la db
apo ʃ . ⌐n chl.
⌐ Aso rfs u l . ld
dlr l hn u ⌐a q ʃ
hlp ⌐ u sp lNscp-
sily ⌐ r dlrs r gld

l cop ⌐ r l = od
Ks , u ⌐a od elr b
Ulfn or b l CE ,
⌐ kv , l nsr Pl
dle e s b ar fra zz
e rsv u od , if usd
v ne qs ab u nu
ak ᵩp gv s . cl ⌐ cu

Intro DC

Key

Abbreviations

merchandise	et cetera	federal
street	question	especially
government	okay	quart
university	represent, representative	incorporate, incorporated
advertise	Christmas	

Brief Forms

k	*k*	*n*
E	*sal*	*ku*
ol	*crc*	*dl*
bo	*pb*	*sal*
nv	*pl*	*kp*
k	*crc*	*E*
pl	*kb*	*opl*
kv	*kv*	*a*
nl	*pv*	*ks*
ak	*ord*	

1

Dear Mr. Davis:

We will be happy to send an engineer to your home to make a complete analysis[1] of your heating and cooling system. The characteristics you described over the phone indicate that your unit[2] is very different from most of the units we see. Because it is not a common unit, we are sending[3] our chief engineer to make the analysis personally. He will plan the visit at your earliest[4] convenience and report his findings promptly.

We can then answer your questions about repairing or replacing[5] the unit. If it becomes necessary to order a new unit, the equipment will be delivered and[6] installed for the purchase price quoted to you originally.

Please call our headquarters to make arrangements for[7] the analysis.

Yours very truly, (147)

2

Dear Miss Roberts:

I am writing in response to your recent letter in which you noted that late charges had been[1] added to your last monthly payment. I am happy to report those charges have been removed because we did[2] receive your payment within the time allowed.

Regarding your request to change the due date on your loan, we understand[3] your need for such a change, and we would like very much to accommodate you. However, we cannot change the[4] payment schedules currently in use. Ordinarily, all of our mortgage arrangements call for a payment on the[5] 20th of each month.

Our advice is that you make two payments within one month. If you can do this, your payment[6] would be automatically received before its due date each month.

I hope this suggestion helps. Please feel free to call[7] whenever you have questions.

Cordially yours, (148)

3

Dear David:

I was pleased to learn of your recent appointment as vice president of Western University.[1] I know the search and screen committee considered many top executives before making a final decision.[2]

As dean of our college, you made many important contributions to our institution. Because of your[3] accomplishments here, we have seen increases in enrollment, improvements in teaching methods, and the start of[4] many needed programs.

We wish to invite you and your family to be our guests at a banquet to be given[5] by our staff, faculty, and student council. This is our way of thanking you for the progress achieved under your[6] direction.

In the future, we will keep you informed on what we are doing here. I hope you will do the same for[7] us. Best wishes in your new position.

Very truly yours, (151)

4

MEMO TO: Fred White

May I propose a new method for recording claims in our central data processing unit?[1] I suggest that claims representatives use a stamp which indicates that the item has been reviewed and should[2] be either accepted or not accepted for processing. When a document comes to a data clerk without[3] this stamp, that item should be returned with the request that it be completed properly.

This method would require[4] very little additional effort and would result in a more efficient and convenient system for[5] everyone. (101)

5

Dear Mr. Johnson:

Thank you for responding to my resumé and letter of application for the position[1] of reporter.

I was very happy to learn that I am under consideration for an opening[2] on your business writing staff. I will gladly send you additional examples of my writing and any[3] other information you desire.

As you requested, I asked two of my college professors to write letters of[4] recommendation. You should receive letters from Dr. Thomas Wilson and Dr. Susan Allen within a[5] few days.

Because of my background in business and economics, I feel certain I could contribute much as a[6] business reporter. Could we set up a meeting to discuss this further?

I would be happy to come to Atlanta[7] and deliver my writing examples in person. I look forward to meeting with you at your convenience.[8]

Sincerely yours, (163)

6

Dear Mrs. James:

Your new credit card is enclosed, and we are pleased to welcome you as a charge customer. Your credit[1] limit is shown at the top of this letter.

The attached brochure gives the information you requested about[2] our rose bushes and other plants that would be appropriate for a warm climate. It also refers you to[3] a local dealer to whom you may go for help with your specific landscaping situation. Our dealers are[4] glad to cooperate with our mail-order customers.

You may order either by telephone or by mail,[5] whichever is more convenient. To ensure prompt delivery, we ship by air freight as soon as we receive your[6] order.

If you should have any questions about your new account, please give us a call.

Cordially yours, (137)

$Cphr\ 5$ *

OUTPUT: TRANSCRIBING SPEEDWRITING NOTES

You have just returned to your work area following a session of dictation. Priority items have been paper clipped, your questions answered, and special instructions ("enclose two copies of new catalog") flagged in colored ink. Now you are ready to transform those notes into an attractive printed document—one that speaks well of you, your supervisor, and the company for which you work. What is the most efficient and reliable way to produce an acceptable transcript?

Begin by following the step-by-step procedures below.

Before Beginning to Type or Keyboard
1. Transcribe in order of priority.
2. Determine letter style, format, and margins.

*Chapter Five

3. Verify spellings of any words you are not certain of—learn to watch for commonly misspelled words that often slip by unnoticed.
4. Elevate your notepad for convenient reading before beginning to type or keyboard.

Before Removing the Document from the Machine
1. Proofread carefully—not once, but twice. Read first against your notes to be certain that your copy is complete and accurate; then read again for typographical errors, spelling errors, and punctuation or grammatical errors you might have overlooked earlier.
2. Make any necessary corrections while the document is in the machine.

Before Presenting the Document for a Signature
1. Cancel your *Speedwriting* notes by drawing a line through the transcribed dictation.
2. Look at your transcript carefully. Is it attractively arranged on the page?

Does it contain noticeable corrections? When your transcribed copy is neat, free of errors, and shows no evidence of corrections, it is ready to be signed and mailed.

3. Type the envelope, giving it the same careful attention you gave the letter.
4. If the letter calls for enclosures, assemble them now to be presented with the letter.
5. Present the letter for your supervisor's signature, submitting the envelope and any specified enclosures along with the transcript.

A Word About Equipment and Supplies

Some supplies and procedures will vary slightly depending upon the printing equipment you use. Let's look first at the items you will always need.

1. Keep these at your work station:
   a. Dictionary—consult it for spellings and definitions.
   b. List of commonly misspelled words—post it nearby.
   c. Office procedures manual.
   d. English usage manual.
2. If you transcribe on a word processor or microcomputer:
   The machine will have many automatic features and will make corrections at your command without the aid of erasing materials. Your keyboarded copy appears on a screen so that you can make corrections before the copy is printed out automatically on paper.
3. If you transcribe on an electric or electronic typewriter:
   These machines often provide self-correcting devices. If your machine doesn't have this feature, choose the most effective agent available—correction film, tape, or fluid, for example—and master the technique of applying it. Your transcript should show no evidence of corrections.

   A beautifully transcribed document is a source of pride for your company. A written communication should act as an ambassador of good will for your employer. Its professional appearance will go a long way toward bringing you a successful career.

LESSON 29

1. Write ╲ for words beginning with the sound of any vowel + *x* (*aks, eks, iks, oks, uks,* or *eggs*).

accident, x-d-nt *vdM*

exist, x-st *ʃ*

explain, x-p-l-n *ypln*

examination, x-min-tion *vmy*

excite, x-ite *vɩ*

excellent, x-l-nt *vlM*

Remember to write *x* for the medial and final sound of *x*.

boxes, b-x-s *bxs*

textbook, t-x-t-b-k *Lxtbc*

tax, t-x *Lx*

relax, re-l-x *rlx*

2. Write *X* for the word beginnings *extr* and *extra*.

extreme, extr-m *X⁀*

extremely, extr-m-ly *X⁀l*

extra *X*

extraordinary, extra-ordinary *Xord*

Write these additional words:

express, x-p-r-s *yprs*

maximum, m-x-mum *⁀xm*

exchange, x-chay-n-j *vCny*

index, nd-x *Nx*

extend, x-t-nd *vtM*

reflex, re-f-l-x *rflx*

Phrases

you will find *ulfM*

as your *zu*

to call *Lcl*

on you *ou*

as you *zu*

on your *ou*

MORE INTRODUCTORY DEPENDENT CLAUSES

Introductory dependent clauses beginning with such words as *after, while,* and *whether* will be highlighted in your reading and writing exercises.

After I study the report, I will write her a memo.

While we were reviewing your account, I noticed that your contract renewal is scheduled for next month.

Whether you are looking for a specific item or gift ideas in general, you'll find our clerks eager to help.

Your Business Vocabulary

copy editor — *cpe edlr* — A person employed to edit written material for publication.

unit price — *unl prs* — The price for an individual item selected from a larger quantity of like merchandise.

PRINCIPLES SUMMARY

1. Write `\` for words beginning with any vowel + *x*: explain, x-p-l-n *vpln*
2. Write `⟋` for the medial and final sound of *x*: boxes, b-x-s *bxs*
3. Write `X` for the word beginnings *extr* and *extra*: extreme, extr-m *X—* ; extraordinary, extra-ordinary *Xord* .

Vocabulary Builder. Practice writing these frequently used words:

export, x-port *vpl*   expert, x-p-r-t *vprl*

excess, x-s *vs*   exception, x-p-tion *vpy*

executed, x-k-ute-ed *vcu—*   explanation, x-p-l-n-tion *vplny*

extent, x-t-nt *vln*   extension, x-t-n-sion *vlny*

Reading and Writing Exercises

-1-

-2-

(shorthand exercises)

Series

Series

Intro DC

Intro DC

-3-

-4-

ho �-vdM ocr-, u
chs ak No, 07-5151.
r rynl chs yr l
cl ou P⌐ll l m ⌐
dy + apv arms
f ⌐c rprs, e rcm
. lM bde sp nr u
⌐C hMls ⌐8 vr
chs, e suq ls fr
ol bcz ⌐ ras hil n
K saly, ⌐lru Cz ls
sp sp or aol fr,
ntrl p lu, p cl cf ur
ne frlr qs, ul

-5-

dvr + ⌐rs h8 ⌐
ak fr v dvs + dvs
⌐so l lk u l bflo,
z nu rzdMs no dol

ur fM ⌐C l lrn ab
r sle, ehp ⌐ encs
n ls L hlp, e l-· p
v sle + ol inf dzn-
l hlp u fl ⌐ hm nu
nu lq, ⌐a e ll u
ab r fr, dvs + dvs
, ⌐ old8 ak fr n ls
sle, e lq ⌐ ⌐m
rzn ev so me Ks
, ⌐ Pl + lyl Svs
e ofr bo bss + Nvs,
ehp ul alo s l hMl
u ak nds, zu lx rep
ec du E= rec inf[Series 9]
kpu lxs[Series 9] + kp ⌐ fs
fu, el l u · nl
nr ⌐ N v yr l rm
u vr Svs, w ⌐ml
dM hzla lcl o s, uvl

Key

1

Dear Ms. Edwards:

I am applying for the position of copy editor with your firm. I believe you will[1] find my background appropriate for the duties described in your newspaper advertisement. Included in the[2] enclosed resumé is a list of books I have edited. I have also written indexes, cover copy,[3] and advertising brochures. During the last four years I have emphasized studies in computer programming.

I am[4] extremely eager to meet with you and learn more about your department. Your company produces excellent[5] books which rate highly in the marketplace. May we discuss this position in person? I will call on June 23[6] to arrange an appointment at your convenience.

I look forward to talking with you then.

Very truly yours,[7] (140)

2

Dear Mr. James:

We have enjoyed serving as your travel agent during the past year. We hope our services[1] resulted in many pleasant memories for you and your family. May we also take this opportunity[2] to remind you we are always ready to help with your travel plans. Whether you are looking ahead to summer[3] or just needing to make last-minute arrangements, we will gladly take care of the details.

Our full line of services[4] makes any trip easier and more relaxing for you. After cold weather sets in, why not consider some[5] fun in the sun? We have several exciting new travel packages to show you. It is not too soon to plan[6] your family outings for summer vacation. An early start ensures you choice accommodations and makes the[7] trip more fun for everyone.

We are looking forward to seeing you this coming year.

Sincerely yours, (158)

3

Gentlemen:

Our shipment of office supplies arrived in excellent condition and on sched-ule this morning. While[1] we were checking our merchandise against the invoice, we discovered an extra order of envelopes. Although[2] we requested only 20 boxes of envelopes, we received 21. Each box contained the full amount[3] of 200 printed envelopes.

We find no mention of the extra envelopes on the invoice, but we see[4] no reason to return the extra package and will add it to our supplies. We have determined that the[5] individual unit price of each box is $8.95, and we are enclosing a check for that[6] amount.

If you feel that this matter requires further discussion, please let me know. Thank you for your promptness in[7] delivering our goods. We are more than satisfied with the attention given our order.

Cordially yours, (159)

4

Dear Mrs. Arnold:

This is in response to your call informing us of the damages to your car. Would you please[1] complete and return the enclosed report within one week following the date of your accident? Please be certain[2] to record all necessary information. Use the additional space provided to explain how the[3] accident occurred.

Your claims account number is 07-5151. Our regional claims manager[4] will call on you promptly to examine the damage and approve arrangements for making repairs.

We recommend[5] an excellent body shop near you which handles most of our claims. We suggest this firm only because it rates[6] highly in customer satisfac-tion. Whether you choose this specific shop or another firm is entirely up[7] to you.

Please call if you have any further questions.

Yours truly, (152)

5

Dear Mr. and Mrs. Hastings:

The accounting firm of Davis and Davis wishes to welcome you to Buffalo.[1]

As new residents, no doubt you are finding much to learn about our city. We hope the enclosures in this[2] letter help. We included a map of the city and other information designed to help you feel at home[3] in your new location.

May we tell you about our firm? Davis and Davis is the oldest accounting firm in[4] this city. We think the main reason we have so many customers is the prompt and loyal service we offer[5] both businesses and individuals.

We hope you will allow us to handle your accounting needs. As your tax[6] representative, we can do everything—record information, compute taxes, and complete the forms for you.[7] We will mail you a note near the end of the year to remind you of our service. In the meantime, don't hesitate[8] to call on us.

Yours very truly, (167)

LESSON 30

1. Write q for the medial or final sound of any vowel + *ng* when the sound is part of the root word and is not a suffix (*ang, eng, ing, ong, ung*).

sang, s-ang *sq*

nothing, n-ith-ing *nlq*

single, s-ing-l *sgl*

long, l-ong *lq*

thing, ith-ing *lq*

young, y-ung *yq*

Brief Forms

already *ar*

next *nx*

immediate *⌒*

experience *vp*

approximate *apx*

Brief Form Development

immediately *⌒l*

approximately *apxl*

| Commonly Misspelled Words | accept | *ac* | (to receive) Tom will be happy to *accept* our service award. |
| | except | *vpl* | (not including) Jane has completed everything *except* the monthly report. |

| Your Business Vocabulary | item breakdown *ıⁿ brcdon* | A classification or division of items within a group or category. |

PRINCIPLES SUMMARY

1. Write q for the medial or final sound of any vowel + *ng* when the sound is part of the root word and is not a suffix (*ang, eng, ing, ong, ung*): long, l-ong *lq* .

Reading and Writing Exercises

-1-

-2-

-3-

-4-

[Page of shorthand outlines — two columns. Legible printed annotations and figures within the shorthand include:]

Intro DC

Series · Series

15 mts

5 yrs

40%

5 = yr

Intro DC

-5-

mo l ~r + sls	~ W cŞ, hrld spN
Psnl erp- l A 2	9 yrs n US ar fş z
nu mbrs l r Sf,	Cf nynr n G v lŞ
~r hrld s~l + ~s	Pg. blĘ hs ~- sls
blĘ ~dsn jyn- r	Pgs n CA, WA, + OR,
dvy o fl 15, bo v lz	blĘ, Ar op- ol v hr
ppl as ~ pzl v	ofs n sn frnssco,
rynl yr f eqpm	+ hrld lb ~v nl
sls + Svs. hrld l	, bŞn ofs ~l. p
cvr ~ NE pl v	jyn ~e n lk- lz v
Nre + blĘ l cvr	nu ppl l r co.

Key

| 1 |

Dear Policyholder:

The insurance benefits described in the attached bulletin bring many improvements[1] to your existing program.

Our new medical plan covers long hospital stays and medical leaves from your job.[2]

In order to help you better understand your new insurance plan, we are enclosing a bulletin containing[3] complete details. Please study it. We encourage you to discuss the new program with your personnel officer[4] soon. Use this individual meeting as an opportunity to ask questions about your coverage.[5] It is important that you fully understand the program in order to use it to your best advantage.

Yours[6] truly, (121)

| 2 |

Gentlemen:

We are happy to tell you we have found the solution to the problem in your engine. After[1] making a complete investigation, our research manager discovered that the problem was caused by a short in[2] the electrical system of the engine. We have replaced the wiring, and your engine is running well. We are[3] confident you will experience no more problems.

We can deliver and install the unit next week. Can you[4] accept delivery on May 7?

Your engine is under warranty, so the repairs will be made free of charge. It[5] will be necessary, however, to present a claim form. Please forward the claim at your earliest convenience.[6]

We are glad to be of service.

Yours very truly, (130)

3

Dear Mr. Stevens:

This is just a reminder to let you know you may now file an exemption on your state[1] property taxes. In order to take advantage of this opportunity, you must file by March 1.

If you have[2] not had experience with filing for a mortgage exemption, you will find the process to be quite easy. Take[3] the enclosed form to your county tax assessor. The entire process takes approximately 15 minutes to[4] complete and will result in a major savings against next year's taxes.

May I emphasize again the importance[5] of filing by March 1. Although the exemption applies to next year's taxes, it must be filed this year.

Please call[6] on me whenever I can be of help.

Cordially yours, (130)

4

Dear Mr. Edwards:

Accompanying this letter is the report you requested presenting long-range plans for[1] our marketing division. The figures represent an item breakdown of gross sales, costs, and percentage of[2] profits over the last five years.

Sales increased sharply in the southern and western regions of the country. Except for[3] two states, sales reached record highs in these regions and represented 40 percent of our total sales last year.

I[4] am also presenting a five-year marketing plan based on past sales and projections for the future.

The overall[5] picture is a pleasant one. I hope the plan meets with your satisfaction.

Very truly yours, (117)

5

MEMO TO: Marketing and Sales Personnel

We are pleased to add two new members to our staff. Mr. Harold Smith[1] and Ms. Betty Madison joined our division on July 15.

Both of these people assume the position[2] of regional manager for equipment sales and service. Harold will cover the northeast part of the country,[3] and Betty will cover the West Coast.

Harold spent nine years in the U.S. Air Force as chief engineer in charge of[4] the testing program. Betty has managed sales programs in California, Washington, and Oregon.

Betty[5] is already operating out of her office in San Francisco, and Harold will be moving into his[6] Boston office immediately. Please join me in welcoming these exciting new people to our company.[7] (140)

LESSON 31

1. Write   *ß*   for the word endings *bil*, *ble (bul)*, or *bly*.

table, t-ble	*lß*	mobile, m-ble	*ß*
double, d-ble	*dß*	eligible, e-l-j-ble	*eljß*
possible, p-s-ble	*psß*	assembly, a-s-m-bly	*asß*
possibly, p-s-bly	*psß*	available, a-v-l-ble	*avlß*

2. Omit the final *t* of a root word after the sound of *k*.

act, a-k	*ac*	object, o-b-j-k	*objc*
elect, e-l-k	*elc*	deduct, d-d-k	*ddc*
instruct, in-st-r-k	*nSrc*	effect, e-f-k	*efc*

Write these additional words:

responsible, response-ble	*rspß*	expect, x-p-k	*pc*
deductible, d-d-k-ble	*ddcß*	elected, e-l-k-ed	*elc-*
probably, prah-b-bly	*Pbß*	impact, im-p-k	*pc*
product, prah-d-k	*Pdc*	protected, pro-t-k-ed	*Plc-*

3. Indicate time in the following way:

ten o'clock	*10°*	8:30 a.m.	*8 ³⁰a*
12 noon	*12 nn*	9:30 p.m.	*9 ³⁰p*

Phrases

as I	*ʒι*	thank you	*lqu*
has been	*hsb*	would like	*dlc*
should be	*sdb*		

USE COMMAS WITH NOUNS OF DIRECT ADDRESS.

A direct address is a specific referral to a person's name, title, and/or other designation. When the direct address occurs in the middle of the sentence, place a comma before and after it. If the direct address occurs at the beginning or at the end of the sentence, use only one comma.

We know, Mary, that you are an excellent administrative assistant.

Professor Jefferson, will you be able to attend the meeting?

You will enjoy working in Washington, Mr. President.

In the reading and writing exercises, the abbreviation **Dir Ad** will be used to highlight nouns of direct address.

Your Business Vocabulary	trust account *lrS ak*	An account established by an individual or organization in the name of another individual or organization to be administered by a trustee (trust company or bank, for example).

PRINCIPLES SUMMARY

1. Write *𝛽* for the word endings *bil, ble (bul),* or *bly*: table, t-ble *ℓ𝛽* .
2. Omit the final *t* of a root word after the sound of *k*: act, a-k *ac* .
3. Indicate time: 7:30 p.m. *7³⁰p* .

Reading and Writing Exercises

-1-

[shorthand outlines]

-2-

[shorthand outlines]

Intro DC

no + r ⌐ ol crds
alrz- fu ak, er A
hpe Ub v hlp. cu

-3-

d ⌐rc o bhf v
prNs ⌐ s d
scl ι ⌐4 l lqu v
⌐C f lN Pq u
kdc- ⌐ lS ⌐os ⌐e,
u kNs re ⌐ scl
brds rsN ack ⌐
. apo L. f loz v
s hu dd n USN
⌐ dlls v nu Pq u
plny hlp-. gr dl,
me v s dlc l nrl
r Cldrn n ly bk
els. ec pln no f
fCr, ⌐ai fsz aq *Dir Ad*,
rc *Dir Ad*, ho C eap-

u l' lk o sC srl
nts. z ly Nca- b ls
rsps af ⌐ Pq *Intro DC*, ⌐ ol
prNs Aso bnfl-
f u pl rrcs.
ihp ⌐ z . ru-e p
fu z l . su

-4-

d r bron vu ks-
opn . lrS ak ⌐r
bq., lrS aks ofr
me Avs l ppl r
dl= l= hu nk rn.
ly Pvd. lq= lr sv=
pln C cb uz- f
dfrN Ppss. f ex.
lrS fN fu Cldrn
Plcs lr f Cr. z ⌐ ak
gros *Intro DC*, bks. bss f
lr cly eyc or ⌐ c

-5-

Key

1

Dear Miss Barnett:

Thank you for the outstanding training sessions you put together this week. The instruction was[1] excellent and should be of great benefit. Please express our appreciation to everyone who helped make such[2] a pleasant experience for us.

The program made such a strong impact on our staff that we wish to plan a[3] similar event for next year. We expect to have approximately 200 people eligible for the[4] program. Would you consider bringing your training group to our city?

We would follow your efficient timetable. By[5] starting the meetings promptly at 8:30 a.m. and ending at 5 p.m., we could complete the sessions in[6] three days. If you approve, I will begin making arrangements now. We already have some suggestions in mind.

I[7] look forward to your reply. Again, you have our thanks for a job well done.

Very truly yours, (156)

2

Dear Ms. James:

Thank you for promptly reporting the loss of your charge card. As I explained during our phone conversation,[1] our computer registered the loss at the time you made the call. That prompt action is especially important[2] for your protection. You are no longer responsible for purchases made by anyone other than authorized[3] persons.

The enclosed cards contain new account numbers. If you have additional copies of your old cards on[4] hand, please dispose of them now. The new cards are in effect now and are the only cards authorized for your account.[5]

We are always happy to be of help.

Cordially yours, (110)

3

Dear Mark:

On behalf of the parents at Smith School, I wish to thank you very much for the excellent program you[1] conducted at last month's meeting.

Your comments regarding the school board's recent action came at an appropriate[2] time. For those of us who did not understand the details of the new program, your explanation helped a great deal.[3]

Many of us would like to enroll our children when they become eligible. We can plan now for the future.[4]

May I emphasize again, Mark, how much we appreciated your willingness to come on such short notice. As[5] they indicated by their responses after the program, the other parents also benefited from your[6] important remarks. I hope it was a rewarding experience for you as well.

Sincerely yours, (138)

4

Dear Mr. Brown:

Have you considered opening a trust account with our bank?

Trust accounts offer many[1] advantages to people in the middle-to-high income range. They provide a long-term savings plan which can be used[2] for different purposes. For example, a trust fund for your children protects their future. As the account grows,[3] it becomes a basis for their college education, or it can fund another investment to give them an[4] especially sound start in life.

There are excellent tax benefits accompanying trust funds. We would be happy[5] to explain them in detail. Why not make an appointment today to learn how these plans operate?

We offer[6] many services designed to help with family and estate planning. We hope you will take advantage of some[7] of the options that are available, Mr. Brown.

Very truly yours, (152)

5

Dear Mr. Smith:

Although your payment which was due September 1 has not been received, we are pleased to tell you that[1] your policy has been kept current through our automatic loan provision. This has resulted in a slight[2] increase in the size of your loan. Please note that the attached statement records this latest action.

As we have explained in[3] the past, it is to your advantage to repay the loan as quickly as possible. By doing so, you renew[4] the full value of your policy. When you make a payment, please return the attached statement with your check. Please write[5] your policy number on the check to help us process your payment quickly.

May we also remind you that we[6] are always happy to answer questions and help in any way we can, Mr. Smith. Do not hesitate to call[7] our toll-free number at any time.

Cordially yours, (150)

LESSON 32

1. Write a small, disjoined, and slightly raised *t* *ℓ* for the word ending *ity* (pronounced *uh-tee*).

quality, q-l-ity   *qℓ ℓ*

authority, a-ith-r-ity   *alr ℓ*

facilities, f-s-l-ity-s   *fslℓs*

majority, m-j-r-ity   *yr ℓ*

possibility, p-s-bil-ity   *psℓℓ*

security, s-k-r-ity   *scr ℓ*

2. Write *ⅇ ⅎ* to indicate parentheses.

Most of our staff (80 %) have had their vacations.

∽8 vr 8f ⅇ 80% ⅎ vh lr vcjs.

Brief Forms

able   *ß*

difficult   *dfc*

opinion   *opn*

contract   *kc*

employ   *⌒p*

Brief Form Development

difficulty   *dfce*

enable   *nß*

responsibility   *rspßℓ*

ability   *ßℓ*

Your Business Vocabulary	term policy *lr plse*	In life insurance, a contract providing benefits for a limited number of years. It pays face value if the owner's death occurs during the time specified in the contract.

PRINCIPLES SUMMARY

1. Write a small, disjoined, and slightly raised *t* *↳* for the word ending *ity (uh-tee)*: quality, q-l-ity *qℓ⁶* .

2. Write *ɇ ⅎ* to indicate parentheses.

Reading and Writing Exercises

-1-

-2-

(Page contains Gregg shorthand outlines, not standard text.)

-3-

Annotations in right column: Series, Series, Intro DC, Dir Ad

l r efls, e pln l
lv / ab 9° (nx
⁀rn⹁ u hlp, Slnl
ap⁔⹁ s

-4-

d⁀s A⁀s ls L ⹁ n
rsp lu rsN nqe
re aplm rNls⹁
Alo ev no aplms
avlB no ⁀e alspa
opn⹀ ⁀n (nx 3
⁀os⹁ l ncrq u
lcp Cç ⌣ s⹁ edu
rq · scr¹ dpzl ⋎
anl ⌵ · f ⁀os rN⹁
ls dpzl lb ret⁃ af
u frnⱦ vb r ⁀⋎⁃
⁃ · nspcq sos la
no d⁀qs ⌵ ocr⁃⹁
e Aso rqȣ 30 ds

nls ⁀n u pln l
⁀⋎ f⁀ (aplm ⹁
u ⁀a Cȥ · 1=yr or
2=yr ls⹁ (2=yr kc
ofrs (Avq ⌵ sv⹀
apxl 20 $ P ⁀o n
rN⹁ eC unl klns
kp lNre + cCn fsl¹⁶⹁
elb hpe l so u ·
aplm⹁ cl r rNl
ofs l sl p · apym⹁
su

-5-

d⁀r lsn hr ⹁ (
rpl u rqȣ⁃⹁ ȥ uc
se⹀ u ern⹀ por ⹁ u
⁀ȣ pl asl⹁ e
agre lau lf ins
plse ᵴd Pvd f⁀
eycql + dl nds vu

fol w evN vu dl, ┌ bnfls + cSs v ls
⌐ dz ⌐ lc l ⌐e sp pln⌐ cf u ⌐ ┼
ls gls⌐ e rcm lau l PCs ┌ plse ⸴ s pl
ins ofr bnfls v p l kp + rel ┌ enc-
6 ⌐ s u P ern = ⌐ sug aplcy⌐ lqf alo ⌐ s
u PCs · 20 = yr br l Avz⌐ u ⸴ v ┌ lsn⌐
plse w a ┌ v 250T $ ⌐ v lu
┌ lB o py 7 lSs

Intro DC

Dir Ad

Key

1

Dear Mr. Webster:

This is to confirm our phone conversation concerning the contract you already have with[1] James Brown.

As I indicated earlier, Mr. Brown has decided to resell the property and has[2] employed me to make the arrangements for him. The proposed new owners wish to purchase his equity and assume the[3] basic contract now in effect.

Please note that the following changes are to be made: The new loan rate[4] will replace the rate paid originally. We will start over with a new ten-year term.

Please ask your attorney to[5] draw up the new agreement with these changes. We will review it before closing. If the agreement requires a[6] title search, the new owners will accept that responsibility.

I appreciate your help in completing[7] the new contract.

Yours truly, (145)

2

Dear Mrs. Allen:

Thank you for your letter, copies of the contract, and related legal information[1] concerning the sale of the property. I was delighted to hear that the closing took place as scheduled without[2] questions or difficulties of any kind.

I wish to call your attention to the enclosed copies of correspondence[3] canceling our original fire insurance policy on that house. I have not yet received anything[4] from the new owners indicating that they have taken out a new policy. Would you be able to determine[5] that adequate coverage has been arranged?

I am also returning your copy of our agreement which[6] we signed as you requested. I assume you can now record the deed and consider the contract completed.

Thanks[7] again for your help.

Cordially yours, (146)

3

Dear Ed:

I am pleased to say I will be visiting Tulsa even sooner than we expected.

I plan to bring[1] our new sales managers on a trip through our western plants during the week of March 6. I want to show them our[2] excellent facilities and the programs currently in effect. We will arrive on Flight 519 at[3] 5:30 p.m. on Wednesday. Could you meet us and have dinner with us that evening?

I would appreciate meeting[4] Thursday morning with you, our new employees, and anyone else you think they should meet.

If it is not too difficult[5] to arrange, Ed, I would like our guests to go through all of the plants. We might consider the possibility of[6] renting a bus for Thursday afternoon. What do you think? Your opinions always contribute greatly to our efforts.[7]

We plan to leave at about 9 o'clock the next morning. Your help is certainly appreciated.

Sincerely,[8] (160)

4

Dear Ms. Adams:

This letter is in response to your recent inquiry regarding apartment rentals. Although[1] we have no apartments available now, we anticipate openings within the next three months. I encourage[2] you to keep checking with us.

We do require a security deposit in the amount of a full month's[3] rent. This deposit will be returned after your furnishings have been removed and an inspection shows that no[4] damages have occurred. We also request 30 days' notice when you plan to move from the apartment.

You may choose[5] a one-year or two-year lease. The two-year contract offers the advantage of saving approximately[6] $20 per month in rent. Each unit contains complete laundry and kitchen facilities.

We will be happy to[7] show you an apartment. Call our rental office to set up an appointment.

Sincerely yours, (156)

5

Dear Mr. Wilson:

Here is the report you requested. As you can see, your earning power is your most important[1] asset. We agree that your life insurance policy should provide for the educational and daily[2] needs of your family in the event of your death.

What does it take to meet these goals? We recommend that your[3] insurance offer benefits of up to six times your present earnings.

I suggest you purchase a 20-year term[4] policy in the amount of $250,000. The table on page 7 lists the benefits[5] and costs of this specific plan. If you wish to purchase the policy, simply complete and return the enclosed[6] application.

Thank you for allowing us to advise you, Mr. Wilson.

Very truly yours, (138)

LESSON 33

1. Write   *U*   for the word beginning *un*.

until, un-t-l *ull*

unfair, un-f-r *ufr*

unpaid, un-p-d *upd*

unchanged,
   un-chay-n-j-duh *uCnj-*

unless, un-l-s *uls*

uncover, un-k-v-r *ucvr*

Brief Form Development.   Use this principle to develop words from brief forms and abbreviations.

unable *uB*

unfortunate *ufCnl*

unsatisfactory *usal*

unnecessary *unes*

More About Phrasing.   An easily recognized word may be omitted from common phrases or compound words. In the following examples, the *Speedwriting* word has been omitted for the italicized word.

nevertheless *nvrls*

time *to* time *Ll*

nonetheless *nnls*

up *to* date *pda*

USE COMMAS WITH APPOSITIVES.

An appositive is a word or group of words that explains, renames, or identifies someone or something that immediately precedes it in the sentence.

Appositives are usually set off by commas from the rest of the sentence. Some examples of appositives are shown below:

His new textbook, *Business Communications,* has now been published.

Please see our sales manager, Sally Stanfield.

Mr. Henry Jackson, the Secretary of State, will deliver our commencement address.

> Appositives will be highlighted in the reading and writing exercises. The abbreviation **Ap** will be highlighted.

| Your Business Vocabulary | computer terminal *kpur lrml* | A device usually consisting of a keyboard and a screen that is used to input/output data to and from a computer. Also called a work station. |
| | questionnaire *qr* | A set of questions assembled for the purpose of making a survey. |

PRINCIPLES SUMMARY

1. Write   *u*   for the word beginning *un*: until, un-t-l *ull* .

Reading and Writing Exercises

-1-

[shorthand notation]

-2-

drs clrc i M

u lno la w bk.

sr ak ayM f nyl

lf inc, z v Ma i

il w l. nu lcy

8 1 9 Ṣ Ṣa Ṣ r l

ku lgv u Psnl Svs

nE und, n od

l brq u plse pda

w enc-. qr asc

f sp inf. d u p

rel f r psy=

fre env Pvd-, p

nl la Ulfn No

555-3100 r ms

uCny-, ull Ma i uc

vzl e, Pofs.

if uv qs (Intro DC) ihp ul

cl n ur n nbrh (Intro DC)

Sp b, assN +

i r A gld l lc

u, uvl

-3-

d rdr ev Ar sM

sv bls f r gzn (Ap)

arl nz (Ap) od- n u n

so fr ev n rsv- ne

pam or plny, n

r cS l asc f pams

ods. e lg r rdrs

ap kv v b B lc

pams nE ly sll

ls ol hoshld or ofs

aks. e ks r rdrs Ub

nf. Nvs hu ac

rspB f kcs ly v

d, eno la lr,

q rzn fu dla n

c pam. l lc ol

fu mls l sll ls

lr = elr. Cc

-4-

-5-

du o ga 10 Intro DC , s no   n rsv . pam bc,

du o ga 1 . / lb du   lz Cnjs l mB s l

r frd d v E o   Pss u pams P ll.

lraf, 3. if u pams   if uv go Intro DC , p cl / bq

r at tcl ddc- f   ofs nrd u or r K

u Cc or os sv ak Intro DC , ul   Svs dpl . cu

Key

1

MEMO TO: Marketing Staff

Our show this year was the best we have ever had. Our products made a favorable[1] impression, and we received many compliments after the show.

We also received some suggestions. For example,[2] many dealers are of the opinion that a 60-day delivery time is too long. It should be reduced[3] to 30 days. If at all possible, we will make that change within the next few months.

Among the compliments[4] received were those referring to our display of cameras connected to computer terminals. We had[5] approximately $1,000,000 worth of merchandise there.

Our employees also made a good impression. Our[6] sincere thanks go to an outstanding staff for an exciting show. (131)

2

Dear Mrs. Clark:

I want you to know that I have become a senior account agent for National Life,[1] Inc.

As of May 1, I will move to a new location at 819 South State Street, where I will[2] continue to give you personal service whenever you need it.

In order to bring your policy up to date,[3] I have enclosed a questionnaire asking for specific information. Would you please return the form in the[4] postage-free envelope provided?

Please note that my telephone number (555-3100)[5] remains unchanged. Until May 1, you can visit me at my present office. If you have questions, I hope you[6] will call. When you are in the neighborhood, stop by. My assistant and I are always glad to talk with you.

Yours[7] very truly, (142)

3

Dear Reader:

We have already sent several bills for our magazine, *Art News,* ordered in your name. So far we[1] have not received any payment or explanation.

It is not our custom to ask for payments with orders. We[2] think our readers appreciate the convenience of being able to make payments whenever they settle their[3] other household or office accounts. We consider our readers to be informed individuals who accept[4] responsibility for contracts they have made.

We know that there is a good reason for your delay in making[5] payment. It will take only a few minutes to settle this matter—either with a check or a few words explaining[6] the delay. Please return your response with the invoice in the accompanying envelope.

Sincerely yours,[7] (140)

4

Dear David:

Thank you for the opportunity to recommend my assistant manager, Jennifer Young, for[1] the position of public relations director. I do so with pleasure.

Jennifer has many fine qualities[2] representative of good management. One strong point is her ability to express her opinions both in[3] speech and in writing. She shows an understanding of company goals along with a sincere concern for our[4] other employees.

Jennifer assumes full responsibility for any job, no matter how difficult.[5] Until she came to the advertising department, Jennifer had no experience in management.[6] Nevertheless, she supervised several projects in the manner of an experienced department head.

In my[7] opinion, Jennifer is ready for increased responsibility. She will bring many fine qualities to the[8] position under consideration.

Yours truly, (169)

5

Dear Customer:

We are converting your billings to a new electronic data processing system which will[1] serve you more efficiently. Here are the basic changes affecting your loan payments:

1. As of[2] January 1, we will employ the use of the enclosed payment book.
2. Your new monthly due date will always be the[3] first day of each month. If your payment was due on January 10, it is now due on January 1. It will[4] be due the first day of every month thereafter.
3. If your payments are automatically deducted from your[5] checking or savings account, you will not receive a payment book.

These changes will enable us to process your[6] payments more promptly. If you have questions, please call the banking office nearest you or our customer service[7] department.

Cordially yours, (144)

LESSON 34

1. Write _ʃl_ for the word ending *cial* or *tial* (shul, chul).

official, o-f-ish-l *ofʃl*   financial, f-n-n-ish-l *fnnʃl*

special, s-p-ish-l *spʃl*   potential, p-t-n-ish-l *ptnʃl*

initial, i-n-ish-l *inʃl*   social, s-ish-l *sʃl*

Abbreviations

volume *vol*   America, American *a*

literature *lil*

Brief Forms

develop *dv*   acknowledge *acy*

organize *og*   associate *aso*

success *suc*   congratulate *kg*

standard *Sd*

Brief Form Development

acknowledgment *acym*   associations *asojs*

organizations *ogjs*   development *dvm*

organizing *og_*   congratulations *kgjs*

standards *Sds*   developing *dv_*

Commonly Misspelled Words	cites *sis*
	questionnaire *qr*

| Your Business Vocabulary | group retirement plan *grp rtrm pln* | A plan to provide income for retired employees; premiums may be paid entirely by the employer or partly by the employer and partly by the employee. |
| | accordingly *acrdl* | Within (according to) a special way. |

PRINCIPLES SUMMARY

1. Write *sl* for the word ending *cial* or *tial* (shul, chul): official, o-f-ish-l *ofsl* ; financial, f-n-n-ish-l *fnnsl* .

Reading and Writing Exercises

-1-

dpl ι ◡ sl l vprs
◡ι spl f nu bns
ssh ofsll adpl-s
dpll ◡e◡ r sls
Psnl v dvo- ◡C
L l dv◡ · dm f r
Pdc ✗ rzlls vb
lM◡z r ◡ cvry
kus l gro◡ods ncrs
acrdl, af P ◡ nu
plse ◡ r rjnl sls
kvny ι rsv- me cls
f sls Psnl ksrn◡

pys ly foN kfz◡ n
od l PvN muSN ι
pln l ιsu · mo ru
a a vpln◡ ◡ plse n
dll◡ z · ιnsl Sp ◡
og◡ · ◡e ◡ A sls
◡rs lq O eC py◡
d ub B l yyn s nx
Fr / 10 a◡ x◡ A n
A ◡ Ppzl hsb l
rsv- ◡r fld◡ ι vpc
lse evn grr suc n
njl sls · su

-2-

ddr ly~s / gvs
~e gr saly l rcm
dr elzbt crlt f rq
v aso Pfsr, z spt
f ls acy i ofr / alC-
fl kln . s~re v hr
p. ~ Aso l 2
artcls se rsNl
pbl+ alg ~ opns
v SdMs + ol fclle,
elzbt jyn- r Sf 3
yrs aq, se hs dv-
nu crss m A hSre
C v kt- C l r
Pq, se sos · re f hu
UC Sds + Pvds ·
lM ex f SdMs +
ol fclle, elzbt , ·
UCr ~ gr plnsl +
· P~s fCr, / s~s
ol apo lae acy hr

kbjs ~ ls P~.
vlu

-3-

d~rs clrc idlc l
lqf ~e ~ ~e o
Mn l Dcs ~ ~pm
SC, Alo ch aq-s
lil o ho l aprC
plnsl ~prs~u Avs
z v spsl hlp, i no
ap ~ fl ~ pl v
~c · q ~py + w
· blr USM v ho l
ak la gl, ~ flo u
Avs + ri Nv Ls
v aplcy lsM ~
eC cpe v ~ rz~a,
i Aso ap ~ rz~a
u gv ~e, ~ dv
~ o rz~a ~ ~ez

+ suc ln ch vpc-,
z · rzll vr e l
no fl la uc c
la insl klc .
kfdN + Pfyl ,
lqu aq fu hlp.
ul

-4-

d r prcr lqu ^{Dir Ad}, r
prcr ^{Dir Ad} f kp r qr
ksrn , ssl scr
rf bl. hr r s
rzlls f la Sva:,
1. yl v ppl Sva-
82% rlu po X
nk l ntn lr Sd
v lv, 2. n srs
v nk af rtrm ks
f grp plns Pvd-
b prs + lbr ogs.

ol srss ll-
Psnl bs or prp ^{Series},
ins dvdNs ^{Series}, + Psnl
sv, 3. S ppl
agre- la ssl scr
bnfls aln r n sfsN
l e fnnsl dms
pz- b nfl, 4. apxl
33% Sa- la · nu Pq
sdb dv- l rpls
S pln, lqu aq f
pp n Sva. ul

-5-

d r dvdsn kgjs
r n od fu + u fl.
u n hsb slc- f
nx vol v yq ppl
n A ^{Ap}, · v spsl
pby, ls Dlgs +
bc lls Nvs U, aq

v 40 hu r ern

olSN rcgny. / sis

r sucs v yq ppl

n A cs v lf = bs,^{Series}

N^{Series} eycq^{Series} gvl^{Series} spls,^{Series}

la^{Series} + dsn, r enc

dla se sps Psnl

+ Pfyl inf Ub d- n

r nx vol. p rd +

rel r inf ne

crcys u + brc,

aq kgjs o rsv lo

spsl aw. cu

Key

1

Dear Paul:

I wish to express my support for the new bonus system officially adopted at the departmental[1] meeting. Our sales personnel have devoted much time to developing a demand for our product, and the[2] results have been excellent. As our market coverage continues to grow, orders increase accordingly.[3]

After presenting the new policy at our regional sales convention, I received many calls from sales[4] personnel concerning points they found confusing. In order to prevent misunderstandings, I plan to issue a[5] memo right away explaining the policy in detail. As an initial step, I am organizing a[6] meeting with all sales managers to go over each point. Would you be able to join us next Friday at 10 a.m.?[7]

All in all, the proposal has been well received in the field. I expect to see even greater success in[8] national sales.

Sincerely yours, (166)

2

Dear Dr. Williams:

It gives me great satisfaction to recommend Dr. Elizabeth Carter for the rank[1] of associate professor. As support for this action, I offer the attached file containing a summary[2] of her experience. I am also including two articles she recently published, along with opinions[3] of students and other faculty.

Elizabeth joined our staff three years ago. She has developed new[4] courses in American history which have contributed much to our program. She shows a regard for high[5] teaching standards and provides an excellent example for students and other faculty.

Elizabeth is[6] a teacher with great potential and a promising future. It seems only appropriate that we acknowledge[7] her contributions with this promotion.

Very truly yours, (151)

3

Dear Mrs. Clark:

I would like to thank you for meeting with me on Monday to discuss my employment search. Although[1] I had acquired some literature on how to approach potential employers, your advice was of special help.[2] I now appreciate more fully the importance of making a good impression, and I have a better[3] understanding of how to accomplish that goal.

I am following your advice and writing individual[4] letters of application to send with each copy of my resumé. I also appreciate the resumé[5] you gave me. I am developing my own resumé with more ease and success than I had expected. As[6] a result of our meeting, I now feel that I can make that initial contact with a confident and[7] professional image.

Thank you again for your help.

Yours truly, (150)

4

Dear Mr. Parker:

Thank you, Mr. Parker, for completing our questionnaire concerning the social security[1] reform bill. Here are some results from that survey:

1. The majority of people surveyed[2] (82 percent) rely upon extra income to maintain their standard of living.
2. The main source[3] of income after retirement comes from group plans provided by employers and labor organizations.[4] Other sources listed were personal business or property, insurance dividends, and personal savings.[5]
3. Most people agreed that social security benefits alone are not sufficient to meet financial[6] demands imposed by inflation.
4. Approximately 33 percent stated that a new program should be[7] developed to replace the existing plan.

Thank you again for participating in the survey.

Yours truly,[8] (160)

5

Dear Mr. Davidson:

Congratulations are in order for you and your family. Your name has been selected[1] for the next volume of *Young People in America,* a very special publication.

This distinguished[2] book lists individuals under the age of 40 who are earning outstanding recognition. It cites the[3] successes of young people in all walks of life—business, industry, education, government, sports, law, and[4] medicine.

The enclosed data sheet specifies personal and professional information to be included[5] in our next volume. Please read and return the information with any corrections you wish to make.

Again,[6] congratulations on receiving this special award.

Cordially yours, (133)

LESSON 35

RECAP AND REVIEW

This review includes the word beginnings, word endings, principles, indications of time, omitted words in phrases, brief forms, and abbreviations that you studied in Lessons 29-34.

1. Since the last review lesson, you learned to write the following word beginnings:

extr and extra   *X*   aks, eks, iks, oks, uks,
                                           eggs   \

un   *u*

2. These word endings were presented:

bil, ble *(bul),* or bly   *B*   ity *(uh-tee)*   *l*

cial, tial *(shul, chul)*   *Al*

3. These words illustrate all of the new principles studied in Lessons 29-34:

accident, x-d-nt   *vdn*   long, l-ong   *lq*

facilities, f-s-l-ity-s   *fslʷ*   exciting, x-ite-ing   *vĿ*

exist, x-st   *ℐ*   until, un-t-l   *ull*

double, d-ble   *dℬ*   relaxing, re-l-x-ing   *rlx*

extremely, extr-m-ly   *X̃l*   effect, e-f-k   *efc*

financial, f-n-n-ish-l   *fnnʃl*   social, s-ish-l   *ssl*

4. You learned to indicate time in the following way:

one o'clock   *1°*   11:30 a.m.   *11 ³⁰a⌐*

12 noon   *12 mn*   10:30 p.m.   *10 ³⁰p⌐*

5. Easily recognized words are omitted from common phrases:

never*the*less   *nvrls*   time *to* time   *Lh*

none*the*less   *nnls*   up *to* date   *pda*

6. Do you recall the following abbreviations?

vol   *lit*   *a*

7. How quickly can you write these brief forms?

always	prove	immediate
consider	next	note
experience	already	approximate
able	opinion	difficult
contract	employ	standard
develop	organize	associate
acknowledge	success	congratulate

Reading and Writing Exercises

-1-

[shorthand exercise]

r avlß ,ul Pbß sa
u cM afd n l b!,
ll s pv , njy ı
fre nı + f uo opns.
L c u rzrvy rel
enc- nl, b hre= r
ofr Ns nx o.
rzrv u da l.
cu

Intro DC

— fló Mn Ma 28
P ll 8 a ,, ılc
fw l ls opl l lrn ,
gro , + bld nu scls.
ıfl Sln pzj l
brg me nu + v
vps, lqf c ls
opl psß. uls ı hr
dfrnl ,ıl rpl lu
ofs ö rn v Ma
28, cu

Series

Series

Intro DC

-2-

d s rbrls hpe
l ac pzj v ex
sec u fr, ı ks
, Clny lb Psn
Czn f rspß⁴⁰ u
dS-, ıdb dlı- l bgn
pm o Ma 21 zu
rqß-, ufCnll r
scl dz n N ull
Ma 25, a ı bgn

-3-

d r bls lqf nqe.
ıblv enc- lıl l
asr u qs, E Dr
ps, f = L Svzr
hu cs sr la r
Psnl r fl lrn- n
Svs r elnc lprers.
r Drs sl p lrn sjs

-5-

[shorthand text]

Intro DC

[shorthand text]

45

corps. *[shorthand]*

Intro DC

Pds- *[shorthand]*

-6-

[shorthand text]

P ✓ sle ksl l
ofsll opn ⌒ srme.
af h spcs _{Intro DC} ulb P-
⌣ · ce l ⌒ sle, Ph
uv ks- kdc lrs ✓
bld⸗ ⅃ lrs r jnl

n pln- _{Intro DC} ls ⸴ no
ord bld⸗ ◟ spsl
crcs sdb sn Ub
fl ap-⸴ ll s no
lf ec hlp ⌒c
nes arms f lr⸗ s

Key

Abbreviations

volume	literature	America, American

Brief Forms

a	*pv*	*⌢*
ks	*nx*	*nl*
vp	*Ar*	*apx*
ß	*opn*	*dfc*
kc	*⌢p*	*Sd*
dv	*oq*	*aso*
acq	*suc*	*kq*

1

Dear Sir:

Here are four reasons why you should keep reading.

1. You are an educated person.
2. You know a bargain[1] when you see it.
3. You believe in saving money when you can.
4. You know how to take advantage of a[2] rare opportunity.

If you need a fifth reason, consider this. You are among only 100 people[3] to receive this offer. As part of a rare marketing program, you and 99 others have been selected[4] to try our vacation homes.

Village Homes is a planned neighborhood already under construction. It is perfect[5] for young families. Village Homes has everything you will want and more. When you see the contracts that are available,[6] you will probably say you can't afford not to buy!

Let us prove it. Enjoy one free night and form your own[7] opinions. To make your reservation, return the enclosed note. But hurry—the offer ends next month. Reserve your[8] date immediately.

Cordially yours, (167)

2

Dear Ms. Roberts:

I am happy to accept the position of executive secretary with your firm. I[1] consider it a challenge to be the person chosen for the responsibilities you described.

I would be[2] delighted to begin employment on May 21 as you requested. Unfortunately, our school does not[3] end until May 25. May I begin the following Monday, May 28, promptly at 8 a.m.?

I[4] look forward to this opportunity to learn, grow, and build new skills. I feel certain the position will bring many[5] new and exciting experiences.

Thank you for making this opportunity possible. Unless I[6] hear differently, I will report to your office on the morning of May 28.

Cordially yours, (139)

3

Dear Mr. Baxter:

Thank you for your inquiry. I believe the enclosed literature will answer your questions.[1]

Every distributor employs a full-time supervisor who makes sure that our personnel are fully trained in[2] servicing our electronic typewriters. Our distributors set up training sessions for staff, dealers, and[3] customers approximately three times per year.

Every distributor is equipped with the machinery and test[4] equipment needed to repair our machines. If it does become necessary to order parts from the factory,[5] those orders are processed and shipped immediately.

If you would like further information, Mr. Baxter,[6] please contact me again. We feel our training is of value not only to new employees but also to[7] continuing personnel as well. We are always glad to answer your questions.

Sincerely yours, (156)

4

Gentlemen:

It is that time of the year when we put away matters of the office to share personal[1] experiences with family and friends. As a contract customer, you already know that our station[2] continues its 24-hour programming during the Christmas holidays. In order to allow our employees[3] as much personal time as possible, we alter our advertising and programming schedules for a few days. From[4] 8 p.m., December 23, until 8 a.m., December 26, we will provide taped programming. All[5] advertising to be broadcast between those dates should be delivered to our offices by 5 p.m., December[6] 20, to allow sufficient time for preparation.

May we also take this opportunity to thank you[7] for your patronage. We have enjoyed serving you during the past year and look forward to continuing our[8] relationship.

Cordially yours, (166)

5

Dear Friends:

When our group meets again next month, we will welcome Shelley Clark as guest speaker. The meeting is being moved[1] back one week to March 8. Shelley was unable to attend on the day regularly scheduled for the meeting.[2]

Shelley is well recognized in our city. She has headed many important committees. Most recently she[3] was elected president of the Chamber of Commerce.

Shelley comes to us immediately following a[4] trip abroad, and she brings exciting news. Traveling on behalf of our city, Shelley met with approximately[5] 45 corporations. Although the mission was a long and difficult one, it produced excellent results.[6] We have already received word that one company plans to send a representative here to investigate[7] building a new plant.

Please note the change on your calendars and plan to be present for the meeting.

Very[8] truly yours, (162)

6

Dear Mr. Harvey:

I want to compliment you on the completion of your new building situated on Park[1] Drive. Our city can be proud of this new addition to our community.

The members of the city council[2] are planning a ribbon-cutting ceremony on the date you requested. The public is invited, and[3] music will be provided by a local high school band. The president of the city council will officially[4] open the ceremony. After he speaks, you will be presented with a key to the city.

Perhaps you have[5] considered conducting tours of the building. While tours are generally not planned, this is no ordinary building.[6] Its special characteristics should be seen to be fully appreciated.

Let us know if we can help[7] make necessary arrangements for the tour.

Sincerely, (150)

Cplr 6 *

WHAT WILL A RESUMÉ DO FOR ME?

Once you have learned skills for today's job market, how will you present them to a prospective employer? An effective way to show what you have learned and what you can do is a resumé.

A resumé lists your educational background, job experience, special skills, and references. If you've not had previous work experience, your resumé is especially important. You must describe all other qualifications that will persuade the interviewer to consider you for employment.

Where to Begin?

List all full-time or part-time jobs you have held, courses studied, awards, activities, and membership in organizations. Then arrange the information in major groups:

*Chapter Six

Personal information: List your name, address, and telephone number. You may list job interests or the position you desire.

Educational background: List schools you've attended (beginning with the most recent), degrees earned, studies emphasized, and special courses. If you received special recognition or awards, include a section for awards and activities.

Employment experience: List any part-time or full-time positions, beginning with the most recent. Specify the name of the employer, beginning and ending dates, and job title. You can strengthen this section by briefly describing your responsibilities.

Special skills: This section tells the employer specifically what you are qualified to do. Drawing from your educational and employment experiences, list all skills. Typing, accounting, art, and French, for example, would all be appropriate here.

References: Include the name, occupation, address, and telephone number of individuals qualified to comment on your abilities, character, or performance. Always ask permission before listing someone as a reference. Choose at least three—usually no more than five—people from different sources. At least one should know you personally; another should know you as an employee or as a student.

Your Resumé Should Be Neat and Well Organized

After you have categorized all information, read, edit, change, correct, and type. Repeat the process until you have the best possible picture of yourself on paper.

Your finished product should do many things. Its primary purpose is to present information that can be quickly and easily analyzed by the interviewer. But it reflects on you in other ways. It sets forth your skills and qualities. It demonstrates your ability to sort, organize, and present information. It becomes a visible example of your work.

Your Completed Resumé

Your finished resumé may surprise even you. Mailed with a well-written application letter, it may persuade an employer to ask for an interview. When the time comes for the interview, your resumé will contribute to the professionalism and self-confidence that give you a winning image.

LESSON 36

1. Write * M* for the sounds of *ance, ence, nce,* and *nse* (pronounced *ence*).

dance, d-nce *dM*   since, s-nce *sM*

balance, b-l-nce *bleM*   defense, d-f-nse *dfM*

expense, x-p-nse *pM*   advance, ad-v-nce *avM*

agency, a-j-nce-e *ajMe*   efficiency, e-f-ish-nce-e *efsMe*

2. Write *s* for the word beginning *sub*.

submit, sub-m-t *s⟍*   subway, sub-w-a *s a*

subscribe, sub-scribe *s S*   substantial,
                                      sub-st-n-ish-l *sSnsl*

subscription,
   sub-scrip-tion *s Sy*   subject, sub-j-k *syc*

Phrases

that you are *laur*   that you will *laul*

Commonly Misspelled Words	congratulate *kq* already *Ar*

Your Business Vocabulary	unpaid balance *upd beM* The total amount of money remaining to be paid on a bill or loan.

PRINCIPLES SUMMARY

1. Write *M* *dM* for the sound of *ance, ence, nce, nse*: dance, d-nce

2. Write *s* for the word beginning *sub*: submit, sub-m-t *s⟍* .

CHAPTER SIX

Reading and Writing Exercises

-1-

[handwritten shorthand]

Intro DC

Intro DC

· 50$ *[handwritten shorthand]*

-2-

[handwritten shorthand]

Intro DC

me vu v asc- ab
pa ncrss, er suq_
· Sd 7% ncrs f A
Psnl, ne ad_l rq_s
f fM _S b rvu- bf
Ap, eap u hlp n
Pvd_ u byl rq_s
z psB.

Intro DC

USN , ul _l · gre_
crd anoM , gfl,
l , crd arv bf
X—s, p sM —e
kfry la , gfl
crds vb _l-,
lqu v —C, ul

-3-

dS , rd — ap
u insl , su v bs_
rvu + — _l L od 3
sSjs Ub gvn , X—s
gfls, _ enc_ ,
m—s + adrss fu
us, L — _l k Avy
vu X—s Dk, _
enc_ · Cc f lol
a—l v 35⁸⁵, ls sd
cvr A hNl_ fes, zi

-4-

d sr n, fu —cs ul
pl a a fnl _s +
bgn · nu lf, L
acy , —pl v ls
evM ev asc- _r
dvd cx_ sec, v Sa_
l dl_ r kNm adrs,
l r dlu _r cx_ hs ac-,
n, brf ln n ofs
_r cx_ hs pv- Ub ·
olSN_ ldr, efl fKnl
lv ls opl lhs h, ehp

[Shorthand notation]

Series

Series

-5-

Intro DC

Intro DC

Intro DC

Intro DC

Key

1

Dear Mrs. Smith:

We have reserved an efficiency apartment for you in Long Beach. The apartment has an[1] excellent view of the ocean and all of the facilities you requested.

Since your vacation falls during the[2] busy season, we recommend that you confirm your reservation. It would be wise to call one week in advance.[3]

Please send a $50 deposit now to reserve this apartment. If you wish us to handle all arrangements[4] for you, we will be happy to forward your check. We will also confirm the dates of your stay.

We feel certain[5] that you will enjoy living in this charming apartment on the beach. Thank you for allowing us to assist you[6] in making your travel plans.

Cordially yours, (128)

2

MEMO TO: All Department Heads

Please note that university budget meetings will begin early next year. It[1] is important that you submit your proposed budgets by January 6. Initial meetings will begin[2] immediately. Final approval is scheduled for the end of April.

Because of large cuts in state allowances,[3] you should make every effort to reduce expenses. Since no new funding is available, it will be[4] impossible to begin new programs. I know that you are all doing your best to keep expenses down.

Many of[5] you have asked about pay increases. We are suggesting a standard 7 percent increase for all personnel.[6]

Any additional requests for funding must be reviewed before April 1. We appreciate your help in[7] providing your budget requests as soon as possible. (150)

3

Dear Sir:

I read with appreciation your initial issue of *Business Review* and wish to order three[1] subscriptions to be given as Christmas gifts. I am enclosing the names and addresses for your use.

I wish to[2] take advantage of your Christmas discount. I am enclosing a check for the total amount of[3] $35.85. This should cover all handling fees.

As I understand it, you will mail a greeting[4] card announcing the gift. Will the card arrive before Christmas? Please send me confirmation that the gift cards have been mailed.[5] Thank you very much.

Yours truly, (105)

4

Dear Senior:

In a few weeks you will put away final exams and begin a new life.

To acknowledge the[1] importance of this event, we have asked Mr. David Cox, Secretary of State, to deliver our commencement[2] address. To our delight, Mr. Cox has accepted.

In his brief term in office, Mr. Cox has proved to be an[3] outstanding leader. We feel fortunate to have this opportunity to hear him. We hope he will share his dreams[4] for a new beginning among nations.

This is the last letter I will write to most of you. As your university[5] president, I wish to congratulate you and thank you for your support. May you be rewarded with the[6] best of health, a stimulating career, and the satisfaction of accomplishment. Above all, enjoy your new[7] life.

Sincerely yours, (144)

5

Dear Mrs. Baxter:

We would like to remind you that your account is past due. Would you take a minute now to mail[1] us a check?

From time to time, we all overlook a payment. Since you have always paid your bills on time, we are certain[2] this delay must be the result of an oversight. If there is some other reason why we have not heard from[3] you, would you drop us a note of explanation?

Perhaps we should point out again that you will save money by[4] submitting your payments in advance. When your payment arrives late, a fee is charged against the unpaid balance.

Thank you[5] for your attention to this matter. If your payment is already in the mail, please disregard this notice.[6]

Sincerely yours, (122)

LESSON 37

1. Write $\mathcal{V}$ for the medial or final sound of *tive*.

active, a-k-tive *acv*   relative, r-l-tive *rlv*

effective, e-f-k-tive *efcv*   objective, o-b-j-k-tive *objcv*

selective, s-l-k-tive *slcv*   positive, p-z-tive *pzv*

Write these additional words:

actively *acvl*   relatively *rlvl*

activity *acv*ᶫ   effectiveness *efcv'*

Brief Forms

usual *uz*   manufacture *ᵧ*

work, world *⌣o*   signature, significant, significance *siq*

Brief Form Development

usually *uzl*   manufacturer *frs*

unusual *uuz*   manufacturing *f-*

working *⌣o̤*

Phrases

I appreciate *ιap*   that I *lαι*

to work *⌣o*

USE COMMAS WITH PARENTHETICAL EXPRESSIONS.

interrupts but doesn't change

A parenthetical expression is a word or group of words that interrupts the natural flow of the sentence. These expressions are often used to add emphasis or show contrast. When removed from the sentence, such expressions do not change the meaning of the sentence.

When the word or phrase occurs in the middle of the sentence, place a comma before and after the expression. If the expression occurs at the beginning or end of the sentence, use only one comma. Some common examples of parenthetical expressions are as follows:

as a rule   furthermore

in other words   for instance

for example   of course

on the other hand   in fact

therefore   however

naturally   nevertheless

Always use commas to separate these words from the rest of the sentence:

We will be happy, *however,* to send you the fabric we have in stock.

We do not, *as a rule,* accept cash payments for merchandise.

Trust funds offer excellent tax benefits, *for example.*

In following lessons, parenthetical expressions will be highlighted. The abbreviation **Paren** will be highlighted.

Your Business Vocabulary

job satisfaction

jb saly

Degree of contentment an employee feels toward his or her employment position.

PRINCIPLES SUMMARY

1. Write ⎐ for the medial or final sound of *tive*: active, a-k-tive 𝒶𝒸𝓋 .

Reading and Writing Exercises

-1-

[shorthand outlines]

-2-

[shorthand outlines]

Series

Series   Paren

-3-

Intro DC

Paren

Paren

-4-

Intro DC

Series ')'

Series ')'

Key

1

MEMO TO: All Department Managers

As usual, each of you will be asked to prepare a performance report[1] on individual employees. However, this year's report will be different. As you can see from the[2] attached copy, we will ask employees their opinions regarding their work productivity, job satisfaction,[3] and career goals.

Please encourage your people to complete these reports as accurately as possible. Be[4] certain that everyone understands the purpose of the report— that it is to help each person achieve his[5] or her goals.

The results of these reports will have a significant effect on future planning. By working[6] together we will increase the efficiency of our organization. (133)

2

Dear Mr. Sharp:

I certainly enjoyed reading the manuscript, *New Developments in Word Processing.* Thank you[1] for allowing me to see the study in advance. I am pleased to offer my opinions on its effectiveness.[2]

I consider this work to be a significant contribution to the field. Mr. Evans gives us an[3] unusual look at the future and its impact on office procedures. As he stated in the first chapter,[4] his objectives are to survey standard equipment in use today and describe products soon to be available.[5]

Mr. Evans is selective in his choice of examples and brief in his descriptions. I found the writing[6] to be clear, well organized, and effective.

Again, I appreciate the opportunity to work with you[7] in reviewing this study. Please call on me if I can be of further help.

Cordially yours, (157)

3

Dear Ed:

Now that all testing is complete, we are authorizing the release of a new product. Effective[1] immediately, we will manufacture engines for small aircraft as well as the appropriate installation[2] equipment.

We received official notice this morning to release the product for the North American market.[3] Please change your records to show the following corrections. We added a new support system and assigned a new[4] code number to reflect the change in pricing.

Orders will be shipped within a maximum of 60 days. We may[5] see a slow start in sales due to problems in the aircraft industry. However, we expect significant[6] increases during the first 18 months. We hope to lead the market within five years.

Please let me know if you have[7] any questions.

Sincerely yours, (146)

4

Dear Charge Customer:

When is a winter sale not just an ordinary sale? When you see our discount prices, you[1] will know. We rarely offer savings like these. Then we make them available only to very special people[2] —our charge customers.

This is not an advertised sale. It is a personal invitation to our regular[3] customers to enjoy special benefits. Please consider it our way of saying thank you for your patronage.[4]

Choose from our top manufacturers—early American, traditional, and contemporary collections.[5] Join us for coffee and browse through our new art displays. You could be the winner of a prize to be given[6] away each day.

Shop at one of our convenient locations today and save. Remember that cash is not necessary.[7] Your signature will reserve the items of your choice.

Sincerely yours, (154)

5

Dear Henry:

We recently invited an expert on writing business letters to teach a course in our plant.

She[1] stressed that a good letter is direct and brief. The information should be well organized. Watch for unnecessary[2] comments. These can distract the reader.

I was impressed by her advice to keep the tone of our letters positive.[3] We can even say no in a positive way.

You can see that I found this course to be extremely important.[4] Would you like to hear more about such a course for your office?

I would be happy to refer you to the instructor.[5] I firmly believe that we can all benefit from such instruction.

Very truly yours, (117)

LESSON 38

1. Write ⟋ for the word ending *ful*.

useful, u-s-ful *usf*   wonderful, w-nd-r-ful *Nrf*

careful, k-r-ful *crf*   helpful, h-l-p-ful *hlpf*

carefully, k-r-ful-ly *crfl*   thankful, ith-ank-ful *Lqf*

Write ⟋ also for the word ending *ify* (pronounced *uh-fi*).

certify, cer-t-ify *SLf*   qualify, q-l-ify *qlf*

justify, j-st-ify *jSf*   classify, k-l-s-ify *clsf*

2. Write ⟋ for the word ending *ification*.

classification,
   k-l-s-ification *clsf₁*   qualification,
   q-l-ification *qlf₁*

identification,
   i-d-nt-ification *idNf₁*   modifications,
   m-d-ification-s *dfjs*

Use these principles to form new words from brief forms:

successful *sucf*   notify *nlf*

notification *nlf₁*   grateful *grf*

cannot *cn*

benefited *bnft-*

Your Business Vocabulary

deductible   *ddcB*   In reference to insurance policies, a set amount of money to be paid by the policyholder toward the total amount of damages on any claim.

PRINCIPLES SUMMARY

1. Write *busf* for the word endings *ful* and *ify (uh-fi)*: useful, u-s-ful ; notify, note-ify *nlf* .
2. Write *bf* for the word ending *ification*: qualification, q-l-ification *qlbf*

Reading and Writing Exercises

-1-

[shorthand outlines]

-2-

[shorthand outlines]

akM, w asd- n
clsf- fnnsl dla z
pl v u rspB us ls,
u no Ppr- rz a
+ Ls v aplcz, sM
ur l glf- l kM o
u eycyl bcgroM Intro DC (9)
a u lS u m z
- rfM, u rcmz
db v hlpf- vlu

-3-

d rs grgre hr, r
bcll u rqs- Ap"cr f (9)
psM, h "ehp u
fM pby nf v +
usf, a e Aso rm
u v f hll cr Svs e
no ofr, e cre- kp
ln v hll cr eqpm
f us N h, uc rM

ne ch no dpzl
rq-, u pa ol la pl v
pM n cvr- b u ins,
n S css Paren (9) u ins
pas f E + rM
eqpm cSs u nlq,
uf uv qs ab u cvrz Intro DC (9)-
Dco h r Pfyl
Sf, ly r spslSs n
fl dcl cho + lb
hpe lgv u asSM,
k l prls f kv
Svs + bS v Pfyl
cr, n ql' ks Intro DC (9) uc
k o s, ul

-4-

d nu pe lk l o,
elncz, N enc- env
ulfM z cho v vlu
ou nu yb, r frS, u

[Shorthand outlines — left column]

pe idNf, crd. p
A u siq + cre r crd
du rglr o hrs. b
Ppr- l so u crd n
u k nl or lv r bld,
r sec ib , u hll
bnfls bcll. rd r
crfl. if uv ne gs
re u hsp or dNl
cvry , cl r Psnl ofs   _[Intro DC]_
l , r 3d ib , u   _[Ap]_
pe hNbc , Pvds .   _[Ap]_
kp gd l r cos Svss
+ plses. p bk f lr
r Psyrs du u frs
c ou nu jb , f uv
ne gs , dN hzla lcl   _[Intro DC]_
o s r ne l , su

-5-

d r edws u m z

[Shorthand outlines — right column]

suq-l e bcz vu
rSC n clsf rr
plNs. d u p ass
s n c . idNf v
enc- lf , , cls
hsb clc lvs du r
p8 2 cs. l v
SdNs brl n ls lf.
r n sn n ne v
bcs n r scl lbrre.
af e d . crf SC v
lil rr ke lbrre , e   _[Intro DC]_
foN r enc- flogrf
la lcs vcl lc r lf.
z uc se , bo lvs v   _[Intro DC]_
r s uuz sp.
hoE , plN rr   _[Paren]_
pcl r groo rr Wrn
Sas + cd n psB
gro ls fr E. or cd
r x , ehp uc idNf

r Davre. ls cls	lrn p f E1. vlu
Pjc hs bk . siq	

Key

1

Dear Mrs. Davidson:

Thank you for notifying us promptly about the items taken from your car on[1] September 5 at approximately 3:30 p.m.

After we examined your policy, we determined[2] that your coverage provides a $150 deductible for losses such as you describe. There[3] are exceptions to the deductible, but they usually concern damages resulting from natural[4] causes. Your losses cannot be classified among them.

Our records show that the total value of the items[5] taken was $178. Therefore, we are enclosing a check for $28. If[6] you have further questions regarding this matter, please feel free to call at any time. We are always ready to[7] explain your policy and give you the best protection offered by it.

Cordially yours, (156)

2

Dear Dr. Jeffries:

I benefited greatly from the information covered in your accounting class and[1] also from the outside projects we completed. I am pleased to say that I have already been able to apply[2] some of that knowledge. For three months I have been working part time in the office of a certified public accountant.[3] I have assisted in classifying financial data as part of my responsibilities there.

I[4] am now preparing a resumé and letters of application. Since you are well qualified to comment on[5] my educational background, may I list your name as a reference? Your recommendation would be very[6] helpful.

Very truly yours, (125)

3

Dear Mrs. Gregory:

Here is the booklet you requested, "Caring for the Patient at Home." We hope you[1] find the publication informative and useful.

May we also remind you of the full health care service we[2] now offer? We carry a complete line of health care equipment for use in the home. You can rent any item[3] with no deposit required. You pay only that part of the expense not covered by your insurance. In most[4] cases, your insurance pays for everything, and the rental equipment costs you nothing.

If you have questions about[5] your coverage, discuss them with our professional staff. They are specialists in filing medical claims and will be[6] happy to give you assistance.

Come to the experts for convenient service and the best of professional care.[7] When quality counts, you can count on us.

Yours truly, (150)

4

Dear New Employee:

Welcome to World Electronics. In the enclosed envelope you will find three items of value[1] on your new job.

The first is your employee identification card. Please add your signature and carry[2] the card during regular working hours. Be prepared to show your card when you come into or leave the building.[3]

The second item is your health benefits booklet. Read it carefully. If you have any questions regarding[4] your hospital or dental coverage, call our personnel office immediately.

The third item, your[5] employee handbook, provides a complete guide to our company's services and policies. Please become familiar[6] with our procedures during your first week on your new job.

If you have any questions, don't hesitate to call on[7] us at any time.

Sincerely yours, (147)

5

Dear Mr. Edwards:

Your name was suggested to me because of your research in classifying rare plants. Would you[1] please assist us in making an identification of the enclosed leaf?

My class has been collecting leaves[2] during the past two weeks. One of my students brought in this leaf. It is not shown in any of the books in our school[3] library. After we made a careful search of the literature in the county library, we found the[4] enclosed photograph that looks exactly like our leaf. As you can see, both leaves have the same unusual shape. However,[5] the plant in the picture grows in the western states and could not possibly grow this far east. Or could it?

We hope[6] you can identify our discovery. This class project has become a significant learning experience[7] for everyone.

Very truly yours, (146)

LESSON 39

1. Write a capital n for the word beginnings *enter*, *inter*, and *intro*.

enterprise, enter-p-r-z *Nprz*

international, inter-n-tion-l *Nnjl*

interest, inter-st *ns*

introduced, intro-d-s-duh *Nds-*

interview, inter-v-u *Nvu*

introductory, intro-d-k-t-r-e *Ndclre*

2. Write *sf* for the word beginning and ending *self*.

self-addressed, self-a-d-r-s-duh *sfadrs-*

himself, him-self *hsf*

self-made, self-m-d *sfd*

herself, h-r-self *hrsf*

self-confidence, self-con-f-d-nce *sfkfdN*

yourself, your-self *usf*

self-assurance, self-a-ish-r-nce *sfasrN*

itself, it-self *sf*

3. Write *svs* for the word ending *selves*.

ourselves, our-selves *rsvs*

yourselves, your-selves *usvs*

themselves, ith-m-selves *hsvs*

Abbreviations

establish *est*

superintendent *S*

Brief Forms

circumstance	*Sk*	once	*on*
particular	*plc*	administrate	*Am*
control	*kl*	sample	*sa*

Brief Form Development

circumstances	*Sks*	particularly	*plcl*
circumstantial	*Sksl*	administration	*Amy*
controlled	*kl-*	samples	*sas*

USE A COMMA TO SET OFF DATES IN SENTENCES.

When naming a day of the week, followed by the date, place a comma after the day of the week and the date. If the date falls at the end of the sentence, place a comma only after the day of the week.

The meeting scheduled for Wednesday, April 2, has been postponed.

The next board meeting will be held on Tuesday, March 7.

In following lessons, commas around dates will be highlighted in your reading and writing exercises. **Date** will be highlighted.

Your Business Vocabulary	international *Nnyl*	Having to do with activities that extend across national boundaries.
	academic programs *acdᴜc Pgs*	Specialized areas of study within a school curriculum.

PRINCIPLES SUMMARY

1. Write a capital n for the word beginnings *enter*, *inter*, and *intro*: interest, inter-st $n\delta$.

2. Write sf for the word beginning and ending *self*: herself, h-r-self $hrsf$.

3. Write svs for the word ending *selves*: yourselves, your-selves $usvs$.

Reading and Writing Exercises

-1-

[shorthand notation]

-2-

[shorthand notation]

-3-

Series

Series

Intro DC

Intro DC

-4-

d r s ر lqf pam
v 40$. ev cr- ر lu
ak, e esp ap u lc‾
ر ᒐ l pln y u
pams vb la. u
ofr l brq ر ak
pda n Jn Stnl lb
sal, e lq eno ho
ر MUSN̄ dv-ksrn‾
u upd blN̄. Ph u
dd n no lau M-
u Ja pam. n u
sN̄. dB pam n
Mr,ₑ apli- ر lu   [Intro DC]
Ja + Ft nSlms. ls
m la uvb ι o
bhN̄. E pam sN̄
ln hsb apli- l ر
 o bf, y ur Sl
pzl- ₉p lt s no.   [Intro DC]
er A NS- n pr‾

K Svs. su

-5-

d r bcr ySrd ch
ر plzr v e‾. NS‾
+ hul qlf- aplcN̄
b. pzj r fr.
dli- lsa la s
yys yq ر no. pe
n r dla Pss‾ dpl,
y prs- b ر rz a
se sN̄ n AvN̄ v
Nvu. af ch lc-
hr n Psn₉ ι nu ر   [Intro DC]
oN̄ la se db ru f
r oqj. se hs. lN̄
bcgroN̄ n ofs Amj
+ se Ps hrsf z.
cpB + sfasr- pe,
ι ofr- s yq ر pzj
S kclj v Nvu +

se cl- ls ⌒rn‾ l   fCr Sks l alo s

ac. er grf lu f rf‾   l rel ⌒ fur. vlu

hr l r fr + hp la

Key

1

Dear Miss Johnson:

Did you know that you are looking at the most powerful credit card in America?

The[1] American Charge Card shown here is more than a credit card. It is your ticket to the world of international[2] business travel. You will find it accepted in major establishments all over the world.

If you wish to apply[3] for membership, simply complete the enclosed form and return it in the self-addressed envelope. If you apply[4] by Monday, May 6, you will receive an executive travel case. This special introductory gift is[5] beautifully styled to organize your personal items.

Why not put your signature on the most useful card[6] in America? Travel in the self-assured manner of experienced business people who are in control[7] and leave the rest to us.

Yours truly, (146)

2

Dear Mr. Evans:

I read with interest your report presenting long-term goals for the college. May I join you in[1] pursuing some of the goals you mentioned? I propose that we arrange a meeting with potential board members.

We[2] might invite the local superintendent of schools along with people from business and industry.

We should meet[3] often to discuss academic programs. How shall we identify the needs of our community? What[4] resources are available to us? You could probably suggest many more questions.

If you agree with this[5] sample plan, I will go to work on it immediately. Would you please send me a list of people you[6] particularly wish to involve?

Yours very truly, (129)

3

Dear Ms. Allen:

Thank you for your interest in the accounting firm of Davis and Davis. Your work experience,[1] educational background, and academic achievements are very impressive.

We do have an opening[2] for an administrative assistant. Your general office skills indicate that you would be highly qualified[3] for this position. Would you be willing to come in for an interview? This position could be an excellent[4] introduction to your career.

If you wish to discuss this opportunity further, please call my office[5] to arrange an interview. I look forward to talking with you.

Very truly yours, (116)

4

Dear Mrs. White:

Thank you for your payment of $40. We have credited it to your account.

We especially[1] appreciate your taking the time to explain why your payments have been late. Your offer to bring the account[2] up to date in June certainly will be satisfactory.

We think we know how the misunderstanding developed[3] concerning your unpaid balance. Perhaps you did not know that you missed your January payment. When you sent[4] a double payment in March, we applied it to your January and February installments. This meant that[5] you have been one month behind. Every payment since then has been applied to the month before.

If you are still puzzled,[6] please let us know. We are always interested in improving customer service.

Sincerely yours, (139)

5

Dear Mr. Baker:

Yesterday I had the pleasure of meeting an interesting and highly qualified[1] applicant for a position with our firm. I am delighted to say that Ms. Joyce Young is now an employee in[2] our data processing department.

I was impressed by the resumé she sent in advance of the interview.[3] After I had talked with her in person, I knew at once that she would be right for our organization. She has[4] an excellent background in office administration, and she presents herself as a capable and self-assured[5] employee.

I offered Ms. Young the position at the conclusion of the interview, and she called this morning[6] to accept. We are grateful to you for referring her to our firm and hope that future circumstances will[7] allow us to return the favor.

Very truly yours, (150)

LESSON 40

1. When a word contains two medial, consecutively pronounced vowels, write the first vowel.

trial, t-r-i-l	*lril*	client, k-l-i-nt	*clin*
annual, an-u-l	*aul*	material, m-t-r-e-l	*trel*
premium, pre-m-e-m	*Pre*	actually, a-k-chay-u-l-ly	*actull*
previous, pre-v-e-s	*Pves*	diagram, d-i-gram	*dig*
various, v-r-e-s	*vres*	period, p-r-e-d	*pred*

2. When a word ends in two consecutively pronounced vowel sounds, write only the last vowel.

area, a-r-a	*ara*	audio, aw-d-o	*ado*
radio, r-d-o	*rdo*	create, k-r-ate	*cra*
idea, i-d-a	*ida*	media, m-d-a	*da*

USE A COMMA BEFORE A COORDINATE CONJUNCTION THAT CONNECTS TWO INDEPENDENT CLAUSES.

When two complete thoughts are connected by *and, or, but, for, nor,* place a comma before the conjunction *and, or, but, for, nor.* Make certain that the conjunction is connecting two complete thoughts—that is, either thought can stand alone without the rest of the sentence.

David will type the report, and Susan will distribute it.

I will be gone on Tuesday, but Ms. Hamilton will be glad to help you.

Do you wish to pay for the item now, or shall we charge it to your account?

In your reading and writing exercises, commas before conjunctions will be highlighted, and the term **Conj** will also be highlighted.

| Your Business Vocabulary | audio-visual $ado = vzul$ | Educational materials (such as filmstrips, movies, videotape programs, and slide/tape programs) that can be seen and heard. |

PRINCIPLES SUMMARY

1. When a word contains two medial, consecutively pronounced vowels, write the first vowel: trial, t-r-i-l trl .
2. When a word ends in two consecutively pronounced vowel sounds, write only the last vowel: area, a-r-a ara .

Reading and Writing Exercises

-1-

-2-

[Shorthand notation]

Intro DC

Intro DC

Intro DC

Conj

-3-

[Shorthand notation]

Conj

Paren

Conj

(Shorthand exercise — left column)

⁓ sr u USN, ur
Ub kg- ou crav ⁓o
n rdo + Uvη, ⁄ db
· Clnη + · plzr Lo
⁓ u· chp Ls opl
Ub psδ ag s⁓
n fCr· s

-4-

d⁓cl me fn sugʒs
vb ⁓d f r nx ara
sls ⁓e· ec ʏc
Lse sv nu fss bcʒ
v rsM adʒs n Psnl·
brf ⁽Paren⁾ cblv · rvu vr
bsc Pg db esp hlpf·
⁄ hs Aso b suq-Lae
D sa⁓ cpes v A
co lil· sC lil d

(Shorthand exercise — right column)

⅃ cals ⁽Series⁾ sls brsrs ⁽Series⁾
+ K hMbcs, ⁓ rcm‾
La A Psnl alM r
nx ara sls ⁓e·
bʒ ⁓e v pv- Ub v
vluδ ⁽Conj⁾ + cdlc L scʒl
⁓ v L· Ph ⁄ db n
E⁏s bδ Nδ ʏf e L
hld s⁓lr sʝs ∫n
v eC pred· Ulb egr
thr ⅃ u lʒ· vlu

-5-

d elʒbl ⁄ aʝNa f
nx ⁓os ara sls
⁓e⁏ no kp· δ frδ
d· mbr vr sls δf
L Pvd ⁓ Pg rvu u
rqδ-⁏ el ɬn alo ⁓

rS v ⌐rn̲ ƒ · q=⫶ =
asr pred, sp Cnys
n S̲ Pdcs lb Dcs-
du̲ ⌐ afnn sp̰, ⌐ ls
L⌐ ⌐ db apo l D
ne nu lil uv re̲
Cnys n prs̲ ⟨Series⟩ Av̲ ⟨Series⟩ or
Dʳ, ⌐ sec d lb

dvo- nlrl l ⌐ Pʳ
v nu Pdcs, r Av̲
dpl ⟩ Ppr̲ ⌐ nu
brsrs C l Pvd
· v̲ adj l r S̲ lil,
ıdb grf ƒ ne sugs
u ⌐a v, cu

Key

1

Gentlemen:

Please send me any literature you have about recreation areas in your state.

I am[1] planning our annual family vacation. We are particularly interested in hotels or[2] apartments located on the beach. Do you have brochures listing rooms available in a middle price range?

We have[3] also heard many good things about your state parks. Please include a catalog describing the parks, their facilities,[4] and the activities provided by each one.

Are there special circumstances we should know about? Are[5] conditions in your area suitable for camping? What is the busy season for your parks?

We would be grateful[6] for any advice you have toward helping us plan a successful vacation. We look forward to hearing from you.[7]

Sincerely yours, (144)

2

Dear Ms. Allen:

If you are like most homemakers, you spend much of your day preparing meals. Shouldn't you have the best[1] possible materials to work with? We think you should. That is why we created our new line of cookware.

We[2] are so convinced of the quality of our product that we make this money-back guarantee. Order your special[3] introductory set and use it on a trial basis. Make your decision at the end of a 30-day[4] period. If you are not completely satisfied, you may return the set. We will then return your money.

What[5] makes us so sure you will love our cookware? We have been manufacturing fine products for over 40 years, and[6] we know what good cooks look for. Once you try this particular set, you will never want to use anything else.

Prove[7] it to yourself. Treat yourself to something special in the kitchen.

Cordially yours, (154)

3

Dear Mr. Miller:

Thank you for offering me the position of audio-visual director of your[1] advertising agency.

I am pleased that you admire my work. I certainly enjoyed meeting you at the[2] convention last month, and it is very tempting to accept your offer. However, I am not ready to leave my[3] work here. I have begun some new programs, and I would like to make sure that they are firmly established and under[4] control before I leave. I am sure you understand.

You are to be congratulated on your creative work[5] in radio and television. It would be a challenge and a pleasure to work with you. I hope this[6] opportunity will be possible again sometime in the future.

Sincerely, (134)

4

Dear Michael:

Many fine suggestions have been made for our next area sales meeting. We can expect to see[1] several new faces because of recent additions in personnel. Therefore, I believe a review of our[2] basic program would be especially helpful. It has also been suggested that we distribute sample copies[3] of all company literature. Such literature would include catalogs, sales brochures, and customer handbooks.[4]

I am recommending that all personnel attend our next area sales meeting. These meetings have proved to[5] be very valuable, and I would like to schedule more of them. Perhaps it would be in everyone's best[6] interest if we were to hold similar sessions at the end of each period. I will be eager to hear what[7] you think.

Very truly yours, (145)

5

Dear Elizabeth:

The agenda for next month's area sales meeting is now complete. On the first day a[1] member of our sales staff will provide the program review you requested. We will then allow the rest of the morning[2] for a question-and-answer period. Specific changes in existing products will be discussed during the[3] afternoon session. At this time it would be appropriate to distribute any new literature you have[4] regarding changes in pricing, advertising, or distribution.

The second day will be devoted entirely[5] to the presentation of new products. Our advertising department is preparing the new brochures which[6] will provide an exciting addition to our existing literature.

I would be grateful for any[7] suggestions you may have.

Cordially yours, (146)

LESSON 41

1. Write   *T*   for the word beginnings *tran* and *trans*.

tranquil, tran-q-l   *Tql*   translate, trans-l-ate   *Tla*

transcribe, tran-scribe   *TS*   transistor, trans-st-r   *TSr*

transfer, trans-f-r   *Tfr*   transportation,
trans-port-tion   *Tply*

2. Always use the word beginnings *trans*, *sur*, and *com* for blending sounds.

transact, trans-a-k   *Tac*   surround, sur-ow-nd   *SoN*

community, com-n-ity   *kn* ᴸ

Otherwise, avoid blending the initial sound of a major accented syllable with a preceding syllable.

indulge, in-d-l-j   *ndly*   entire, en-t-r   *nlr*

addition, a-d-tion   *ady*   allow, a-l-ow   *alo*

Writing Unusual Words. Those proper nouns, technical terms, or unusual words that might be misspelled or transcribed incorrectly may be written in full. In addition, abbreviations or writing shortcuts familiar to the *Speedwriting* writer may be used in recording notes. An example would be as follows:

Mr. Aillet is head of the word processing department at Yazoo Industries.

~r aillet, hd √ wp dpt / Yazoo Ng.

USE COMMAS WITH INTRODUCTORY PHRASES.

(a) An introductory infinitive phrase (a verb preceded by *to*) is followed by a comma.

To get our proposal completed, we had to work for three months after closing hours.

(b) An introductory participial phrase (a verb form used as an adjective) is followed by a comma.

Leaving her umbrella at the office, the secretary got wet while running to catch her bus.

(c) An introductory prepositional phrase or phrases consisting of five or more words, or an introductory prepositional phrase containing a verb form is followed by a comma.

In two or three days, I will be finished with the inventory.

At the beginning of our employment with Brown and Company, we were required to complete a training course.

After giving considerable thought to your suggestion, we have decided to adopt the proposal.

In the reading and writing exercises, the abbreviation **Intro P** will be used to highlight introductory phrases.

Your Business Vocabulary	transaction *Tac*	The completion or carrying out of an exchange of things of value, frequently preceded by negotiation.
	premiums *Prems*	In reference to insurance, the payments on an insurance policy.

PRINCIPLES SUMMARY

1. Write T for the word beginnings *tran* and *trans*: transfer, trans-f-r *Tfr* .
2. Always use the word beginnings *trans*, *sur*, and *com* for blending sounds; otherwise, avoid blending the initial sound of a major accented syllable with a preceding syllable.

Reading and Writing Exercises

-1-

[Shorthand outlines]

Jl 1 [Date] ul rsv · rdo-
ra rzrv- f drvrs
hu vm p- · vdM O
· 5 = yr pred. ls ,
r a v rw sf
drv hbls, er a
rde lb v Svs. vlu

e l lq E, hu
hlp- m Ppr rdo
+ nzppr Avms [Series] m
Pvd Tply [Series] + m c
Hs v cls, u hlp-
c ls drv · suc [Conj]
+ er grf lu f pl
u B ls lo f s. uvl

-2-

d k mbrs ur a
Mrf! p ac r
kgjs f c ls yrs
fM drv r bgS +
bS E, e rC- r gl
2 cs ahd v L,
m r drv N- o
Oc 4 [Intro DC] eh vd- a pcjs,
l lr r no trel
rws aso- vlnlr
o [Intro DC] eno u sr r
fl v aCvm + saly.

-3-

d s evns r enc-
rl eSa kc hsb
rvz- l e r lrs
e agre- po. p nl
S alC- dcq la r
nu prp ln hsb
clrl dfn- r c no
lgr b kfz- SoM
aras. cpes v ls
rvj dl- l r nu
ors ySrd [Conj] + ly gv r

(shorthand outlines)

Intro P

Intro DC

Intro DC

Paren

-4-

(shorthand outlines)

inf _{Intro P} u fnl cpe ✓ lS
l ndd pv Ub vluß.
s

-5-

dS r aɟNe hsb
alrz- b ⌐ fed gvl
l Ppr · rpl o Tpḷ
Svss. elb Sva +
sa ⌐ sles ⌣ I HT
or ⌒ rzdNs. u
sle qlfo _{Conj} b er NS-
m v u pp f rzns
ol ln sz. u Amɟ hs
bk nn f s ⌐drn
cdas + ldrs. bcz

e ks u kn^b Ub Xord,
er asc u l Sv ʒ.
⌐dl f r Sde, ⌐ enc-
f ascs f dll- inf.
p rel , b ⌐ da sp-.
cd u Aso spli s ⌣
lil ou Tpḷ coo,
edlc lno ab
scɟls _{Series} frs _{Series} ✓
No v clcNs uʒ-
⌐ Svss o · dl
bss, ʒʒ ⌐ rzlls
vb pbls- _{Intro DC} el ⌐l
Nv cpes l A pp
sles. su

Key

1

Dear Mr. Ames:

Thank you for your inquiry about transferring your current automobile insurance to a[1] different car. The process is quite simple. In order to do so, just give me the model, year, make, and registration[2] number of your new car. I will take care of everything else.

There will be a slight increase in your annual[3] premium. The amount of the increase will depend on the kind of new car you purchase. Please notify me[4] as soon as you buy your new car. Becoming effective immediately, the change in your new policy will[5] provide you with continued coverage. I will mail you a copy of the revised policy for your signature.[6]

Here is good news. Effective Tuesday, July 1, you will receive a reduced rate reserved for drivers who have[7] not experienced an accident over a five-year period. This is our way of rewarding safe driving[8] habits.

We are always ready to be of service.

Very truly yours, (173)

2

Dear Committee Members:

You are all wonderful! Please accept our congratulations for making this year's fund drive[1] the biggest and best ever.

We reached our goal two weeks ahead of time. When the drive ended on October 4,[2] we had exceeded all expectations.

While there are no material rewards associated with volunteer[3] work, we know you share our feelings of achievement and satisfaction. We wish to thank everyone who helped in[4] preparing radio and newspaper advertisements, in providing transportation, and in making hundreds[5] of calls.

You helped to make this drive a success, and we are grateful to you for putting your abilities to work[6] for us.

Yours very truly, (125)

3

Dear Ms. Evans:

The enclosed real estate contract has been revised to meet the terms we agreed upon. Please note on[1] the attached diagram that the new property line has been clearly defined. It can no longer be confused with[2] surrounding areas. Copies of this revision were delivered to the new owners yesterday, and they gave[3] it their immediate approval.

After adding your signature to all three copies of the contract, you will[4] need to return them to me. Once you have signed the forms, the contract becomes final. The title to your property[5] is then transferred to the new owners.

You have my congratulations on handling this matter so well. A[6] transaction such as this ordinarily takes several weeks. This matter has been resolved quickly and conveniently[7] because of the help of everyone involved.

I hope you will call on me again if I can be of assistance.[8]

Cordially yours, (163)

4

Dear Jeffrey:

Could you please prepare a new list of all companies we are currently supplying? Because we wish[1] to add information, the format may differ from the one you have followed in the past. We ordinarily[2] group all customers by size of account. However, our marketing department produces a similar[3] document listing all customers by the area served. It would be more efficient to create one list that is[4] equally beneficial to both departments.

Why don't you meet with our marketing director to establish[5] a new format? Please continue to show the dollar amount received from each customer on an annual[6] basis. It would also be helpful to give an item breakdown of the products purchased.

As a source of vital[7] information, your final copy of the list will indeed prove to be valuable.

Sincerely, (156)

5

Dear Sir:

Our agency has been authorized by the federal government to prepare a report on transportation[1] services. We will be surveying and sampling cities with 100,000 or more residents. Your[2] city qualifies, but we are interested in having you participate for reasons other than size.[3] Your administration has become known for its modern ideas and leadership. Because we consider your[4] community to be extraordinary, we are asking you to serve as a model for our study.

The enclosed[5] form asks for detailed information. Please return it by the date specified. Could you also supply us with[6] literature on your transportation companies? We would like to know about schedules, fares, and the number of[7] clients using the services on a daily basis.

As soon as the results have been published, we will mail[8] individual copies to all participating cities.

Sincerely yours, (174)

LESSON 42

RECAP AND REVIEW

You have now completed all of the principles lessons in this text. Let's review the principles, brief forms, and abbreviations presented in the last six lessons.

1. You learned to write the following word beginnings:

sub	*S*	tran, trans	*T*
enter, inter, intro	*n*	self	*sf*

2. You also learned these word endings:

ful	*b*	self	*sf*
ify	*b*	selves	*svs*
ification	*bʏ*		

3. Write these words that illustrate all of the new principles you studied in Lessons 36-41:

effective, e-f-k-tive	*efcv*	himself, him-self	*hsf*
grateful, grate-ful	*grf*	ourselves, our-selves	*rsvs*
qualify, q-l-ify	*qlf*	trial, t-r-i-l	*lril*
qualification, q-l-ification	*qlfʏ*	idea, i-d-a	*ida*
interview, inter-v-u	*nvu*	transcribe, tran-scribe	*TS*
self-addressed, self-a-d-r-s-duh	*sfadrs-*	since, s-nce	*sn*

4. Do you recall the following abbreviations?

esl   *S*

5. How quickly can you write these brief forms?

usual	once	work
circumstance	manufacture	administrate
world	significance	signature
significant	particular	sample
control		

Reading and Writing Exercises

-1-

[The following is handwritten shorthand notation, transcribed as best as legible]

d rs jcsn r rgS
f fMs hsb apv-.
l Sv r sle + SoN
ara ⸲ ec no esl   *(Intro P)*
r Ppz- ldrs Pg. ⌐
srs u USN r ssl
siq v ls Pg. clMs
Czn l pp lb lrn-
n ldrs lds.
oN r clMs v
kp- r crs ⸲ ly lb   *(Intro DC)*
ncry- l dr ol
s ls Pgs n r kn'⸴
r obycv no ⸴ l
lca · yp- Psn l ld
r lrn sys. eblv

u lb r S qlf- Psn
bcz vy aCvms n
vlnlr o⸴ d ub
l l Sv z Px⸴ v
crs ⸲ ul s lgv   *(Paren)*
ls lr crf ksy. p
alo e l asr ne
qs u a v / ls
h. s

-2-

d rs lsn u
anoNm k z Nrf
mz. sC. Pq ⸴ Sln
lb sucf n ls kn'⸴
dd ι USN crcl la

· grM hsb aw- f ls
Pjc, ⌐ grM sf, qc
· akm, kgjs q lu ⩛
ol Nvs hu s⌐l- ⌐
Ppzl, cdb hpe l
Sv ou brd v drrs _{Conj}
b ccn ac ⌐ pzj v
P, ⌐ Amv dles d
rq ⌐ l ln ⌐ c P
Sks alo. hoE _{Paren} cc
lq v sv ppl hu v
⌐d scq kbjs n
vlnlr ⌐ o. d u
lc ⌐ l rcm loj
hu ⌐ b NS- n bk
P, cfl p- Ub ks- f
ls pzj. lqf vo v
kfdM, cu

-3-

d ble · fu ⌐ cs aq

u vprs- NS n ⌐ o
f r co, ⌐ la ⌐ eh
no opn lofr u.
sM Sks v Cny- _{Intro DC} cc
no rf u l · pzj
⌐ C bk avlS ol
ySrd, ⌐ enc · jb
dSj f ofs v Amv
sec, A aplcNs
⌐S v Pves vp n
ofs ⌐ o ⩛ scl n
srlhM l qlf f ls
pzj. zj rcl _{Intro DC} uv
Ar esl- · ⌐prsv
bcgroM C ⌐s
rc ⩛ TS spdrc
PjsMl, cf u ⌐sl
apli _{Intro DC} p cl ⌐c ofs
b Fr afnn, ec ln
ar · Nvu l Dcs ⌐
pzj frlr, uvl

-4-

[Gregg shorthand outlines]

-5-

[Gregg shorthand outlines]

Printed annotations appearing among the shorthand: Paren, Conj, Intro DC, Paren, Paren, Conj, Intro DC, Conj, Intro P, Conj

rsNl se hs Sv- ʒ
ad alɜ n r Nnɟl
dvɟ, ɔ sr p lɑ
l lk u assN n gl
est- n hr nu ofs.
se ɔ lc fw Lo ⌣
eC vu.

-6-

dɯs le n evN
v · dN nvlv s ɩ
n u f l ud N
hlp l arv ⌒l.
r sle ɔ n nd v nu
erɟNe eqpm^{Conj} +
es asc u l kb l r
fN drv, e N r

eqpm l cor l ⌐
Sds crc v ol sles
⌐ sʒ v rs. ⌣ ncrs-
dms f us vr lx $^{Intro P}
me f nu eqpm ,
jɜ n avlB. e lɟ ec
Ok ls dfc suy b
gn ⌐ spl v ksrn-
sljns lc u n r vres
nbrhs, r crN gl ,
l rʒ enf me f i nu
a blN. N u sN
s · dnɟ n enc- env.
Ln u^{Paren} l^{Paren} l hlp n
ffl · vll nd n r
kn⌐. su

Key

Abbreviations
establish   superintendent

Brief Forms

1

Dear Ms. Jackson:

Our request for funds has been approved. To serve our city and surround-ing area, we can now[1] establish our proposed leadership program. I am sure you understand the social significance of this program.[2] Clients chosen to par-ticipate will be trained in leadership methods. Once the clients have com-pleted our course,[3] they will be encouraged to direct other similar programs in our community.

Our objective now is[4] to locate an experienced person to lead our training sessions. We believe you to be the most qualified[5] person because of your achievements in volunteer work. Would you be willing to serve as president?

Of course, you[6] will wish to give this matter careful consideration. Please allow me to answer any questions you may have[7] at this time.

Sincerely, (145)

2

Dear Mr. Wilson:

Your announcement came as wonderful news. Such a program is certain to be successful in[1] this community. Did I understand correctly that a grant has been awarded for this project? The grant itself[2] is quite an accomplishment. Congratulations go to you and the other individuals who submitted[3] the proposal.

I would be happy to serve on your board of directors, but I cannot accept the position[4] of president. The administrative duties would require more time than my present circumstances allow.[5] However, I can think of several people who have made significant contributions in volunteer work.[6] Would you like me to recommend those who might be interested in becoming president?

I feel pleased to be[7] considered for this position. Thank you for your vote of confidence.

Cordially yours, (156)

3

Dear Betty:

A few weeks ago you expressed interest in working for our company. At that time we had no[1] openings to offer you. Since circumstances have changed, I can now refer you to a position which became[2] available only yesterday.

I am enclosing a job description for the office of administrative[3] secretary. All applicants must have previous experience in office work and skill in shorthand[4] to qualify for this position. As I recall, you have already established an impressive background which[5] includes writing and transcribing Speedwriting proficiently.

If you wish to apply, please call my office by Friday[6] afternoon. We can then arrange an interview to discuss the position further.

Yours very truly, (139)

4

Dear Mr. Roberts:

I have a question regarding our usual procedure for paying insurance claims for[1] medical visits.

We ordinarily advise the employee to present the form for the doctor's signature[2] during the visit. In some cases, the doctor requests additional time for entering information[3] relative to that visit. The form is then mailed to the employee, and the employee submits it to our office.[4]

This procedure adds several days between the time the employee pays for the visit and the date the form[5] arrives in our office. Once the forms come in, we process them immediately and issue a check to the[6] employee. By that time, however, the total transaction has taken up to three weeks.

There must be a way to save[7] processing time. I would be grateful for your ideas on this subject.

Yours truly, (155)

5

MEMO TO: All Employees

Pamela Carlson will become general manager of our manufacturing[1] division as of July 1.

When the change becomes effective, the manufacturing division will be[2] expanded to include two new departments. The office of industrial research will be responsible for[3] long-range planning, and a systems control department will ensure continued excellence for our product. You will be[4] hearing more about both of these developments in the near future.

Having joined our staff as an engineer,[5] Pamela brought many fine ideas to our operation. She has acted as superintendent for special[6] projects, and most recently she has served as worldwide analyst in our international division.

I am[7] sure Pamela will welcome your assistance in getting established in her new office. She is looking forward[8] to working with each of you. (165)

| 6 |

Dear Mrs. Lee:

In the event of an accident involving someone in your family, you would want help to[1] arrive immediately. Our city is in need of new emergency equipment, and we are asking you[2] to contribute to our fund drive.

We want our equipment to correspond to the standards characteristic of[3] other cities the size of ours. With increased demands for the use of our tax dollars, money for new equipment[4] is just not available. We think we can overcome this difficult situation by gaining the support[5] of concerned citizens like you in our various neighborhoods.

Our current goal is to raise enough money for[6] one new ambulance. Won't you send us a donation in the enclosed envelope? Then you, too, will help in fulfilling[7] a vital need in our community.

Sincerely yours, (151)

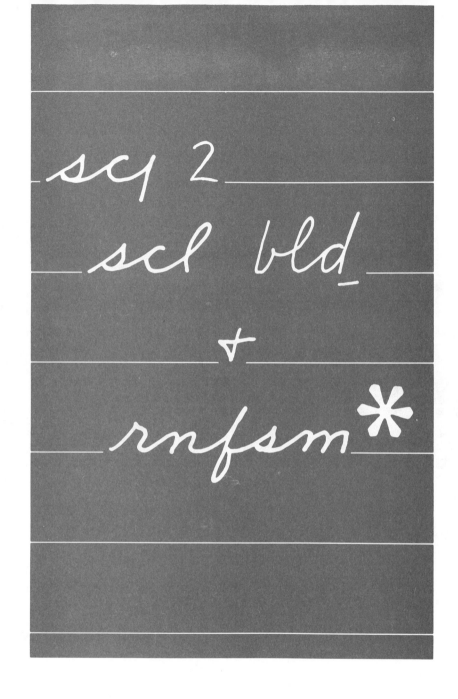

Cplr 7*

WHAT MAKES AN EMPLOYMENT INTERVIEW SUCCESSFUL?

Employment interviews have two main purposes: to exchange information and to make a favorable impression. The information you give and receive will help you and the employer decide if you and the job are right for each other.

Before the Interview

Know your facts. Learn about the company in advance—its size, products, and locations. Know the position title for which you are interviewing and the salary range for that position. (School counselors and the classified pages of newspapers are excellent sources for obtaining such information.)

Anticipate questions. Be ready to answer routine interview questions: What

*Chapter Seven

attracted you to this position? What do you know about the company? What are your career goals and salary expectations for this job?

Have questions ready. Be prepared to ask specific questions related to the job: What are the primary duties? What performance evaluation procedures are utilized? What are the advancement opportunities? What are the insurance and vacation benefits? What is the salary range for the position being discussed?

Dress appropriately. Your attire and personal grooming reflect your attitude, judgment, and personality. For a polished and professional image, dress conservatively and neatly.

Psych yourself up. Enthusiasm is infectious. Allow yourself to enjoy the pride and excitement that come from entering the work force. You are a trained individual with marketable skills and talents—a trait to be proud of! The enthusiasm you feel for yourself and your future will have a positive impact on the interviewer. People who feel good about themselves and their company are usually happy and well-liked employees.

Take what you'll need for the interview. Have these aids easily accessible: two reliable pens, a notepad (with possible notes or questions for the interview), a pocket-size dictionary, and an extra copy of your resumé.

Leave home in time to arrive early. Before announcing yourself to the receptionist, visit a nearby lounge or dressing room to be certain you are well groomed. Knowing you look your very best will give you confidence during the interview. Announce yourself to the receptionist ten to fifteen minutes before the interview. You may be given application forms to complete during this time.

During the Interview

Once inside the interviewer's office, try to relax. While this interview is important, it should also be enjoyable. Remember, you are a skilled individual about to exchange information with another professional. Also expect the interviewer to be friendly and professional. Also expect the interviewer to look for an employee with those same qualities—friendliness and professionalism.

Be professional. Greet your interviewer with a smile and a firm handshake.

Be poised but comfortable. Arrange yourself comfortably on the chair to avoid stiffness, fidgeting, fatigue, and awkwardness. Avoid nervous habits. Never chew gum, tap your fingers, or smoke during an interview.

Listen carefully. Listen attentively to the interviewer's description of the company, job, and related information. Save your questions until the interviewer has completed his or her initial explanation.

Answer questions. Always answer questions directly, honestly, politely, and briefly. Phrase statements positively—"I enjoy working in a small office," rather than "I don't like large offices." Be courteous—respect and friendliness are always admired traits. Be honest—don't try to flatter or mislead the interviewer. Be specific—give the interviewer the information he or she wants, but do not overwhelm the interviewer with long, complicated explanations.

Ask intelligent questions. When the interviewer asks for questions, ask anything not covered in his or her initial explanation: When will the decision for hiring be made; what kind of training or orientation program is planned for the job, for example.

Be positive. Even if you are not impressed by what you learn during the interview, maintain a polite and positive attitude throughout the meeting.

After the Interview

Thank the interviewer warmly and exit as soon as he or she signals that the interview has come to a close. If additional information is expected of you (skill tests, academic information, or a follow-up call), be certain you understand when and how you are to proceed.

Once away from the office, mentally evaluate the interview. Were there questions you didn't anticipate? What areas would you improve upon for future interviews?

What were your impressions of the company, the interviewer, and the position described? If you were strongly attracted to the job, write a follow-up letter thanking the interviewer and stating that you would enjoy working for the company in that capacity.

While you're waiting for the job offer, send other applications and schedule other interviews. Expect to interview several times—as many times as necessary—before acquiring that special first job. The job search is often just that—a search. Through repeat performances, you will not only sharpen your interviewing skills, but you will also increase your knowledge about different working environments, thereby giving you a greater basis for comparing jobs and companies.

Of course, when you do accept a job, notify those companies to whom you made application that you have accepted employment elsewhere. Tell them where you will be working and what you will be doing. They may want to keep this information with your original application for future reference.

LESSON 43

Brief Form Review

appropriate	*apo*	accept	*ac*	
necessary	*nes*	during	*du̲*	
determine	*dl*	other	*ol*	
perhaps	*Ph*	after	*af*	
include	*-l*	part	*pl*	
market	*-r*	full	*b*	
manage	*-y*	very	*V*	
letter	*L*	why	*y*	

Abbreviation Review

attention	*all*	north	*N*	
Christmas	*X-s*	south	*S*	
enclose	*enc*	east	*E*	
second	*sec*	west	*W*	
junior	*jr*	senior	*sr*	

Commonly Misspelled Words	schedule	*scjl*
	receiving	*rsv̲*

Reading and Writing Exercises

-1-

Intro DC

Series   Series

Intro P

-2-

Intro P

Intro DC

Conj

Intro P

Intro P   Paren

-3-

-4-

Ap

Paren

-5-

Conj

Paren

Intro DC

Paren

n grds ı lru 6 ͺ	lp + kpur clss fl-
scl ofsls ‿ alspa_	frꝺ [Conj] b nꝺ ᴣ Aso
· Srq rsp [Conj] b evn	Srq n arl + dr‿a ͵
ly ‿ Sprᴣ- lse la	M ⁄ rw_ l pla ·
me clss ‿ f af ⌒	pl n pl_ ls fn Pq
frꝺ hr v rꝺrɉ ͵ ⌒	lglꞃ ˯ ul

1

MEMO TO: All Secretarial and Clerical Staff

Many of you have expressed interest in the training[1] sessions now being scheduled. The purpose of these sessions is to introduce all staff members to the changes made[2] necessary by additions to our office information system.

These workshops will begin in the early[3] part of July. The subjects to be covered include new procedures in managing workflow, distributing[4] information, and keying and coding copy. We will also discuss advanced methods for distributing office[5] reports and for transmitting other forms of interoffice mail.

The enclosed paper provides a list of dates and[6] times for specific work sessions. Please note that we are asking you to choose your preferred times. After you have determined[7] your first and second choices, please fill in the appropriate information and return the form to us.

To[8] complete our schedule on time, we will need all responses by the end of this week. Your immediate attention[9] would be appreciated. (185)

2

Dear Mr. Carson:

This letter is in response to your recent article on corporate growth and planning.

Having[1] also done research in that area, I would like to point out the following ideas for your consideration.[2] While growth may have leveled off in the East for the time being, many business executives expect this[3] condition to last a very short time. We see many new firms being built in the South, but we should also look[4] at the reasons why in order to view this result with appropriate emphasis.

For many years such growth was[5] prevented by a shortage of certain necessary resources. With the development of industries[6] using high technology, however, both the western and southern parts of the country have enjoyed an upward[7] swing in their economies. This shift in markets means a better distribution for the nation as a whole.

I[8] enjoyed your writing and wish you continued success.

Sincerely, (171)

3

Dear Mrs. Hester:

After reading your report on developing a writing lab for use in our high school, I[1] must add my congratulations to the many others you are receiving.

The proposed lab offers many[2] wonderful additions to our writing program here. Do I understand correctly that the lab will be open to[3] students in the junior class as well as those in the senior class?

You have asked for suggestions on how to fund this[4] important plan. I can certainly advise you on grants that might be available. The enclosed listing gives the[5] names of contributing organizations and full details on how to contact them.

There will be much to do in[6] submitting a final proposal. Please accept my sincere offer to help make this dream a reality.

Yours[7] truly, (141)

4

MEMO TO: James Olson, Shipping Department Manager

Thank you for your inquiry regarding our schedule for[1] shipping and receiving during the holidays. The answer to your question is yes—we will keep someone on[2] duty throughout the holidays with the exception of Christmas Day.

It is reasonable to assume that shipments[3] will be minimal during this period. Therefore, all unused shipping platforms will be closed with the exception[4] of one. The north platform should be maintained at all times for loading and receiving goods.

Most departments will be closed[5] or operating on a part-time basis during the last week of December. Perhaps you should talk directly[6] with the data processing department to work out a plan for the immediate recording and processing[7] of invoices. (143)

5

Dear Committee Member:

The results of our fund drive are in, and we have gone over our original goal.[1] Therefore, all of the projects chosen this year can be funded as planned.

When you attend next month's meeting, please bring the[2] project proposals with you. I will have a full report on the fund drive and how the money is to be spent.

In[3] addition, I have heard many nice comments on the summer program we are offering to students in grades one through[4] six. School officials were anticipating a strong response, but even they were surprised to see that many classes[5] were full after the first hour of registration. The typing and computer classes filled first, but interest[6] was also strong in art and drama.

Isn't it rewarding to play a part in putting this fine program together?[7] Yours truly, (143)

LESSON 44

Brief Form Review

manufacture	⟍ƒ	employ	⟋p
appreciate	ap	world	⟍o
individual	nv	would	d
complete	kp	point	py
standard	ßd	about	ab
industry	n	work	⟍o
develop	dv	both	bo
present	p	am	⌒

Abbreviation Review

merchandise	⟍dse	example	ex
information	inf	catalog	cal
department	dpl	America	a⟍
economic	eco	credit	cr
question	q	Ms.	⟍s

Commonly Misspelled Words

efficiency	efßne
identifying	idnf-

Reading and Writing Exercises

-1-

ddr dvdsn ~ ru
o bhf vr ecos cls
l lqf fn Pf o nCrl
rsrss aroN ~ o,
u ~d . lM py ab
~ grl v N la hlp-
s se ho ~ nrje
Pbl dv. Wrn
cMres no dpM po
yl + nCrl gs f ~s
v ls nrje nds. n
A ~ f ex lz Pdcs   _(Paren) (Paren)_
spl O hf v nrje
ks ~ , dv cMres
bgn l rl ~ po N,   _(Intro DC)_
ls nds l gro. el
ln fs evn grs srys
v gs + yl, ll s
rmbs Aso la r
srss v ls dzrv

eql cr + Plcf. lz
r gfls v lM. esd
A lrn l ap ~ z pl
v ~ os ll. ul

-2-

mo l A dpl hds
es Nds . nu ~ld
f us n ~ c Pf ~ M
evluys, p nl la ~
alC- f ~ dz n Cny
r Sds f ~ zr ~ o
efs Ne b l dz asc   _(Conj)_
f ~ inf f ~ pe.
ls inf l Sv me
Ppss n r ogf, rzlls
lb hlpf n idNf
aras v ~ pvm o .
Nv lvl + Aso o .
dpll lvl. ~ Sva

lb uz-z · bss f dl
y ncrss + P—ys,/
l Aso U s ab (crr
gls + lvl v jb saly
p-b —pes, p P(gr
(bgn v eC Nvu
l alo Aql h f Dcy
√ kp-f—, elb hpe
l asr ne qs u —a
v,

-3-

dS — ru l rqS
inf ou kp ln v
c—p eqpm, lS c
ι alN-, lrvl so
—ι sa u Pdcs o
Dpla, yz —prs-bo
— (ql' vu cos —o
+ — (ecol prss √
—dse, sM — pln

· s —ι c —p f by
scols ⌢, / —a pls sv   *Intro DC*
ods, — ptcl NS-n
bcpcs + cc eqpm,
cd u Aso l cS
fgrs f Ms lry enf
l akda 4 ppl, if
u co —fs ιhs f
lr spls ⌢ p so —e   *Intro DC*
l uv avlб, ιdlc
(cal —l-l —ιh
adrs sn abv, bcz
cS, · —pl fcr ⌢ p py   *Intro DC*
ol ne Dk u ofr l
scol grps, ul

-4-

dhs jsn cd ι suq
ι — lpc f r aul
pln —e ×, ιblv

ed A bnfl f . Dcy
v ho Nvs + grps
c dsys + arv
yyms, dsy = c ,
acv n inf Pss. eC
v s cs dsys E d
vs lvs. SdN
dsds po. crr. yb
aplcN Czs f avlB
opn. pe dls ho
C o l Pds U
. nu ss , r Dcy
cdb bs. o lz qs: l
inf dz. Nv uz n
c. dsy. l ,
lvl v pt pls. 6
inf. ho dz r Psn
uz la inf n arv
. Cys. yf u lc ls
ida il gldl hlp dv

Intro DC

drel f sC. Dcy. su

-5-

drs rfe er dli-
l lk u z. Cy K.
edlc l lc . m
l U u ab r me
bnfls n Sr fu, u
Cy crd l opn r
dr l opls C r
n avlB l rglr
Ks. f ex oN . o
e hld . sl rzrv- f
cr = crd PCss. ul
rsv . blln prir
l lz evNs lS chs
prss + dpls. l cd
c sp ezer os
ecol. ul Aso rsv
AvN nls v A ol

Paren

Series

Series

sls n ady l · hld | e pln lgv u, las

cal P gfl idas f E | r ⌣a v sa er hpe

mbr √ fl. hoE, r | l -l u n r spol

bo lons ev lofr, ⌣rs | fl v G Ks, cu

⌣rfe, (prl Svs

1

Dear Dr. Davidson:

I am writing on behalf of our economics class to thank you for your fine presentation[1] on natural resources around the world.

You made an excellent point about the growth of industry[2] that helped us see how the energy problem developed. Western countries now depend upon oil and natural[3] gas for most of their energy needs. In America, for example, these products supply over half of the[4] energy consumed. As developing countries begin to rely more upon industry, their needs will grow.[5] We will then face even greater shortages of gas and oil.

Let us remember also that our sources of water[6] deserve equal care and protection. These are gifts of the land. We should all learn to appreciate them as part of[7] the world's wealth.

Yours truly, (144)

2

MEMO TO: All Department Heads

We are introducing a new method for use in making performance[1] evaluations.

Please note that the attached form does not change our standards for measuring work efficiency, but it[2] does ask for more information from the employee. This information will serve many purposes in our[3] organization.

The results will be helpful in identifying areas of improvement on an[4] individual level and also on a departmental level. The survey will be used as a basis for[5] determining wage increases and promotions. It will also tell us about the career goals and level of job[6] satisfaction experienced by employees.

Please present the questionnaire at the beginning of each interview[7] to allow adequate time for discussion of the completed form.

We will be happy to answer any[8] questions you may have. (163)

3

Dear Sir:

I am writing to request information on your complete line of camping equipment.

Last week I[1] attended a travel show where I saw your products on display. I was impressed both with the quality of your[2] company's work and with the economical prices of the merchandise. Since I am planning a summer camp for[3] Boy Scouts, I may place several orders.

I am particularly interested in backpacks and cooking equipment.[4] Could you also include cost figures for tents large enough to accommodate four people? If your company[5] manufactures items for water sports, please show me what you have available.

I would like the catalog[6] mailed to my home address shown above. Because cost is an important factor, please point out any discount you[7] offer to scout groups.

Yours truly, (145)

4

Dear Ms. Jason:

Could I suggest one more topic for our annual planning meeting?

I believe we would all[1] benefit from a discussion of how individuals and groups make decisions and arrive at judgments.[2]

Decision-making is an activity in information processing. Each of us makes decisions every day[3] of our lives. The student decides upon a career. A job applicant chooses from available openings.[4] An employee determines how much work to produce under a new system.

Our discussion could be based on these[5] questions: What information does an individual use in making a decision? What is the level[6] of importance placed on the information? How does the person use that information in arriving at a[7] choice?

If you like this idea, I will gladly help develop the material for such a discussion.[8]

Sincerely yours, (163)

> **5**
>
> Dear Mrs. Murphy:
>
> We are delighted to welcome you as a charge customer. We would like to take a moment[1] to tell you about the many benefits in store for you.
>
> Your charge card will open the door to opportunities[2] which are not available to regular customers. For example, once a month we hold a sale reserved[3] for credit-card purchases. You will receive a bulletin prior to these events listing items, prices, and[4] departments. What could make shopping easier or more economical?
>
> You will also receive advance notice[5] of all other sales in addition to a holiday catalog presenting gift ideas for every member[6] of the family. However, the best bonus we have to offer, Mrs. Murphy, is the expert service we[7] plan to give you.
>
> That's our way of saying we are happy to include you in our special family of charge[8] customers.
>
> Cordially yours, (165)

LESSON 45

Brief Form Review

administrate	Am	please	p
correspondence	cor	between	btn
opportunity	opt	next	nx
signature	sig	over	O
participate	pp	business	bs
approximate	apx	already	Ar
contribute	kt	able	B
opinion	opn	as	3

Abbreviation Review

corporation	$corp$	amount	$a\!\!\downarrow$
executive	ex	volume	vol
secretary	sec	total	tol
establish	esl	Miss	M
number	No	day	d

Commonly Misspelled Words

exceeded	$vd-$
procedures	$Psjrs$

Reading and Writing Exercises

-1-

-2-

hnc , bl Cyss + Sl   kv clgres + Pss—⌣
⌢nln · efsN flo   s uz kpur Pg, a
v ⌣o, sN ⌐ vol v   dB = Cc ⌐ klN vu
kncys , ncrs rlr   Sva⸱ , eC q nes⸱
ln dcrs_ ofss ⌢S   , , sıq l ⌐ Pps v
 _Intro DC_⑨   Sde⸱ dz , Dlg⌐
uz alhc ⌢ms v   bln fc + opn⸱ rmbr _Paren_⑨
Pss inf⸱ elnc eqpm   aso _Paren_⑨ la fnl suc dpNs
ofrs · fSr _Series_⑨ ⌢ ecol _Series_⑨ +   po K rsp⸱ p dzn ⌐
 ⌢ acrl ⌣a l kl   dcm so la ppy nd
Sd rpls + cor, chp   n b · dfc lsc, oq_⸱
 ⌣ı brf kNs v hlp⸱⸜   efcv qr , · qr akm
p klc ⌢e of ıc kb   n sf⸱ pS vps v Nca-
frlr⸱ s   la ⌐ ⌢S sucf Pycs
   ⌣ loz la cdb kp— n

-3-   · fu mls ⌣ · rzynB
mo l drs v av⸜ r   dgre v ez⸱
nx asnm f NWrn
corp , l dv · qr
Ub uz— n lr ⌢r rSC,   -4-
p oq u dla so la ⌐   dfrN ⌐ da fr fl'
asrs ⌢a b grp— n   fSvl , dra_ nr⸱ ⌐

| u P ~ rsp l no u | u cN afd l M. cu |
| l lc avy v · bs opl | |

1

Dear Ms. Ramsey:

Each summer our community presents a festival for the arts. As part of the program, we[1] invite well-known people to visit our city and participate in the productions.

Performances are held[2] every Friday evening during the month of July on the front lawn of our courthouse. Our guests appear before a[3] group of approximately 500 people. The evening program includes our guest performer and is followed[4] by an informal reception.

We are cordially inviting your client, Mark Logan, to participate in[5] this year's event. He has established a long and successful history in the film industry and is well[6] recognized for his support of the performing arts.

As the official representative of Mr. Logan, would[7] you consider the enclosed dates and give us your response within 30 days?

Very truly yours, (157)

2

Dear Miss Miller:

Thank you for your inquiry about modern office procedures.

The most serious problem[1] managers face is the shortage of time. If decisions are made too quickly or without adequate consideration[2] of all the facts involved, misunderstandings may develop.

Time shortage is caused by a problem we refer[3] to as overload. Supervisors complain of being burdened with paperwork. They are unable to give the[4] proper amount of thought needed to make the best choices and still maintain an efficient flow of work.

Since[5] the volume of communications is increasing rather than decreasing, offices must use automatic means of[6] processing information. Electronic equipment offers a faster, more economical, and more[7] accurate way to control standard reports and correspondence.

I hope my brief comments have helped. Please contact me if[8] I can contribute further.

Sincerely, (167)

3

MEMO TO: Director of Advertising

Our next assignment for Northwestern Corporation is to develop[1] a questionnaire to be used in their market research.

Please organize your data so that the answers may be[2] grouped in convenient categories and processed with our usual computer program.

Always double-check the[3] content of your survey. Is each question necessary? Is it significant to the purpose of the study?[4] Does it distinguish between fact and opinion? Remember, also, that final success depends upon customer[5] response. Please design the document so that participation need not be a difficult task.

Organizing[6] an effective questionnaire is a great accomplishment in itself. Past experiences have indicated[7] that the most successful projects were those that could be completed in a few minutes with a reasonable[8] degree of ease. (163)

4

Dear Friend:

The date for our fitness festival is drawing near. The events planned for Saturday include a two-mile[1] jog and a cross-country run. The agenda for Sunday will be limited to our traditional bicycle[2] race.

The total number of entries received so far has already exceeded the figures from last year. Fortunately,[3] many people have already contacted our planning committee about helping. However, more volunteers[4] are needed to ensure that the events are managed well. We need help in registering participants,[5] judging, timing, and maintaining records. There will also be opportunities for helping in the general[6] administration of the event.

Will you be available to assist in this cause? If you can participate,[7] please telephone me at home any time after 5 p.m. or contact our secretary, Mary Nelson.[8]

Sincerely yours, (163)

5

Dear Business Graduate:

Are you eager to get ahead in the business world? Then you need a publication that[1] tells you exactly what is going on in businesses around the world every day of the week.

You need to know[2] the latest in news and developments, and you want that information as it happens—not after the event[3] has been changed, edited, and almost forgotten. Right?

That's why executives everywhere are subscribing to our[4] daily bulletin, *America Today.* On those pages they read about major issues facing management[5] at all levels.

Here's how you can form your own opinion. Add your signature to the enclosed form and receive[6] a sample subscription completely free of charge.

Don't just think it over—look it over. Your prompt response will[7] enable you to take advantage of a business opportunity you can't afford to miss.

Cordially yours,[8] (160)

LESSON 46

Brief Form Review

circumstance	_Sk_	contract	_kc_
experience	_ᵧp_	customer	_K_
advantage	_Avy_	suggest	_sug_
immediate	_⌒_	success	_suc_
difficult	_dfc_	specify	_sp_
property	_prp_	public	_pb_
against	_ag_	once	_oN_
sample	_sa_	buy	_b_

Abbreviation Review

representative	_rep_	advertise	_Av_
government	_gvl_	American	_A_
literature	_lil_	federal	_fed_
especially	_esp_	million	_M_
represent	_rep_	okay	_ok_

Commonly Misspelled Words		
	believe	_blv_
	among	_ag_

Reading and Writing Exercises

-1-

-2-

(Shorthand exercises with annotations: "Intro DC", "Intro DC", "Intro P", "Intro DC", "Paren")

-3-

-4-

-5-

Intro P

Paren

Intro DC

Intro DC

Intro DC

Sva e lrn— la	rzlls lc h₂ ⁹ ✓ eze
· lpcl a ∨ 3 lns	lse y Ks ku l lc
rsvs · avy rsp ∨	avy vr Svss. e ⌒ 4
23 cls + Pdss · sl	u ⌒ s⌒ suc. cu
6 ⌒ flo d₂ ⌣ sal	

1

Dear Henry:

I would like to suggest a change in your investment plan for the coming year.

New circumstances have[1] caused me to revise my views on purchasing public stock. There now seem to be several advantages for[2] people who buy shares in public utilities. Here are the reasons why.

The federal government has taken steps[3] to help power companies get more capital and is providing generous tax benefits for stockholders.[4] When you buy shares in large electric utilities, you can apply your dividends toward additional[5] purchases of stock at a sizable discount.

As additional encouragement to invest revenue, the[6] government allows you to deduct much of those dividends against your taxable income. If you hold your stocks for[7] a period of five years, your earnings are taxed at a rate considerably less than the standard percentage.[8]

Perhaps we should meet again to go over these new developments. Most days next week are okay with me.

Yours[9] truly, (181)

2

Dear Homeowner:

If you enjoy your home, you probably have no plans to move and have not bothered to find out its[1] current worth. However, do you realize that your house can be a valuable source of income even while you[2] live in it?

That's right. You don't have to sell your home in order to cash in on its value.

Once you have applied for[3] an equity loan, your property is appraised by our representative. We then subtract the unpaid balance[4] of your mortgage from its current market value. You can then borrow up to the full amount of your equity.[5]

Millions of Americans are taking advantage of this new source of credit. Some use the extra money for investments, for[6] special purchases, or even for monthly income.

A[7] simple telephone call will give you all the details you need. As your savings and loan company, we take pride in[8] presenting these opportunities.

Sincerely yours, (169)

3

Dear Mr. Morgan:

I must thank you again for your patience. I had promised to report to you in three weeks, but[1] your book proposal was very detailed and required more time than I had thought it would.

I would be glad to represent[2] your work and already have some publishers in mind. I found your manuscript to be interesting, well written,[3] and especially rich in original material. Based on the past sales of similar kinds of[4] literature, there is every reason to believe that this book will have good market appeal.

Although your sample[5] chapters were quite representative of your writing style, my usual procedure is to present the entire[6] manuscript in order to secure the best possible contract. Can you let me know when you expect to have the[7] material completed?

I look forward to hearing from you and serving as your agent.

Very truly yours,[8] (160)

4

MEMO TO: Pamela Webb

The printing agency just called to say there could be a delay in getting the[1] budget revisions to our office by the specified time.

Would you please handle this matter? It is essential that[2] we have this material for the Ways and Means Committee on Tuesday. We expect the final corrections to[3] be approved early that morning and introduced into the House of Representatives on the following day.[4]

The state budget must take priority over all other business in the legislature. Therefore, I am[5] authorizing you to make special arrangements to complete the job on time.

Although I will be in conference all[6] afternoon, I am leaving a message with my secretary to forward your call. If you experience[7] difficulty of any kind, please contact me immediately. (151)

5

Dear Customer:

Welcome to our family of advertisers. You made a wise choice when you decided to[1] advertise in the classified pages.

The want ads reach more consumers on a daily basis than any other[2] local means of communication. The classified section is among the most read parts of the newspaper. In[3] a recently conducted survey, we learned that the readership of these pages is second only to the front[4] page.

While the want ads have long been recognized as a low-cost and convenient means of advertising, many[5] people may not realize their effectiveness. In that same survey we learned that a typical ad of three lines[6] receives an average response of 23 calls and produces a sale by the following day.

With satisfying[7] results like these, it is easy to see why customers continue to take advantage of our services.[8] We wish you the same success.

Cordially yours, (168)

LESSON 47

Brief Form Review

characteristic	*crc*	hospital	*hsp*
significance	*sig*	response	*rsp*
convenience	*kv*	operate	*op*
acknowledge	*acj*	satisfy	*sal*
particular	*plc*	doctor	*dr*
accomplish	*ak*	they	*ly*
associate	*aso*	come	*k*
specific	*sp*	too	*l*

Abbreviation Review

incorporate	*inc*	record	*rec*
insurance	*ins*	avenue	*ave*
president	*P*	month	*~o*
thousand	*T*	Mrs.	*~rs*
et cetera	*elc*	Mr.	*~s*

Commonly Misspelled Words		
receipt	*rse*	
experiencing	*yp-*	

Reading and Writing Exercises

-1-

-2-

-4-

-5-

Intro DC

Intro P

Paren Paren

Paren Paren

Intro DC

Intro DC

(shorthand notes — not transcribable as text)

1

Dear Mrs. Parker:

This letter is to acknowledge your payment of January 8. We have credited your[1] account with the amount submitted, and we are enclosing a receipt for your records.

Thank you for writing to[2] explain why you have fallen behind in making your monthly installments. We greatly appreciate your taking[3] the time to let us know the reason for your delay.

We understand that you and your family are experiencing[4] a difficult situation and are doing your best to resolve the problem. Because of these particular[5] circumstances, the minimum payment you suggested will be satisfactory until the balance[6] has been paid in full.

Helping customers has always been a characteristic that we proudly associate[7] with our firm. Please come to us again when you are in need of special arrangements.

Very truly yours, (158)

2

Dear Mr. and Mrs. Henderson:

We are especially pleased to welcome you as a new policyholder.[1] Now that you've decided to trust your health benefits to us, we hope you will experience the security[2] and peace of mind that have come to thousands of other clients who enjoy the full protection of our insurance.[3]

The enclosed card entitles you to major medical coverage at any hospital in America.[4] The card contains your claim number, account number, and social security number. To file a claim for hospital[5] expenses or for doctors' fees, please be prepared to produce all three numbers.

The enclosed pamphlet provides general[6] information. I hope you will allow me to answer specific questions as they come up. If for some reason[7] you cannot reach me, my associates are ready and eager to help. They are qualified individuals[8] who take their responsibilities seriously.

Cordially yours, (174)

3

Dear Mr. Jackson:

When the Transportation Commission met last evening, several things came to my attention.[1]

Our airport property includes several buildings on Airline Avenue which are rented to individuals.[2] In order to satisfy federal requirements, we must introduce new terms effective this year. My advisers[3] say it will not be difficult to incorporate the new terms into the existing contracts.

Although it[4] has never been our objective to earn profits from this property, I am well aware of the rising costs[5] required to operate expensive equipment, to employ staff, to house aircraft, etc. Any extra[6] revenue will be used to cover other necessary administrative expenses.

Because this is a[7] matter of substantial significance to our city budget, I am appointing a subcommittee to[8] determine what the rent increases should be.

Yours very truly, (171)

4

Dear Dr. Richards:

I wish to congratulate you on your appointment to the rank of professor. Your associates[1] in the department tell me that this is a promotion which is well deserved and will prove to be an exciting[2] development for the university as well as for you.

I am very interested in the[3] particular research in which you are now involved. Do I understand correctly that you have completed a[4] new translation of early Eastern writings?

If this is the case, I would be grateful for the opportunity[5] to discuss your findings further. I, too, have long been interested in man's earliest writings.

After I heard[6] a detailed description of your findings, I thought we might be able to help each other. Could we arrange a time[7] to meet at your convenience?

Sincerely yours, (148)

| | 5 |

Dear Joy:

While attending a national conference last week, I received a nice compliment that I wish to pass[1] on to you.

One of our largest customers said wonderful things about the changes you have accomplished since[2] assuming your new responsibilities. He pointed out several areas that have undergone great[3] improvement in the few months since your transfer to the regional office. I, too, am impressed with your accomplishments.[4] While we have experienced a significant increase in sales, we have also seen a major reduction in[5] expenses.

In my early years with this company, a supervisor once told me that it was characteristic[6] of good management to reward outstanding effort. Therefore, it is appropriate to authorize a special[7] bonus payable to you.

We are grateful for your continued good work.

                              Cordially yours, (156)

LESSON 48

Brief Form Review

distribute	$\mathcal{D}$	every	$\mathcal{E}$
character	crc	again	aq
consider	ks	those	Loz
continue	ku	ever	$\mathcal{E}$
ordinary	ord	note	nl
situate	sil	from	f
deliver	dl	own	o
control	kl	was	3

Abbreviation Review

university	U	hundred	H
envelope	env	billion	B
company	co	regard	re
invoice	inv	cents	¢
return	rel	hour	hr

Commonly Misspelled Words	immediately	~l
	neighborhood	nbrh

Reading and Writing Exercises

-1-

-2-

Conj

-3-

Intro P

Intro DC

Intro DC

br da sp- so lau
cvry l ku ol
Npj. ul

-4-

dS O 2H yrs
ag sv uhpe slzns
d hSre b lro.
Sprz ple n bSn, f
ppl hu lv q le, l   *Intro P*
. sd d la S vb!,
prls sa Dagrem
h ldu lxs + n
gl' le, e Slnl
hp so, z Drs v fn
le, ev lrn- la s rl   *Intro P*
Ks cb v plc + N
sll f ne ls ln
dlcl flvr e ofr, v
crs, ord Pdc flo   *Paren*
aroN bSn, n r

brM. l edu n
ch lno C ab
lxs + repj, edu   *Intro DC*
no r le, r spsl
dr Pss ylds sC.
lN flvr la nobde
d E d p, Obrd=
n evn bc. bq
pllcl spls, ou nx
vzl lu nbrh r   *Intro P*
pv l usf. lc.
lp f bSn + lro
u old brN Obrd.
fu X $ u a
pa l dfnll b rl
. gr lS n le, cu

-5-

dM gra l rd
NS u nzppr artcl
asc f nmys f aul

Intro P

Intro P

Intro DC

1

Gentlemen:

This letter is to acknowledge your order of August 7.

In accordance with your request, we[1] are printing 600 copies of the letterhead and extra envelopes to accompany the stationery.[2] Those items will be printed at your regular contract rate and delivered to your office at no additional[3] charge.

Again, I wish to explain why your last shipment arrived late. As shown on your copy of the invoice, we[4] shipped everything on schedule. Unfortunately, all of the interstate highways were later closed due to[5] unanticipated bad weather. I apologize for any inconvenience you may have experienced,[6] but the situation was caused by circumstances beyond our control.

Our shipping supervisor is Edward Brown.[7] If you need personal service, contact him immediately. He has an extraordinary skill for solving[8] problems on a moment's notice.

Sincerely yours, (169)

2

Dear Mrs. Webster:

Thank you for your letter of inquiry regarding our apartments. Our planned community[1] offers many advantages to young families.

We are located next to a relatively new subdivision.[2] Our apartments are situated on a beautiful site surrounded by large trees. We are within walking[3] distance of a major shopping center, a health club, and a golf course. The schools in our neighborhood are among[4] the best in this city.

Transportation arrangements are easy to make. Buses leave every hour for downtown, and[5] the train station is only a few minutes away by automobile. Interstate highways make it convenient[6] to drive anywhere in the city.

Residents say that our apartments provide an extraordinarily[7] enjoyable experience. Will you allow us to prove them right? Model apartments are open every day. Please[8] telephone our office to arrange an appointment in advance.

Sincerely, (174)

3

Dear Mr. Fields:

I am sending this note as a reminder that your service contract is due to expire at the[1] end of this month.

Like many other fine investments, this contract becomes more valuable with age. Although your[2] appliance is still in excellent condition and should yield many more years of good service, the chances of it[3] needing repairs increase with every year that goes by. Even when you own the best of equipment, there is always the[4] possibility that one service call will cost as much as an entire year of protection under our agreement.[5]

Our plan protects you against that possibility. For your convenience we have prepared a new contract for[6] your signature. Please sign and return both copies by the date specified so that your coverage will continue[7] without interruption.

Yours truly, (146)

4

Dear Sir or Madam:

Over 200 years ago several unhappy citizens made history by throwing[1] a surprise party in Boston. For people who love good tea, what a sad day that must have been!

Experts say the[2] disagreement had to do with taxes and not with the quality of the tea. We certainly hope so. As[3] distributors of fine tea, we have learned that smart customers can be very particular and won't settle for[4] anything less than the delicate flavor we offer.

Of course, the ordinary product floating around Boston[5] was not our brand. While we do not claim to know much about taxes and representation, we do know our tea. Our[6] special drying process yields such an excellent flavor that nobody would ever dump it overboard—not[7] even to make a big political splash.

On your next visit to your neighborhood market, prove it to yourself.[8] Take a tip from Boston and throw your old brand overboard. The few extra cents you may pay will definitely be[9] worth a great taste in tea.

Cordially yours, (187)

5

Dear Miss Gray:

I read with interest your newspaper article asking for nominations for the annual[1] community service award. After considering all of the areas of service described, I wish to[2] recommend Michael Boyd for this award.

His credits are many. He once served on the faculty of a major[3] university and recently was a member of the committee responsible for revising and[4] updating our state laws. When an addition was suggested for the hospital, he was the first to organize[5] and distribute information for the fund drive.

During his residency in this city, he has made numerous[6] significant contributions. He continues to serve our community whenever the need develops.

There[7] is an old expression used to describe outstanding character. I would make a slight change to make my point about[8] Michael: In this town we consider him to be one in a billion.

Cordially yours, (176)

LESSON 49

Brief Form Review

importance	*pl*	usual	*uz*
correspond	*cos*	prove	*pv*
convenient	*kv*	order	*od*
committee	*k*	under	*U*
organize	*og*	ship	*A*
arrange	*ar*	port	*pl*
several	*sv*	came	*k*
charge	*Cj*	up	*p*

Abbreviation Review

superintendent	*S*	dollars	*$*
incorporated	*inc*	street	*S*
agriculture	*agr*	inch	*in*
economy	*eco*	yard	*yd*
percent	*%*	and	*+*

Commonly Misspelled Words	
annually	*aull*
achievement	*aCvm*

Reading and Writing Exercises

-1-

dS ⌐ njs lrjS fr
v kpurs⌒ elncs inc⌒
, Nds . ss la, ab
l Cnj ⌐ N, ev cra-
· S nu ptℬ kpur, ⌐
Nprz , kvl sl enf
l pls nsd · alsa cs⌒
yl s Xord n s
ℬls, s gcl bk · fwrl
f us n ejcyl clsr s⌒
bss, + Pfyl ofss, no
ol co ks cls l ⌐C
s gc + prl Svs · e
op rpr sNrs Q O
⌐ o + ⌐p apxl
30T ppl, f ur lg v
PCs · nu kpur, dM
M ls l · ⌐a b ⌐
kpur uvb ⌐a f. uvl

-2-

ds ⌐rln lqf ar
l dl ⌐ rt sm e
rgS b llfn, p nf
u dle Psn la s
lb hr lrsv ⌐ gs S
b v arvl, r bld
S l ⌐c Sln la s
, P S W here S
NrN dy ⌐ 24 = hr
pred u sp bgn,
12 nn o Mn, Nv 9,
e op U · Sd Psjr v
Cc eC crln, ls Pss
lcs ol · fu mls +
uzl elmas MUSN
la cd dv, f ne ths
r n n agrem ⌐s
cpe v od, · sp nly
lb ⌐d 5 inv, er

~S grf fu l'l hlp
n ls ~pl ~lr. su

-3-

d ~r ~dsn , ~ ↲
l kq u ɟ syc Czn
fu rsN Sde o Nnyl
afrs. u evluys ofr
lN gdlns f fCr
v agr n rly l ~o
eco, iz ncry- l
rd ab ⌐ nu ~lds
b̲ ~p- l ncrs ⌐
spli v fd n Udv-
pls v ~o. lil
rsNl pbls- b ls
U Sas la srlys cb
kl- sucfl uf e ~pv
~lds v Tply + Dy,
n u ks la sv Bs
v $ r spN aull ɟ

fed ad, ᵍ⁽Intro DC⁾ ⌐ cS v Dy
sNrs s ~s s~l
n kprsn. n lrns
v $ + ¢ ⁽Intro P⁾, / db · q
nv𝓁m l oq r aɟNes
u dS-, ul

-4-

d k mbs e rspcfl
s~l ⌐ alC- Pjc
Ppzl fu apvl, ⌐
Ppzl Ps · nlNv
aprC l clsr~
lrn. U ⌐ pln olln-
hr, ⁽Intro P⁾ sp SdNs lb
slc- ɟ bss v Pves
aCvm. ls pln
reps . ~yr Sp v
gs ~pl l r scl
sS~. ⌐ Pq dS-,
⌐ rzll v me ~os

[Shorthand outlines — Gregg shorthand]

Intro DC

Conj

-5-

Intro P

1

Dear Sir or Madam:

The nation's largest manufacturer of computers, Electronics Incorporated,[1] is introducing a system that is about to change the industry.

We have created a super new[2] portable computer. The ENTERPRISE is conveniently small enough to place inside an attaché case, yet[3] it is extraordinary in its abilities. It is quickly becoming a favorite for use in[4] educational classrooms, businesses, and professional offices.

No other company comes close to matching[5] our quick and expert service. We operate repair centers all over the world and employ approximately[6] 30,000 people.

If you are thinking of purchasing a new computer, don't miss this one. It may be the[7] computer you have been waiting for.

                              Yours very truly, (149)

2

Dear Ms. Martin:

Thank you for arranging to deliver the rush shipment we requested by telephone.

Please inform[1] your delivery person that someone will be here to receive the goods at the time of arrival. Our building[2] superintendent will make certain that someone is present at the West Hickory Street entrance during the[3] 24-hour period you specified beginning at 12 noon on Monday, November 9.

We operate[4] under a standard procedure of checking each carton. This process takes only a few minutes and usually[5] eliminates misunderstandings that could develop. If any items are not in agreement with our[6] copy of the order, a specific notation will be made on the invoice.

We are most grateful for your[7] willingness to help in this important matter.

                              Sincerely yours, (151)

3

Dear Mr. Madison:

I wish to congratulate you on the subject chosen for your recent study on[1] international affairs. Your evaluations offer excellent guidelines for the future of agriculture[2] in relation to world economy.

I was encouraged to read about the new methods being employed to[3] increase the supply of food in underdeveloped parts of the world. Literature recently published by this[4] university states that shortages can be controlled successfully if we improve methods of transportation[5] and distribution.

When you consider that several billions of dollars are spent annually for federal[6] aid, the cost of distribution centers seems small in comparison. In terms of dollars and cents, it would be[7] a good investment to organize the agencies you described.

Yours truly, (154)

4

Dear Committee Member:

We respectfully submit the attached project proposal for your approval.

The[1] proposal presents an intensive approach to classroom learning. Under the plan outlined here, specific students[2] will be selected on the basis of previous achievement. This plan represents a major step of great[3] importance to our school system. The program described is the result of many months of study and is based upon[4] recommendations by the superintendent of our school district.

Such a program will contribute much to the[5] excellence already in existence at this junior high school. We are grateful that this community continues[6] to demonstrate interest in maintaining our high quality of education, and we appeciate the[7] opportunity to submit this formal request.

Cordially yours, (152)

5

Dear Mrs. Evans:

I am pleased to inform you that the fabric chosen for your chair covering has been ordered[1] at the 20 percent discount we discussed and will be charged to your account. Your order is scheduled to arrive[2] the first week of April. Since the labor will require approximately two weeks, I think we can have the chairs[3] recovered and ready for delivery by May 1.

Our measurements indicate that we will need a total of[4] eight yards of the 60-inch material. According to my revised estimate, that will leave one additional[5] yard for the matching pillows.

A new shipment of materials which would be appropriate for your new drapes[6] came in yesterday. There are several colors and patterns that would correspond well with your overall design.[7] Could you stop by the store sometime this week to make a selection?

Sincerely yours, (154)

LESSON 50

Brief Form Review

congratulate	*kg*	refer	*rf*
satisfactory	*sal*	great	*gr*
significant	*sig*	firm	*fr*
important	*pl*	good	*g*
general	*jn*	more	*⌢*
respond	*rsp*	that	*la*
always	*a*	has	*hs*
direct	*dr*	go	*g*

Abbreviation Review

vice president	*VP*	ounce	*oz*
boulevard	*blvd*	pound	*lb*
enclosure	*enc*	quart	*ql*
dollar	*$*	square	*sq*
cent	*¢*	feet	*fl*

Commonly Misspelled Words		
privilege	*prvlg*	
assistance	*assn*	

Reading and Writing Exercises

-1-

-2-

[Shorthand exercises]

Intro DC

Intro P

sa ⟋ acCull
aprs l rSr nCrl
clr l old flbrcs,
l pv r py ₉ e nvr
u l kpr ql¹⟍ ⟋ enc-
cpns nlll u l · 50¢
Dk ou nx PCs ⌄
2 = lb bx + · 1$
Dk 6 4 = lb bx,
ln kpr prss, ⟋n
⟋ ks l cln por [Intro DC ₉]
r 2 = lb eco sz l
olll l ql ⌄ ld
lqd· yl ⟋ cSs 60¢
ls, ⟋ ⟋cs q sM
l b · ql¹ Pdc +
sv me ⟋ s ⟋
⟋⟍ · ul

-3-

d mbr ⌄ brd ⟋

hsb brl l ⟋
all la ⟋ P ⌄ brd
⌄ drrs lb ol ⌄
lon nx ⟋ c, bcz
ls ⟋ e l ⌄ · sig
⟋ pc o fCs acj [Intro DC ₉]
⟋ sug lae dla
⟋ ⟋ e ull ⟋ flo
Wd, z ⟋ evdN 6
enc- ayNa⟋r ⟋m [Intro DC ₉]
syc ⌄ Dcj lb ⟋
Ppz- PCs ⌄ prp o
⟋r a blvd, ⟋
l · cpe vr pln-
adj l ⟋ Sry bld
⟋C Ss o la prp·
yf ⟋ nu fsl¹, bll
acrd l lz spjsel [Intro DC ₉]
⌄ · lol ⌄ 25T sq
fl n ⟋rhos sps,
⟋ X⟋l ⟋pl lae

k l · dfnl dsy o
ls ~dr + kfr arms
du_ r nx ~e, ulc
fw lse_ u ln, ru

-4-

y lqf dmSra_ u
kfdN n r ~ntnN
Svss, S · prvly lvu
z · nu kc K, z Pfjls
n ls bo[Intro P,]e A Srv
f hu Sds, n O 40
yrs v bo[Intro P,]ev nvr
ls · K bcz v pr
Svs, e lq S fr lcl
La gu · akm, l rzn
fr suc, r frNl
rlyt e njy ~eC
clM, uf usd E fM
La ne jb, ls ln
sal[Intro DC,]i N u l

klc ~e PsnLL, ul
se la r suly, crc-
~l, z sr VP v
ls co~ic asr u la
er s~l enf l dl
Psnl Svs b ery
enf lgl r jb dn
lu saly, su

-5-

d brbra kgys! u
rmbr r d ~n u
mrl- n frS grd,
no ~ p- l lrn
laul rsv u dgre
fr cly n ls ln ·
~o, ~r dd r h
qx, u flr lls ~e
lau pln l bgn ·
crr n Psnl ~ym,
ndls lsa[Paren,]uv ~d

1

MEMO TO: Walter Carson

Soon our advertising department will announce our new product to the general[1] public. Because direct mail may offer greater advantages in promotion, we are considering a[2] recommendation that we distribute free samples in addition to sponsoring an extensive advertising[3] campaign.

Packages would be delivered to every home in major residential neighborhoods. Each package would[4] include an 8-ounce sample and a cover letter introducing the product. It would also include a coupon[5] offering 50¢ off the retail price of the 2-pound box and a $1 coupon for the 4-pound[6] size.

The distribution would be timed so that the samples would arrive on the fifth day following our initial[7] advertisement.

Would you please read and respond to the attached sample letter? (154)

2

Dear Resident:

Inside this package you will find a surprising enclosure. We are including a free sample[1] of an exciting new laundry soap.

Why is our product surprising? Because of a significant discovery,[2] we have developed a new process and created a new formula which resulted in extra cleaning[3] ability. Our soap offers more cleaning power than any other product on the market. Customers say[4] it actually appears to restore natural color to old fabrics.

To prove our point, we invite you to[5] compare quality. The enclosed coupons entitle you to a 50¢ discount on your next purchase of the[6] 2-pound box and a $1 discount on the 4-pound box.

Then compare prices. When it comes to cleaning power,[7] our 2-pound economy size will outlast one quart of the leading liquid. Yet it costs 60¢ less.

It makes[8] good sense to buy a quality product and save money at the same time.

Yours truly, (175)

3

Dear Member of the Board:

It has been brought to my attention that the president of the Board of Directors will[1] be out of town next week. Because this meeting will have a significant impact on future action, I am[2] suggesting that we delay the meeting until the following Wednesday.

As is evident on the enclosed agenda,[3] our main subject of discussion will be the proposed purchase of property on Waterway Boulevard. I am[4] including a copy of our planned addition to the storage building which exists on that property. If the[5] new facility is built according to these specifications, we will have a total of 25,000 square[6] feet in warehouse space.

It is extremely important that we come to a definite decision on this[7] matter and confirm arrangements during our next meeting.

I look forward to seeing you then.

Respectfully[8] yours, (161)

4

Gentlemen:

Thank you for demonstrating your confidence in our maintenance services. It is a privilege to[1] have you as a new contract customer.

As professionals in this business, we always strive for high standards.[2] In over 40 years of business, we have never lost a customer because of poor service. We think it is[3] fair to call that quite an accomplishment.

One reason for our success is the friendly relationship we enjoy[4] with each client. If you should ever find that any job is less than satisfactory, I want you to contact[5] me personally. I will see that the situation is corrected immediately.

As senior vice[6] president of this company, I can assure you that we are small enough to deliver personal service but[7] large enough to get the job done to your satisfaction.

Sincerely yours, (152)

5

Dear Barbara:

Congratulations! I remember the day when you enrolled in the first grade. Now I am pleased to learn[1] that you will receive your degree from college in less than a month. Where did the time go?

Your father tells me that you[2] plan to begin a career in personnel management. Needless to say, you have made a wise choice. There are many[3] fine opportunities available, and a person with your ability is certain to do well.

If I[4] can be of assistance in your job search, I hope you will let me know. I have always thought highly of you. You are[5] a fine example of a friend and a dedicated student. I would be most happy to serve as a reference[6] for you.

You will always have my best wishes for every success.

Cordially yours, (135)

PREPARING TO GIVE DICTATION

Administrative assistants and secretaries may frequently have occasion to dictate material to others. Whether a person dictates "live" to another individual or to a machine for transcription at a later time, proper dictation techniques can enhance the quality of the transcription.

In planning for dictation, the material to be transcribed immediately should be designated top priority. Material that could be transcribed at any time within the next few days should be designated low priority.

Prior to responding to correspondence, organize your thoughts by underlining and making marginal notations on the original correspondence regarding the most important points of each letter or memorandum being answered. Also, attach other material to the correspondence being answered when such attachments would help in preparing the response.

Immediately before the actual dictation of each piece of correspondence begins, indicate any special instructions. If there is a special letter style to be used or if more than one file copy is needed, make such notations at this time.

When dictation begins, speak distinctly in a relaxed, natural manner. Give instructions for special capitalization and punctuation such as hyphens, dashes, colons, apostrophes, and paragraph endings. Material to be typed in all capitals or material to be underscored should be designated. Difficult words and "sound-alike" words should be spelled in order to avoid confusion. Unusual spellings should also be dictated; i.e., the name Smythe might be spelled—s-m-y as in yesterday-t-h-e.

At the completion of the dictation, indicate any special mailing instructions; and if other individuals are to receive a copy of the correspondence, give their names and addresses.

Effective dictation and transcription skills are indeed complementary abilities. The ability to dictate competently and transcribe accurately can do much to increase the productivity of any office.

DEVELOPING AND MEASURING SPEEDWRITING READING SKILLS

The ability to read *Speedwriting* notes rapidly will help you to record and transcribe those notes more efficiently. To develop your reading ability most effectively, set a reading-rate goal. As a general rule, you should be able to read from *Speedwriting* notes at approximately twice your dictation-recording goal. That is, if you are striving to write in *Speedwriting* at a minimum of 80 words per minute, the reading-rate goal (from material you have practiced) should be at least 160 words per minute. The reading-rate chart on the following pages has been designed to assist you in measuring your ability to read from any letter or memorandum in the text.

Reading rates in words per minute are indicated horizontally across the top of the chart. The number of words in a letter is indicated vertically down the left side of the chart. The body of the table gives the amount of time required to read a certain length of letter at a given rate. For example, a 130-word letter would need to be read in 49 seconds to achieve a reading rate of 160 words per minute.

The reading-rate chart can be used in two ways:
1. You can determine the number of minutes and seconds needed to reach a specified reading-rate goal.
2. You can read a letter, determine the amount of time elapsed, and then determine the rate at which you read the letter.

When you are reading for practice and hesitate over a word, follow these three steps:
1. Immediately sound-spell the word.
2. If sound-spelling does not reveal the word, read a few words ahead to see if the word can be determined by context. (This skill will prove extremely valuable in transcription.)
3. Consult the printed key to determine the correct word.

READING-RATE CHART

Words in Letter	Reading Rate (words per minute)												
	80	90	100	110	120	130	140	150	160	170	180	190	200
82	1:01	0:55	0:49	0:45	0:41	0:38	0:35	0:33	0:31	0:29	0:28	0:26	0:25
84	1:03	0:56	0:50	0:46	0:42	0:39	0:36	0:34	0:31	0:29	0:28	0:27	0:25
86	1:04	0:57	0:52	0:47	0:43	0:40	0:37	0:34	0:32	0:31	0:29	0:27	0:26
88	1:06	0:59	0:53	0:48	0:44	0:41	0:38	0:35	0:33	0:31	0:29	0:28	0:26
90	1:08	1:00	0:54	0:49	0:45	0:42	0:39	0:36	0:34	0:32	0:30	0:28	0:27
92	1:09	1:01	0:55	0:50	0:46	0:42	0:39	0:37	0:34	0:32	0:31	0:29	0:28
94	1:10	1:03	0:56	0:51	0:47	0:43	0:40	0:38	0:35	0:33	0:31	0:30	0:28
96	1:12	1:04	0:58	0:52	0:48	0:44	0:41	0:38	0:36	0:34	0:32	0:30	0:29
98	1:13	1:05	0:59	0:53	0:49	0:45	0:42	0:39	0:37	0:35	0:32	0:31	0:29
100	1:15	1:07	1:00	0:55	0:50	0:46	0:43	0:40	0:38	0:35	0:34	0:32	0:30
102	1:16	1:08	1:01	0:56	0:51	0:47	0:44	0:41	0:38	0:36	0:34	0:32	0:31
104	1:18	1:09	1:02	0:57	0:52	0:48	0:45	0:42	0:39	0:37	0:35	0:33	0:31
106	1:19	1:11	1:04	0:58	0:53	0:49	0:45	0:42	0:40	0:37	0:35	0:33	0:32
108	1:21	1:12	1:05	0:59	0:54	0:50	0:46	0:43	0:40	0:38	0:36	0:34	0:32
110	1:23	1:13	1:06	1:00	0:55	0:51	0:47	0:44	0:41	0:39	0:37	0:35	0:33
112	1:24	1:15	1:07	1:01	0:56	0:52	0:48	0:45	0:42	0:40	0:37	0:35	0:34
114	1:25	1:16	1:08	1:02	0:57	0:53	0:49	0:46	0:43	0:40	0:38	0:36	0:34
116	1:27	1:17	1:10	1:03	0:58	0:54	0:50	0:46	0:43	0:41	0:38	0:37	0:35
118	1:28	1:19	1:11	1:04	0:59	0:54	0:51	0:47	0:44	0:41	0:40	0:37	0:35
120	1:30	1:20	1:12	1:05	1:00	0:55	0:51	0:48	0:45	0:43	0:40	0:38	0:36
122	1:31	1:21	1:13	1:07	1:01	0:56	0:52	0:49	0:46	0:43	0:41	0:39	0:37
124	1:33	1:23	1:14	1:08	1:02	0:57	0:53	0:50	0:46	0:44	0:41	0:39	0:37
126	1:34	1:24	1:16	1:09	1:03	0:58	0:54	0:50	0:47	0:44	0:42	0:40	0:38
128	1:36	1:25	1:17	1:10	1:04	0:59	0:55	0:51	0:48	0:45	0:43	0:40	0:38
130	1:38	1:27	1:18	1:11	1:05	1:00	0:56	0:52	0:49	0:46	0:43	0:41	0:39
132	1:39	1:28	1:19	1:12	1:06	1:01	0:57	0:53	0:49	0:47	0:44	0:42	0:40
134	1:40	1:29	1:20	1:13	1:07	1:02	0:57	0:54	0:50	0:47	0:44	0:42	0:40
136	1:42	1:31	1:22	1:14	1:08	1:03	0:58	0:54	0:51	0:48	0:46	0:43	0:41
138	1:43	1:32	1:23	1:15	1:09	1:04	0:59	0:55	0:52	0:49	0:46	0:44	0:41
140	1:45	1:33	1:24	1:16	1:10	1:05	1:00	0:56	0:53	0:49	0:47	0:44	0:42

(Chart is continued on the next page.)

Words in Letter	Reading Rate (words per minute)												
	80	90	100	110	120	130	140	150	160	170	180	190	200
142	1:47	1:35	1:25	1:17	1:11	1:06	1:01	0:57	0:53	0:50	0:47	0:45	0:43
144	1:48	1:36	1:26	1:19	1:12	1:06	1:02	0:58	0:54	0:51	0:48	0:45	0:43
146	1:50	1:37	1:28	1:20	1:13	1:07	1:03	0:58	0:55	0:52	0:49	0:46	0:44
148	1:51	1:39	1:29	1:21	1:14	1:08	1:03	0:59	0:56	0:52	0:49	0:47	0:44
150	1:53	1:40	1:30	1:22	1:15	1:09	1:04	1:00	0:56	0:53	0:50	0:47	0:45
152	1:54	1:41	1:31	1:23	1:16	1:10	1:05	1:01	0:57	0:54	0:51	0:48	0:46
154	1:56	1:43	1:32	1:24	1:17	1:11	1:06	1:02	0:58	0:54	0:51	0:49	0:46
156	1:57	1:44	1:34	1:25	1:18	1:12	1:07	1:02	0:59	0:55	0:52	0:49	0:47
158	1:59	1:45	1:35	1:26	1:19	1:13	1:08	1:03	0:59	0:56	0:53	0:50	0:47
160	2:00	1:47	1:36	1:27	1:20	1:14	1:09	1:04	1:00	0:56	0:53	0:51	0:48
162	2:02	1:48	1:37	1:28	1:21	1:15	1:09	1:05	1:01	0:57	0:54	0:51	0:49
164	2:03	1:49	1:38	1:29	1:22	1:16	1:10	1:06	1:02	0:58	0:55	0:52	0:49
166	2:05	1:51	1:40	1:31	1:23	1:17	1:11	1:06	1:02	0:59	0:55	0:52	0:50
168	2:06	1:52	1:41	1:32	1:24	1:18	1:12	1:07	1:03	0:59	0:56	0:53	0:50
170	2:08	1:53	1:42	1:33	1:25	1:18	1:13	1:08	1:04	1:00	0:57	0:54	0:51
172	2:09	1:55	1:43	1:34	1:26	1:19	1:14	1:09	1:05	1:01	0:57	0:54	0:52
174	2:11	1:56	1:44	1:35	1:27	1:20	1:15	1:10	1:05	1:01	0:58	0:55	0:52
176	2:12	1:57	1:46	1:36	1:28	1:21	1:15	1:10	1:06	1:02	0:59	0:56	0:53
178	2:14	1:59	1:47	1:37	1:29	1:22	1:16	1:11	1:07	1:03	0:59	0:56	0:54
180	2:15	2:00	1:48	1:38	1:30	1:23	1:17	1:12	1:08	1:04	1:00	0:57	0:54
182	2:17	2:01	1:49	1:39	1:31	1:24	1:18	1:13	1:08	1:04	1:01	0:57	0:55
184	2:18	2:03	1:50	1:40	1:32	1:25	1:19	1:14	1:09	1:05	1:01	0:58	0:55
186	2:20	2:04	1:52	1:41	1:33	1:26	1:20	1:14	1:10	1:06	1:02	0:59	0:56
188	2:21	2:05	1:53	1:43	1:34	1:27	1:21	1:15	1:11	1:06	1:03	0:59	0:56
190	2:23	2:07	1:54	1:44	1:35	1:28	1:21	1:16	1:11	1:07	1:03	1:00	0:57
192	2:24	2:08	1:55	1:45	1:36	1:29	1:22	1:17	1:12	1:08	1:04	1:01	0:58
194	2:26	2:09	1:56	1:46	1:37	1:30	1:23	1:18	1:13	1:08	1:05	1:01	0:58
196	2:27	2:11	1:58	1:47	1:38	1:30	1:24	1:18	1:14	1:09	1:05	1:02	0:59
198	2:29	2:12	1:59	1:48	1:39	1:31	1:25	1:19	1:14	1:10	1:06	1:03	0:59
200	2:30	2:13	2:00	1:49	1:40	1:32	1:26	1:20	1:15	1:11	1:07	1:03	1:00

(Chart is continued on the next page.)

Words in Letter	Reading Rate (words per minute)												
	210	220	230	240	250	260	270	280	290	300	310	320	330
82	0:23	0:22	0:21	0:21	0:20	0:19	0:18	0:18	0:17	0:16	0:16	0:15	0:15
84	0:24	0:23	0:22	0:21	0:20	0:19	0:19	0:18	0:17	0:17	0:16	0:16	0:15
86	0:25	0:23	0:22	0:22	0:21	0:20	0:19	0:18	0:18	0:17	0:17	0:16	0:16
88	0:26	0:24	0:23	0:22	0:21	0:20	0:20	0:19	0:18	0:18	0:17	0:17	0:16
90	0:26	0:25	0:23	0:23	0:22	0:21	0:20	0:19	0:19	0:18	0:17	0:17	0:16
92	0:27	0:25	0:24	0:23	0:22	0:21	0:20	0:20	0:19	0:18	0:18	0:17	0:17
94	0:27	0:26	0:25	0:24	0:23	0:22	0:21	0:20	0:19	0:19	0:18	0:18	0:17
96	0:28	0:26	0:25	0:24	0:23	0:22	0:21	0:21	0:20	0:19	0:19	0:18	0:17
98	0:29	0:27	0:26	0:25	0:24	0:23	0:22	0:21	0:20	0:20	0:19	0:18	0:18
100	0:29	0:27	0:26	0:25	0:24	0:23	0:22	0:21	0:21	0:20	0:19	0:19	0:18
102	0:29	0:28	0:27	0:26	0:24	0:24	0:23	0:22	0:21	0:20	0:20	0:19	0:19
104	0:30	0:28	0:27	0:26	0:25	0:24	0:23	0:22	0:22	0:21	0:20	0:20	0:19
106	0:30	0:29	0:28	0:27	0:25	0:24	0:24	0:23	0:22	0:21	0:21	0:20	0:19
108	0:31	0:29	0:28	0:27	0:26	0:25	0:24	0:23	0:22	0:22	0:21	0:20	0:20
110	0:31	0:30	0:29	0:28	0:26	0:25	0:24	0:24	0:23	0:22	0:21	0:21	0:20
112	0:32	0:31	0:29	0:28	0:27	0:26	0:25	0:24	0:23	0:22	0:22	0:21	0:20
114	0:33	0:31	0:30	0:29	0:27	0:26	0:25	0:24	0:24	0:23	0:22	0:21	0:21
116	0:33	0:32	0:30	0:29	0:28	0:27	0:26	0:25	0:24	0:23	0:22	0:22	0:21
118	0:34	0:32	0:31	0:30	0:28	0:27	0:26	0:25	0:24	0:24	0:23	0:22	0:21
120	0:34	0:33	0:31	0:30	0:29	0:28	0:27	0:26	0:25	0:24	0:23	0:23	0:22
122	0:35	0:33	0:32	0:31	0:29	0:28	0:27	0:26	0:25	0:24	0:24	0:23	0:22
124	0:35	0:34	0:32	0:31	0:30	0:29	0:28	0:27	0:26	0:25	0:24	0:23	0:23
126	0:36	0:34	0:33	0:32	0:30	0:29	0:28	0:27	0:26	0:25	0:24	0:24	0:23
128	0:37	0:35	0:33	0:32	0:31	0:30	0:28	0:27	0:26	0:26	0:25	0:24	0:23
130	0:37	0:35	0:34	0:33	0:31	0:30	0:29	0:28	0:27	0:26	0:25	0:24	0:24
132	0:38	0:36	0:34	0:33	0:32	0:30	0:29	0:28	0:27	0:26	0:26	0:25	0:24
134	0:38	0:37	0:35	0:34	0:32	0:31	0:30	0:29	0:28	0:27	0:26	0:25	0:24
136	0:39	0:37	0:35	0:34	0:33	0:31	0:30	0:29	0:28	0:27	0:26	0:26	0:25
138	0:39	0:38	0:36	0:35	0:33	0:32	0:31	0:30	0:29	0:28	0:27	0:26	0:25
140	0:40	0:38	0:37	0:35	0:34	0:32	0:31	0:30	0:29	0:28	0:27	0:26	0:25

(Chart is continued on the next page.)

Words in Letter	Reading Rate (words per minute)												
	210	220	230	240	250	260	270	280	290	300	310	320	330
142	0:41	0:39	0:37	0:36	0:34	0:33	0:32	0:30	0:29	0:28	0:27	0:27	0:26
144	0:41	0:39	0:38	0:36	0:35	0:33	0:32	0:31	0:30	0:29	0:28	0:27	0:26
146	0:42	0:40	0:38	0:37	0:35	0:34	0:32	0:31	0:30	0:29	0:28	0:27	0:27
148	0:42	0:40	0:39	0:37	0:36	0:34	0:33	0:32	0:31	0:30	0:29	0:28	0:27
150	0:43	0:41	0:39	0:38	0:36	0:35	0:33	0:32	0:31	0:30	0:29	0:28	0:27
152	0:43	0:41	0:40	0:38	0:36	0:35	0:34	0:33	0:31	0:30	0:29	0:29	0:28
154	0:44	0:42	0:40	0:39	0:37	0:36	0:34	0:33	0:32	0:31	0:30	0:29	0:28
156	0:45	0:43	0:41	0:39	0:37	0:36	0:35	0:33	0:32	0:31	0:30	0:29	0:28
158	0:45	0:43	0:41	0:40	0:38	0:36	0:35	0:34	0:33	0:32	0:31	0:30	0:29
160	0:46	0:44	0:42	0:40	0:38	0:37	0:36	0:34	0:33	0:32	0:31	0:30	0:29
162	0:46	0:44	0:42	0:41	0:39	0:37	0:36	0:35	0:34	0:32	0:31	0:30	0:29
164	0:47	0:45	0:43	0:41	0:39	0:38	0:36	0:35	0:34	0:33	0:32	0:31	0:30
166	0:47	0:45	0:43	0:42	0:40	0:38	0:37	0:35	0:34	0:33	0:32	0:31	0:30
168	0:48	0:46	0:44	0:42	0:40	0:39	0:37	0:36	0:35	0:34	0:33	0:32	0:31
170	0:49	0:46	0:44	0:43	0:41	0:39	0:38	0:36	0:35	0:34	0:33	0:32	0:31
172	0:49	0:47	0:45	0:43	0:41	0:40	0:38	0:37	0:36	0:34	0:33	0:32	0:31
174	0:50	0:47	0:45	0:44	0:42	0:41	0:39	0:37	0:36	0:35	0:34	0:33	0:32
176	0:50	0:48	0:46	0:44	0:42	0:41	0:39	0:38	0:36	0:35	0:34	0:33	0:32
178	0:51	0:49	0:46	0:45	0:43	0:41	0:40	0:38	0:37	0:36	0:34	0:33	0:32
180	0:51	0:49	0:47	0:45	0:43	0:42	0:40	0:39	0:37	0:36	0:35	0:34	0:33
182	0:52	0:50	0:47	0:46	0:44	0:42	0:40	0:39	0:38	0:36	0:35	0:34	0:33
184	0:53	0:50	0:48	0:46	0:44	0:42	0:41	0:39	0:38	0:37	0:36	0:35	0:33
186	0:53	0:51	0:49	0:47	0:45	0:43	0:41	0:40	0:38	0:37	0:36	0:35	0:34
188	0:54	0:51	0:49	0:47	0:45	0:43	0:42	0:40	0:39	0:38	0:36	0:35	0:34
190	0:54	0:52	0:50	0:48	0:46	0:44	0:42	0:41	0:39	0:38	0:37	0:36	0:35
192	0:55	0:52	0:50	0:48	0:46	0:44	0:43	0:41	0:40	0:38	0:37	0:36	0:35
194	0:55	0:53	0:51	0:49	0:47	0:45	0:43	0:42	0:40	0:39	0:38	0:36	0:35
196	0:56	0:53	0:51	0:49	0:47	0:45	0:44	0:42	0:41	0:39	0:38	0:37	0:36
198	0:57	0:54	0:52	0:50	0:48	0:46	0:44	0:42	0:41	0:40	0:38	0:37	0:36
200	0:57	0:55	0:52	0:50	0:48	0:46	0:44	0:43	0:41	0:40	0:39	0:38	0:36

BRIEF FORMS BY ORDER OF PRESENTATION

The numeral in the upper left corner of a box indicates the lesson in which the brief forms were introduced. To use the table as a reference for brief forms in the order of their presentation, read from left to right across each numbered row.

	A	B	C	D	E	F	G	H
1	[1]	/	)	*m*	(	*l*	*e*	*l*
2	[2]	*c*	♭	v	∧	[4]	↗	∠
3	⌐	∼	o	*pl*	*Ph*	*d*	*u*	[6] *ac*
4	*af*	*apo*	*b*	*dl*	*du*	*nes*	*y*	[9] *ar*
5	3	*jn*	*gr*	*hsp*	*la*	⌣	[11] *bln*	*op*
6	*pp*	*py*	*prp*	*rf*	*rsp*	*A*	*sil*	*suq*
7	*loz*	[13] ⌢	*G*	*dr*	*q*	*h*	*ly*	[16] *ap*
8	*cor*	*D*	*p*	*P*	*sp*	[18] *ab*	*K*	*hs*
9	*I*	*od*	*O*	*U*	[20] *Avn*	*aq*	*bs*	*sv*
10	[22] *crc*	*E*	*n*	*ol*	*sal*	[24] *ak*	*k*	*kp*
11	*ku*	*kb*	*kv*	*dl*	*opl*	[26] *bo*	⌐*pl*	*Nv*
12	*pb*	[27] *a*	*ks*	*nl*	*ord*	*pv*	[30] *as*	*apx*
13	*yp*	⌢	*nx*	[32] *B*	*kc*	*dfc*	⌐*p*	*opn*
14	[34] *acy*	*aso*	*kq*	*dv*	*oq*	*Sd*	*suc*	[37] *f*
15	*siq*	*uz*	*o*	[39] *am*	*Sk*	*kl*	*oN*	*plc*
16	*sa*							

ABBREVIATIONS BY ORDER OF PRESENTATION

The numeral in the upper left corner of a box indicates the lesson in which the abbreviations were introduced. To use the table as a reference for abbreviations in the order of their presentation, read from left to right across each numbered row.

	A	B	C	D	E	F	G	H
1	[2] ⊦	cal	co	inf	p	rel	VP	[4] m
2	⌢r	⌢rs	⌢s	[6] corp	E	enc	N	S
3	W	[9] a⌢l	all	cr	no	%	tot	[11] dpt
4	env	ins	inv	re	[13] p	sec	sr	[16] ave
5	blvd	d	ex	hr	⌢o	rec	[18] B	¢
6	$	H	in	M	og	lb	T	[20] agr
7	eco	ft	sq	yd	[22] esp	etc	⌢dse	qt
8	g	U	[24] fed	gvt	inc	ok	rep	s
9	[27] av	X⌢s	[34] a⌢	lit	vol	[39] est	S	

PHRASES
BY ORDER OF PRESENTATION

The numeral in the upper left corner of a box indicates the lesson in which the phrases were introduced. To use the table as a reference for phrases in the order of their presentation, read from left to right across each numbered row.

	A	B	C	D	E	F	G	H
1	[13] ⌒	ʋc	ᴄh	ʋʋ	ʋl	ʋlʋ	eɔ	ec
2	eʋ	ehp	ed	edʋ	uɔ	uc	uʋ	uno
3	ul	ud	Uʋ	ʟq	Lʋ	Lʋu	Lʋu	Lno
4	Lpa	Lqf	Lqf	Lqfℒ	[15] ʋcd	ᴄhp	Lse	ʄ
5	✓	Lau	Lau	eʋ	dʋ	◠	[16] ʋd	ʋdap
6	ʋdʋ	eɲd	el	edap	ucʋ	udlc	↴	ʃ
7	Lae	[17] ʋblʋ	udu	uɲd	Lcp	cdʋ	ʄu	ʄu
8	ɲ	ʋu	ʋu	lu	lu	[18] edu	eʄl	und
9	Lʋc	ʋʋ	ʋɔ	lu	lu	[19] eap	eh	e
10	u	luʒ	ʋh	♂	[20] ʋno	eɔn	elʋ	ulʋ
11	Lgl	Lhɔ	LsN	cʋ	[22] ʋʋb	ʋɲd	⁴ʒ	eblʋ
12	eno	ʒlʒ	[23] ʋdlc	eɔp-	ucn	ucd	Lɔʋ	Lsa
13	[24] ʄl	udʋ	ʒʒ	ʒe	[25] ʋlc	ecd	eʋʋ	edlc
14	ʋdu	Lgʋ	Lʋʒl	[26] Lk	Lofɔ	Ldl	[29] ulfN	Lcl
15	ʒu	ʒu	ou	ou	[31] ʒe	hsʋ	ɲdʋ	Lqu
16	dlc	[33] nʋɔls	nnls	⌒⌒	pda	[36] Lauɔ	Laul	[37] ʋap
17	Lo	Laɪ	appendix ʋcʋ	ʋcn	ʋdu	ʋh	ʋɲl	ecʋ
18	ecn	eʋh	eɲl	uh	uʋʋ	uʋh	ʒl	ʄcla
19	ʋn	ʋu	ʋu					

KEY TO BRIEF FORMS

	A	B	C	D	E	F	G	H
1	[1] a an	it at	is his	in not	the	to too	we	will well
2	[2] are our	can	for full	of have very	us	[4] firm	from	letter
3	manage	market	on own	part port	perhaps	would	your	[6] accept
4	after	appropriate	be, but, been buy, by	determine	during	necessary	why	[9] arrange
5	as was	general	great grate	hospital	that	were with	[11] between	operate
6	participate	point	property	refer	respond response	ship	situate	suggest
7	those	[13] am more	charge	doctor direct	go good	he had him	they	[16] appreciate
8	correspond correspon- dence	distribute	please up	present	specific specify	[18] about	customer	has
9	include	order	over	under	[20] advantage	again against	business	several
10	[22] character characteristic	ever every	industry	other	satisfy satisfactory	[24] accomplish	come came committee	complete
11	continue	contribute	convenient convenience	deliver	opportunity	[26] both	important importance	individual
12	public	[27] always	consider	note	ordinary	prove	[30] already	approximate
13	experience	immediate	next	[32] able	contract	difficult	employ	opinion
14	[34] acknowledge	associate	congratulate	develop	organize	standard	success	[37] manufacture
15	signature significant significance	usual	work world	[39] administrate	circumstance	control	once	particular
16	sample							

KEY TO ABBREVIATIONS

	A	B	C	D	E	F	G	H
1	[2] and	catalog	company	information	president	return	vice president	[4] Miss
2	Mr.	Mrs.	Ms.	[6] corporation	east	enclose enclosure	north	south
3	west	[9] amount	attention	credit	number	percent	total	[11] department
4	envelope	insurance	invoice	regard	[13] junior	second secretary	senior	[16] avenue
5	boulevard	day	example executive	hour	month	record	[18] billion	cent cents
6	dollar dollars	hundred	inch	million	ounce	pound	thousand	[20] agriculture
7	economic economy	feet	square	yard	[22] especially	et cetera	merchandise	quart
8	question	university	[24] federal	government	incorporate incorporated	okay	represent representative	street
9	[27] advertise	Christmas	[34]America American	literature	volume	[39] establish	superintendent	

KEY TO PHRASES

	A	B	C	D	E	F	G	H
1	[13] I am	I can	I had	I have	I will	I will be	we are	we can
2	we have	we hope	we would	we would be	you are	you can	you have	you know
3	you will	you would	to be	to go	to have	to have you	to have your	to know
4	to pay	thank you for	thank you for your	thank you for your letter	[15] I could	I hope	to see	for the
5	of the	that you	that your	will be	would be	it is	[16] I would	I would appreciate
6	I would be	we should	we will	we would appreciate	you can be	you would like	and the	at the
7	that we	[17] I believe	you do	you should	to keep	could be	for you	for your
8	in the	of you	of your	will you	will your	[18] we do	we feel	you need
9	to make	have been	of our	to you	to your	[19] we appreciate	we had	we were
10	you were	to use	have had	on the	[20] I know	we are not	we will be	you will be
11	to get	to hear	to send	can be	[22] I have been	I should	I was	we believe
12	we know	as well as	[23] I would like	we are pleased	you cannot	you could	to receive	to say
13	[24] I feel	you would be	as soon as	as we	[25] I look	we could	we have been	we would like
14	to do	to give	to visit	[26] to come	to offer	to determine	[29] you will find	to call
15	as you	as your	on you	on your	[31] as I	has been	should be	thank you
16	would like	[33] nevertheless	nonetheless	time to time	up to date	[36] that you are	that you will	[37] I appreciate
17	to work	that I	appendix I can be	I cannot	I do	I have had	I shall	we can be
18	we cannot	we have had	we shall	you had	you have been	you have had	as to	fact that
19	have not	have you	have your					

BRIEF FORMS BY ALPHABETICAL ORDER

To use the table as a reference for brief forms in alphabetical order, read from left to right across each numbered row.

	A	B	C	D	E	F	G	H
1	·	ß	ab	ac	ak	acy	am	avy
2	af	aq	ar	a	⌒	ap	apo	apx
3	r	ar	3	aso	b	bln	bo	bo
4	c	crc	G	Sk	k	kp	kq	ks
5	ku	kc	kb	kl	kv	cor	K	dl
6	dl	dv	dfc	D	dr	du	↗	ε
7	yp	fr	b	f	fn	q	gr	hs
8	h	hsp	⌢	pl	n	L	nv	n
9	,	/	L	⌐	f	r	nes	nx
10	nl	v	o	m	op	opn	opl	od
11	ord	oq	ol	O	pl	pp	plc	ph
12	p	py	p	prp	pv	pb	rf	rsp
13	sa	sal	sv	A	suq	sil	sp	sd
14	suc	suq	la	⌐	ly	loz	l	U
15	s	uz	e	⌣	y	l	o	d
16	u							

ABBREVIATIONS
BY ALPHABETICAL ORDER

To use the table as a reference for abbreviations in alphabetical order, read from left to right across each numbered row.

	A	B	C	D	E	F	G	H
1	av	agr	a	and	+	all	ave	B
2	blvd	cal	¢	Xs	co	corp	cr	d
3	dpt	$	E	eco	enc	env	esp	est
4	etc	ex	fed	ft	gvt	hr	H	in
5	inc	inf	ins	inv	jr	lit	mdse	M
6	m	o	r	rs	s	N	No	ok
7	oz	%	lb	p	qt	q	rec	re
8	rep	rel	sec	sr	S	sq	s	S
9	T	tot	U	VP	vol	W	yd	

PHRASES BY ORDER OF CATEGORY

To use the table as a reference for phrases in alphabetical segments, read from left to right across each numbered row.

	A	B	C	D	E	F	G	H
1	⌣	ιap	ιblv	ιc	ιcb	ιcn	ιcd	ιdu
2	ιfl	ιh	ιv	ιvb	ιvh	ιhp	ιno	ιlc
3	ιsl	ιsd	ιʒ	ιl	ιlb	ιd	ιdap	ιdb
4	ιdlc	eap	er	ern	erp-	eblv	ec	ecb
5	ecn	ecd	edu	efl	eh	ev	evb	evh
6	ehp	eno	esl	esd	⌣	el	elb	ed
7	edap	edb	edlc	ur	uc	ucn	ucb	ucd
8	udu	uh	uv	uvb	uvh	uno	und	usd
9	u	ul	ulb	ulfη	ud	udb	udlc	lb
10	lcl	lk	ldl	ldu	lgl	lgv	lg	lv
11	lvu	lvu	lhr	lcp	lno	lvc	lofr	lpa
12	lrsv	lsa	lse	lsη	luʒ	lvʒl	lo	ᴌ
13	ʒι	ʒl	ʒe	ʒlʒ	ʒu	ʒu	ʃ	cb
14	cdb	fcla	f	fu	fu	hsb	vb	vh
15	vn	vu	vu	η	⌒	vr	√	vu
16	vu	ƌ	ou	ou	sdb	lgu	lai	lae
17	lau	laur	laul	lau	lu	lu	lb	lu
18	lu	db	dlc	ʒʒ	nvrls	nnls	lgf	lgf
19	lgfℒ	⌐⌐	pda					

KEY TO
BRIEF FORMS

	A	B	C	D	E	F	G	H
1	a an	able	about	accept	accomplish	acknowledge	administrate	advantage
2	after	again against	already	always	am more	appreciate	appropriate	approximate
3	are our	arrange	as was	associate	be, but been buy, by	between	both	business
4	can	character characteristic	charge	circumstance	come came committee	complete	congratulate	consider
5	continue	contract	contribute	control	convenient convenience	correspond correspon- dence	customer	deliver
6	determine	develop	difficult	distribute	doctor direct	during	employ	ever every
7	experience	firm	for full	from	general	go good	great grate	has
8	he had him	hospital	immediate	important importance	in not	include	individual	industry
9	is his	it at	letter	manage	manufacture	market	necessary	next
10	note	of have very	on own	once	operate	opinion	opportunity	order
11	ordinary	organize	other	over	part port	participate	particular	perhaps
12	please up	point	present	property	prove	public	refer	respond response
13	sample	satisfy satisfactory	several	ship	signature significant significance	situate	specific specify	standard
14	success	suggest	that	the	they	those	to too	under
15	us	usual	we	were with	why	will well	work world	would
16	your							

KEY TO ABBREVIATIONS

	A	B	C	D	E	F	G	H
1	advertise	agriculture	America American	amount	and	attention	avenue	billion
2	boulevard	catalog	cent cents	Christmas	company	corporation	credit	day
3	department	dollar dollars	east	economic economy	enclose enclosure	envelope	especially	establish
4	et cetera	example executive	federal	feet	government	hour	hundred	inch
5	incorporate incorporated	information	insurance	invoice	junior	literature	merchandise	million
6	Miss	month	Mr.	Mrs.	Ms.	north	number	okay
7	ounce	percent	pound	president	quart	question	record	regard
8	represent representative	return	second secretary	senior	south	square	street	superinten-dent
9	thousand	total	university	vice president	volume	west	yard	

KEY TO PHRASES

	A	B	C	D	E	F	G	H
1	I am	I appreciate	I believe	I can	I can be	I cannot	I could	I do
2	I feel	I had	I have	I have been	I have had	I hope	I know	I look
3	I shall	I should	I was	I will	I will be	I would	I would appreciate	I would be
4	I would like	we appreciate	we are	we are not	we are pleased	we believe	we can	we can be
5	we cannot	we could	we do	we feel	we had	we have	we have been	we have had
6	we hope	we know	we shall	we should	we were	we will	we will be	we would
7	we would appreciate	we would be	we would like	you are	you can	you cannot	you can be	you could
8	you do	you had	you have	you have been	you have had	you know	you need	you should
9	you were	you will	you will be	you will find	you would	you would be	you would like	to be
10	to call	to come	to determine	to do	to get	to give	to go	to have
11	to have you	to have your	to hear	to keep	to know	to make	to offer	to pay
12	to receive	to say	to see	to send	to use	to visit	to work	and the
13	as I	as to	as we	as well as	as you	as your	at the	can be
14	could be	fact that	for the	for you	for your	has been	have been	have had
15	have not	have you	have your	in the	it is	of our	of the	of you
16	of your	on the	on you	on your	should be	thank you	that I	that we
17	that you	that you are	that you will	that your	to you	to your	will be	will you
18	will your	would be	would like	as soon as	nevertheless	nonetheless	thank you for	thank you for your
19	thank you for your letter	time to time	up to date					

IDENTIFICATION INITIALS FOR UNITED STATES AND TERRITORIES

Alabama (AL)	*AL*	Maryland (MD)	*MD*
Alaska (AK)	*AK*	Massachusetts (MA)	*MA*
Arizona (AZ)	*AZ*	Michigan (MI)	*MI*
Arkansas (AR)	*AR*	Minnesota (MN)	*MN*
California (CA)	*CA*	Mississippi (MS)	*MS*
Colorado (CO)	*CO*	Missouri (MO)	*MO*
Connecticut (CT)	*CT*	Montana (MT)	*MT*
Delaware (DE)	*DE*	Nebraska (NE)	*NE*
District of Columbia (DC)	*DC*	Nevada (NV)	*NV*
Florida (FL)	*FL*	New Hampshire (NH)	*NH*
Georgia (GA)	*GA*	New Jersey (NJ)	*NJ*
Hawaii (HI)	*HI*	New Mexico (NM)	*NM*
Idaho (ID)	*ID*	New York (NY)	*NY*
Illinois (IL)	*IL*	North Carolina (NC)	*NC*
Indiana (IN)	*IN*	North Dakota (ND)	*ND*
Iowa (IA)	*IA*	Ohio (OH)	*OH*
Kansas (KS)	*KS*	Oklahoma (OK)	*OK*
Kentucky (KY)	*KY*	Oregon (OR)	*OR*
Louisiana (LA)	*LA*	Pennsylvania (PA)	*PA*
Maine (ME)	*ME*	Rhode Island (RI)	*RI*

South Carolina (SC)   *SC*   West Virginia (WV)   *WV*

South Dakota (SD)   *SD*   Wisconsin (WI)   *WI*

Tennessee (TN)   *TN*   Wyoming (WY)   *WY*

Texas (TX)   *TX*

Utah (UT)   *UT*

Vermont (VT)   *VT*   Guam (GU)   *GU*

Virginia (VA)   *VA*   Puerto Rico (PR)   *PR*

Washington (WA)   *WA*   Virgin Islands (VI)   *VI*

CANADIAN PROVINCES AND TERRITORIES

Alberta (AB)   *AB*   Nova Scotia (NS)   *NS*

British Columbia (BC)   *BC*   Ontario (ON)   *ON*

Labrador (LB)   *LB*   Prince Edward Island (PE)   *PE*

Manitoba (MB)   *MB*   Quebec (PQ)   *PQ*

New Brunswick (NB)   *NB*   Saskatchewan (SK)   *SK*

Newfoundland (NF)   *NF*   Yukon Territory (YT)   *YT*

Northwest Territories (NT)   *NT*

INDEX OF CITIES

American Cities

City		City	
Albany	*Abne*	Miami	
Atlanta	*allna*	Minneapolis	*mepls*
Austin	*asn*	Mobile	
Baltimore	*bel*	Nashville	*nsvl*
Boston	*bsn*	Oakland	*oclN*
Buffalo	*bflo*	Phoenix	*fnx*
Chicago	*scg*	Portland	*plln*
Cleveland	*clvln*	Shreveport	*srvpl*
Columbus	*clbs*	Tacoma	*lca*
Dallas	*dls*		
Denver	*dnvr*	**Canadian Cities**	
Detroit	*dlryl*	Calgary	*clgre*
El Paso	*el pso*	Edmonton	*edmln*
Fresno	*frzno*	Halifax	*hlfx*
Houston	*hsn*	Montreal	*mlrel*
Jacksonville	*jcsnvl*	Quebec	*qbc*
Little Rock	*lll rc*	Toronto	*lrNo*
Los Angeles	*ls agls*	Vancouver	*vncvr*
Memphis	*mfs*	Windsor	*nzr*
		Winnipeg	*npg*

METRIC TERMS

	(length) meter m	(capacity) liter ℓ	(weight) gram g
kilo	$k\ell$ /meter	$k\ell$	kg
hecto	hm	$h\ell$	hg
deca	dam	$da\ell$	dag
deci	dm	$d\ell$	dg
centi	cm	$c\ell$	cg
milli	mm	$m\ell$	mg
micro	$\sim cm$	$\sim c\ell$	$\sim cg$
nano	nm	$n\ell$	ng

SPELLING STUDY

All individuals who write business communications need to spell correctly frequently used words. In fact, the ability to spell well consistently ranks among the traits most desired by employers.

Surprisingly, a large number of spelling errors occurs from a relatively small number of words. Each of the six Spelling Checks that follow consists of 100 common words that tend to cause spelling problems. Mastery of the words in the Spelling Checks will enable you to spell correctly most of the words in which spelling errors frequently occur. Although the lists are not long, time devoted to the spelling study of the words on each list will certainly be time well spent.

SPELLING CHECK NUMBER 1

1. ability	26. congratulations	51. interest	76. pursuant
2. access	27. consumer	52. irrelevant	77. questionnaire
3. accounting	28. cooperation	53. lease	78. receipts
4. acknowledgment	29. counseling	54. liability	79. recommend
5. adaptable	30. curriculum	55. lose	80. referring
6. admissible	31. definitely	56. marriage	81. repetition
7. advise	32. determine	57. meant	82. restaurant
8. allotted	33. disappoint	58. merge	83. salary
9. alternative	34. distribution	59. modifications	84. security
10. analyze	35. edition	60. necessary	85. sewer
11. applicants	36. eligible	61. objectives	86. sincerely
12. approximate	37. enrollment	62. offered	87. software
13. ascertain	38. especially	63. opinion	88. stationary
14. assure	39. exaggerate	64. organization	89. subject
15. audit	40. executive	65. parallel	90. sufficient
16. ballot	41. expenses	66. participation	91. surprise
17. believable	42. facilities	67. percentage	92. taxable
18. brilliant	43. fascinate	68. personally	93. termination
19. calendar	44. filed	69. physical	94. through
20. capacity	45. foreign	70. possibility	95. transmitted
21. categories	46. general	71. preliminary	96. truly
22. changeable	47. growth	72. presently	97. union
23. clients	48. human	73. prior	98. usually
24. commitment	49. incidentally	74. professional	99. valve
25. competitor	50. installation	75. proprietary	100. versus

SPELLING CHECK NUMBER 2

1. abrupt	15. authorization	29. courses	43. field
2. accessible	16. bankruptcy	30. customer	44. forty
3. accrual	17. believe	31. delegate	45. generally
4. acquaintance	18. brochure	32. develop	46. guarantee
5. addition	19. campus	33. disastrous	47. imagine
6. admittance	20. capital	34. district	48. incompatible
7. advisory	21. category	35. education	49. institution
8. allowable	22. choose	36. embarrass	50. internal
9. among	23. closing	37. entered	51. issue
10. anxious	24. committee	38. essential	52. juvenile
11. appointment	25. complaint	39. exceed	53. led
12. aptitude	26. conscientious	40. exhibit	54. library
13. assessed	27. continuing	41. experience	55. mailable
14. athlete	28. coordinator	42. facility	56. material

57. media	68. personnel	79. recommendations	90. survey
58. microcomputer	69. plausible	80. registration	91. technical
59. monitoring	70. practical	81. replacement	92. than
60. nickel	71. premises	82. retrieval	93. throughout
61. obsolete	72. prevalent	83. schedules	94. transportation
62. officer	73. privilege	84. seize	95. university
63. opponent	74. professor	85. shining	96. utilization
64. orientation	75. provided	86. specifically	97. variable
65. parcel	76. pursue	87. stationery	98. vice
66. particularly	77. quotient	88. subsequent	99. warranty
67. perform	78. receive	89. suggested	100. whose

SPELLING CHECK NUMBER 3

1. absence	26. conscious	51. issued	76. pursuing
2. accidentally	27. continuous	52. knowledge	77. rapport
3. accumulate	28. corporate	53. ledger	78. received
4. acquire	29. courteous	54. license	79. recommended
5. address	30. debatable	55. maintenance	80. relieve
6. adolescent	31. delinquent	56. mathematics	81. representative
7. affect	32. development	57. medical	82. rhythm
8. allowed	33. discuss	58. miniature	83. scheduling
9. amounts	34. divide	59. moral	84. sense
10. apologies	35. effect	60. ninth	85. similar
11. appraisal	36. emphasis	61. occasion	86. specifications
12. argued	37. entitled	62. omission	87. stockholder
13. assessment	38. established	63. opportunity	88. substantial
14. attendance	39. excellence	64. original	89. suggestions
15. authorized	40. existence	65. parity	90. surveyor
16. banquet	41. explanation	66. passed	91. techniques
17. beneficial	42. facsimile	67. performance	92. their
18. brought	43. finally	68. persuade	93. together
19. cancellation	44. friend	69. pleasant	94. treasurer
20. carried	45. government	70. practice	95. unnecessary
21. ceiling	46. handicapped	71. premium	96. utilized
22. chose	47. immediately	72. previously	97. varies
23. collateral	48. increase	73. probably	98. video
24. committees	49. instruction	74. projects	99. weather
25. compliance	50. international	75. providing	100. withdrawal

SPELLING CHECK NUMBER 4

1. abundance
2. accommodate
3. accurate
4. acquisition
5. adequate
6. advantageous
7. affluent
8. almost
9. analyses
10. apologize
11. appreciable
12. arguing
13. assistance
14. attention
15. available
16. basis
17. benefited
18. bureaus
19. candidate
20. cashier
21. census
22. cite
23. column
24. communications
25. conceive
26. consensus
27. contractors
28. correspondence
29. criteria
30. decision
31. describe
32. different
33. discussed
34. divine
35. efficient
36. employee
37. entry
38. estate
39. excellent
40. exists
41. extension
42. faculty
43. financial
44. fulfill
45. governor
46. hardware
47. implementation
48. indicates
49. insurance
50. interpret
51. it's
52. labeling
53. legible
54. limited
55. manageable
56. matrix
57. medicine
58. minimum
59. morale
60. nominal
61. occasionally
62. omit
63. opposite
64. paid
65. partial
66. password
67. permanent
68. persuasive
69. plotter
70. precede
71. preparation
72. primitive
73. procedures
74. prominent
75. provisions
76. pursuit
77. realize
78. receiving
79. reconcile
80. reluctant
81. required
82. ridiculous
83. secretaries
84. separate
85. specified
86. strength
87. substantially
88. summary
89. susceptible
90. technology
91. then
92. toward
93. tries
94. until
95. validate
96. variety
97. villain
98. warehouse
99. weird
100. writing

SPELLING CHECK NUMBER 5

1. academic
2. accomplish
3. achieve
4. across
5. adjournment
6. advertisement
7. all right
8. already
9. analysis
10. apparent
11. appreciated
12. argument
13. associated
14. attorneys
15. beginning
16. benefits
17. business
18. cannot
19. cassette
20. certainly
21. claimants
22. coming
23. comparative
24. concern
25. consistent
26. controlled
27. council
28. criticism
29. deductible
30. description
31. disability
32. disease
33. division
34. either
35. employees
36. environment
37. estimated
38. except
39. expenditure
40. extraordinary
41. familiar
42. fiscal
43. function
44. grammar
45. height
46. implemented
47. industrial
48. integrated
49. interrupt
50. itinerary
51. laboratory
52. leisure

53. loneliness
54. manufacturing
55. maximum
56. mentioned
57. miscellaneous
58. mortgage
59. noticeable
60. occurred
61. omitted
62. optical
63. participant
64. pamphlet
65. past
66. permissible
67. pertinent
68. position
69. preferred
70. prepared
71. principal
72. proceed
73. property
74. psychology
75. quantity
76. reason
77. recent
78. reference
79. remittance
80. requirement
81. role
82. secretary
83. sequential
84. site
85. speech
86. studies
87. succeed
88. supersede
89. system
90. temporary
91. there
92. tragedy
93. useful
94. valuable
95. various
96. visible
97. whether
98. wholly
99. written
100. yield

SPELLING CHECK NUMBER 6

1. accelerate
2. accordance
3. achievement
4. activities
5. administrative
6. advisable
7. allotment
8. alter
9. analyst
10. appearance
11. appropriate
12. arrangement
13. assumption
14. audio
15. balance
16. behavior
17. binary
18. businesslike
19. capabilities
20. casualty
21. certificate
22. clientele
23. commission
24. competitive
25. conference
26. consultant
27. convenience
28. counsel
29. currently
30. defendant
31. despair
32. disappear
33. diskette
34. dissatisfied
35. document
36. electrical
37. enclosing
38. equipped
39. evaluate
40. excess
41. expense
42. extremely
43. family
44. follows
45. further
46. grateful
47. heroes
48. important
49. initial
50. intelligence
51. inventories
52. its
53. laid
54. letterhead
55. loose
56. marketable
57. means
58. menu
59. misspell
60. notify
61. occurrence
62. operating
63. optimism
64. paragraph
65. participate
66. patient
67. personal
68. phase
69. possession
70. prejudiced
71. prescription
72. principle
73. production
74. proposal
75. purpose
76. quarter
77. reasonable
78. recognize
79. referred
80. renewable
81. resolution
82. safety
83. sector
84. services
85. situation
86. station
87. studying
88. successful
89. supervisor
90. tariff
91. terminal
92. thorough
93. transferred
94. undoubtedly
95. using
96. valuation
97. vendor
98. volume
99. while
100. wholesale

SUMMARY OF SPEEDWRITING PRINCIPLES

BY ORDER OF PRESENTATION

1. Write what you hear | high | *hi*

2. Drop medial vowels | build | *bld*

3. Write initial and final vowels | office | *ofs* | fee | *fe*

4. Write *c* for the sound of *k* | copy | *cpe*

5. Write a capital *C* for the sound of *ch* | check | *Cc*

6. Write ⌒ for the sound of *m* | may | *⌒a*

7. Write ⌣ for the sound of *w* and *wh* | way | *⌣a* | when | *⌣n*

8. Underscore the last letter of any word to add *ing* or *thing* as a word ending | billing | *bl̲* | something | *s⌒*

9. To form the plural of any word ending in a mark of punctuation, double the last mark of punctuation | savings | *sv̲*

10. Write *ѕ* to form the plural of any word, to show possession, or to add *ѕ* to a verb | books | *bcs* | runs | *rns*

11. Write *m* for the sounds of *mem* and *mum* | memo | *mo*

12. Write *m* for the sounds of *men, min, mon, mun* | menu | *mu* | money | *me*

13. Write *m* for the word endings *mand, mend, mind, ment*

demand *dm*   amend *am*

remind *rm*   payment *pam*

14. Write a capital *n* for the sound of *nt*

sent *sN*

15. Write *A* for the sound of *ish* or *sh*

finish *fns*

16. Write a capital *a* for the word beginnings *ad, all, al*

admit *ad*   also *aso*

17. Write *m* for the initial sound of *in* or *en*

indent *ndN*

18. Write *o* for the sound of *ow*

allow *alo*

19. Write a printed capital *S* (joined) for the word beginnings *cer, cir, ser, sur*

certain *Sln*   survey *Sva*

20. To form the past tense of a regular verb, write a hyphen after the word

used *uz-*

21. Write *l* for the sound of *ith* or *th*

them *L*

22. Write *l* for the word ending *ly* or *ily*

family *fl*

23. Write a capital *D* for the word beginning *dis*

discuss *Dcs*

24. Write a capital *M* for the word beginning *mis*

misplace *Mpls*

25. Retain beginning or ending vowels when building compound words

payroll *parl* headache *hdac*

26. Retain root-word vowels when adding prefixes and suffixes

disappear *Dapr* payment *pam*

27. Write a capital *P* (disjoined) for the word beginnings *per, pur, pre, pro, pro* (prah)

person *Psn*   prepare *Ppr*

provide *Pvd*   problem *Pbl*

28. Write *g* for the word ending *gram*

telegram *Ulg*

29. Write *y* for the sound of *oi*

boy *by*

30. For words ending in a long vowel + *t*, omit the *t* and write the vowel

rate *ra*   meet *e*

31. Write *a* for the word beginning *an*

answer *asr*

32. Write *q* for the medial or final sound of any vowel + *nk*

bank *bq*   link *lq*

33. Write a capital *S* (disjoined) for the word beginning *super* and for the word endings *scribe* and *script*

supervise *Svz*   describe *dS*

manuscript *mS*

34. Write *el* for the word beginning *electr*

electronic *elnc*

35. Write *w* for the word ending *ward*

backward *bcw*

36. Write *h* for the word ending *hood*

boyhood *byh*

37. Write *1* for the word ending *tion* or *sion*

vacation *vy*

38. Write *a* for the initial and final sound of *aw*

law *la*   audit *adl*

39. Write *q* for the sound of *kw*

quick *qc*

40. Write a capital *n* for the sound of *nd*

friend *frn*

41. Write *⌒* for the initial sound of *em* or *im*

emphasize *fsz*   impress *prs*

42. Omit *p* in the sound of *mpt* — prompt — *P~ᴸ*

43. Write *k* for the sounds of *com,* — common — *kn* — convey — *kva*
con, coun, count
— counsel — *ksl* — account — *ak*

44. Write *S* for the sound of *st* — rest — *rS*

45. Write *q* for the word ending — require — *rq*
quire

46. Write *ʒ* for the sound of *zh* — pleasure — *plʒr*

47. Write *ʹ* for the word ending — kindness — *cN'*
ness

48. Write ** for words beginning — explain — *\pln* — accident — *\dN*
with the sound of any vowel + *x*

49. Write *⤬* for the medial and final — boxes — *bⅹs* — relax — *rlx*
sound of *x*

50. Write *X* for the word beginnings — extreme — *X~*
extr and *extra*
— extraordinary — *Xord*

51. Write *q* for the medial or final — rang — *rq* — single — *sgl*
sound of any vowel + *ng*

52. Write *ß* for the word endings — possible — *psß* — probably — *Pbß*
bil, ble, bly

53. Omit the final *t* of a root word after — act — *ac*
the sound of *k*

54. Write a small, disjoined, and slightly — quality — *ql ᴸ*
raised *t* for the word ending *ity*

55. Write *U* for the word beginning — until — *ull*
un

56. Write *sl* for the word ending *cial* — financial — *fnnsl*
or *tial* (shul, chul)

57. Write _ⁿ_ for the sounds of *ance,*
    ence, nce, nse   expense

58. Write _s_ for the word beginning
    sub   submit

59. Write _v_ for the medial and final
    sound of *tive*   effective

60. Write _ƒ_ for the word endings
    ful and *ify*   careful   justify

61. Write _ƒ_ for the word ending
    ification   qualifications

62. Write a capital _n_ for the word
    beginnings *enter, inter, intro*   enterprise

    introduce   interest

63. Write _sƒ_ for the word beginning
    and ending *self*   self-made   myself

64. Write _svs_ for the word ending
    selves   ourselves

65. When a word contains two medial,
    consecutively pronounced vowels,
    write the first vowel   trial

66. When a word ends in two
    consecutively pronounced vowels,
    write only the last vowel   idea

67. Write _T_ for the word beginnings
    tran and *trans*   transfer

SUMMARY OF SPEEDWRITING PRINCIPLES

BY SYSTEM CATEGORY

Simple Sounds			**Lesson**
1. Write what you hear	high	*hi*	1
2. Write C for the sound of k	copy	*cpe*	2
3. Write ⌒ for the sound of m	may	*⌒a*	2
4. Write ⌣ for the sound of w	way	*⌣a*	2
5. Write ∂ to form the plural of any word, to show possession, or to add ∂ to a verb	books	*bcs*	
	runs	*rns*	2
6. Omit p in the sound of *mpt*	empty	*⌒e*	22
7. Write ⤴ for the medial and final sound of x	boxes	*bxs*	
	tax	*lx*	29
8. Omit the final t of a root word after the sound of k	act	*ac*	31

Vowels			
1. Drop medial vowels	build	*bld*	1
2. Write initial and final vowels	office	*ofs*	
	fee	*fe*	1
3. Retain beginning or ending vowels when building compound words	payroll	*parl*	
	headache	*hdac*	9

4. Retain root-word vowels when adding prefixes and suffixes

    disappear   *Dapr*

    payment   *pam*   9

5. For words ending in a long vowel + *t*, omit the *t* and write the vowel

    rate   *ra*

    meet   *⌣e*   12

6. When a word contains two medial, consecutively pronounced vowels, write the first vowel

    trial   *Lril*   40

7. When a word ends in two consecutively pronounced vowels, write only the last vowel

    idea   *ida*   40

Vowel Blends

1. Write   O   for the sound of *ow*   allow   *alo*   5

2. Write   *y*   for the sound of *oi*   boy   *by*   11

3. Write   *a*   for the initial and final sound of *aw*   law   *la*

    audit   *adl*   19

Consonant Blends

1. Write a capital   C   for the sound of *ch*   check   *Cc*   2

2. Write   ⌣   for the sound of *wh*   when   *⌣n*   2

3. Write a capital   *n*   for the sound of *nt*   sent   *sn*   3

4. Write   *A*   for the sound of *ish* or *sh*   finish   *fnA*   4

5. Write   *l*   for the sound of *ith* or *th*   them   *⌐*   8

6. Write *q* for the medial or final sound of any vowel + *nk*

bank   *bq*

link   *lq*   13

7. Write *q* for the sound of *kw*

quick   *qc*   19

8. Write a capital *N* for the sound of *nd*

friend   *frN*   20

9. Write *S* for the sound of *st*

rest   *rS*   23

10. Write *z* for the sound of *zh*

pleasure   *plzr*   25

11. Write *q* for the medial or final sound of any vowel + *ng*

rang   *rq*

single   *sgl*   30

12. Write *M* for the sounds of *ance, ence, nce, nse*

balance   *belM*   36

Compound Sounds

1. Write *m* for the sounds of *mem* and *mum*

memo   *mo*   3

2. Write *m* for the sounds of *men, min, mon, mun*

menu   *mu*

money   *me*   3

3. Write *k* for the sounds of *com, con, coun, count*

common   *kn*

convey   *kva*

counsel   *ksl*

account   *ak*   23

Word Beginnings

1. Write a capital $\mathcal{A}$ for the word beginnings *ad, all,* and *al*

   admit   *a—l*

   also   *Aso*   4

2. Write $\mathcal{M}$ for the initial sound of *in* and *en*

   indent   *ndM*   4

3. Write a printed capital $\mathcal{S}$ (joined) for the word beginnings *cer, cir, ser, sur*

   certain   *Sln*

   survey   *Sva*   5

4. Write a capital $\mathcal{D}$ for the word beginning *dis*

   discuss   *Dcs*   8

5. Write a capital $\mathcal{M}$ for the word beginning *mis*

   misplace   *Mpls*   8

6. Write a capital $\mathcal{P}$ (disjoined) for the word beginnings *per, pur, pre, pro, pro* (prah)

   person   *Psn*

   prepare   *Ppr*

   provide   *Pvd*

   problem   *Pbl*   10

7. Write $\mathcal{a}$ for the word beginning *an*

   answer   *asr*   13

8. Write a capital $\mathcal{S}$ (disjoined) for the word beginning *super*

   supervise   *Sv3*   15

9. Write $\mathcal{el}$ for the word beginning *electr*

   electronic   *elnc*   15

10. Write ⌐ for the initial sound of *em* or *im*

    emphasize   *faz*

    impress   *prs*   22

11. Write ＼ for words beginning with the sound of any vowel + *x*

    explain   *pln*

    accident   *dM*   29

12. Write X for the word beginnings *extr* and *extra*

extreme

extraordinary   29

13. Write U for the word beginning *un*

until   33

14. Write S for the word beginning *sub*

submit   36

15. Write a capital η for the word beginnings *enter, inter, intro*

enterprise

interest

introduce   39

16. Write sf for the word beginning *self*

self-made   39

17. Write T for the word beginnings *tran* and *trans*

transfer   41

Word Endings

1. Underscore the last letter of the word to add *ing* or *thing* as a word ending

billing

something   2

2. To form the plural of any word ending in a mark of punctuation, double the last mark of punctuation

savings   2

3. To form the past tense of a regular verb, write a hyphen after the word

used   6

4. Write m for the word endings *mand, mend, mind, ment*

demand

amend

remind

payment   3

5. Write *l* for the word ending *ly* or *ily*

family *fl* 8

6. Write *q* for the word ending *gram*

telegram *Ulq* 10

7. Write a capital *S* (disjoined) for the word endings *scribe* and *script*

describe *dS*

manuscript *mS* 15

8. Write *w* for the word ending *ward*

backward *bcw* 16

9. Write *h* for the word ending *hood*

boyhood *byh* 16

10. Write *↗* for the word ending *tion* or *sion*

vacation *vcy* 17

11. Write *q* for the word ending *quire*

require *rq* 25

12. Write *'* for the word ending *ness*

kindness *cM'* 26

13. Write *B* for the word endings *bil, ble, bly*

possible *psB*

probably *PbB* 31

14. Write a small, disjoined, and slightly raised *t* for the word ending *ity*

quality *ql^t* 32

15. Write *Al* for the word ending *cial* or *tial* (shul, chul)

financial *fnnAl* 34

16. Write *V* for the medial and final sound of *tive*

effective *efcv* 37

17. Write *l* for the word endings *ful* and *ify*

careful *crf*

justify *jSf* 38

18. Write *by* for the word ending *ification*

qualifications *qlfys* 38

19. Write ![self symbol] for the word ending
    self   myself   ![myself shorthand]   39

20. Write ![selves symbol] for the word ending
    selves   ourselves   ![ourselves shorthand]   39

Marks of Punctuation

1. Underscore the last letter of the word   billing   ![billing shorthand]
   to add *ing* or *thing* as a word ending
                                             something   ![something shorthand]   2

2. To form the plural of any word
   ending in a mark of punctuation,
   double the last mark of punctuation   savings   ![savings shorthand]   2

3. To form the past tense of a regular
   verb, write a hyphen after the word   used   ![used shorthand]   6

4. Write ![ness symbol] for the word ending
   ness   kindness   ![kindness shorthand]   26

5. To show capitalization, draw a small
   curved line under the last letter of the
   word   Bill   ![Bill shorthand]   1

6. Write ![period symbol] to indicate a period at
   the end of a sentence   1

7. Write ![question mark symbol] to indicate a question
   mark   1

8. Write ![paragraph symbol] to indicate the end of a
   paragraph   1

9. Write ![exclamation symbol] to indicate an
   exclamation mark   5

10. Write ![dash symbol] to indicate a dash   5

11. Write ![hyphen symbol] to indicate a hyphen   5

12. To indicate solid capitalization, double
    the curved line underneath the last
    letter of the word   5